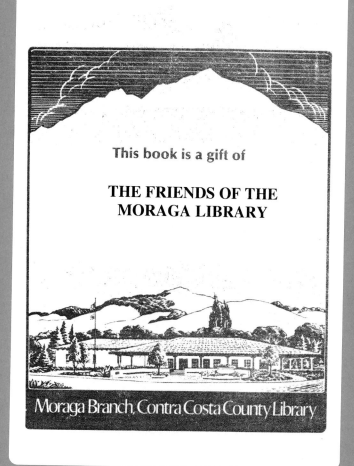

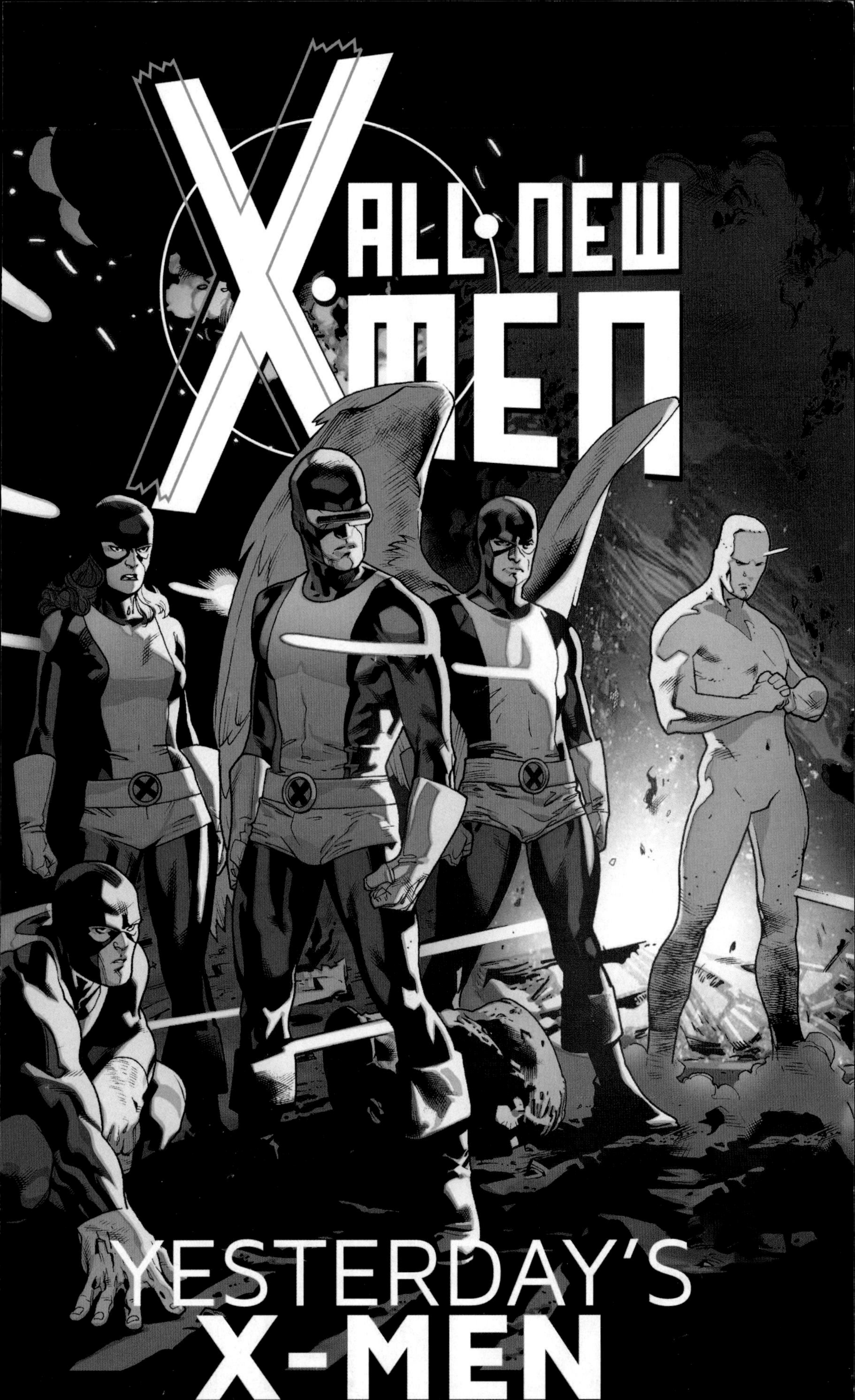
ALL-NEW
X-MEN
YESTERDAY'S
X-MEN

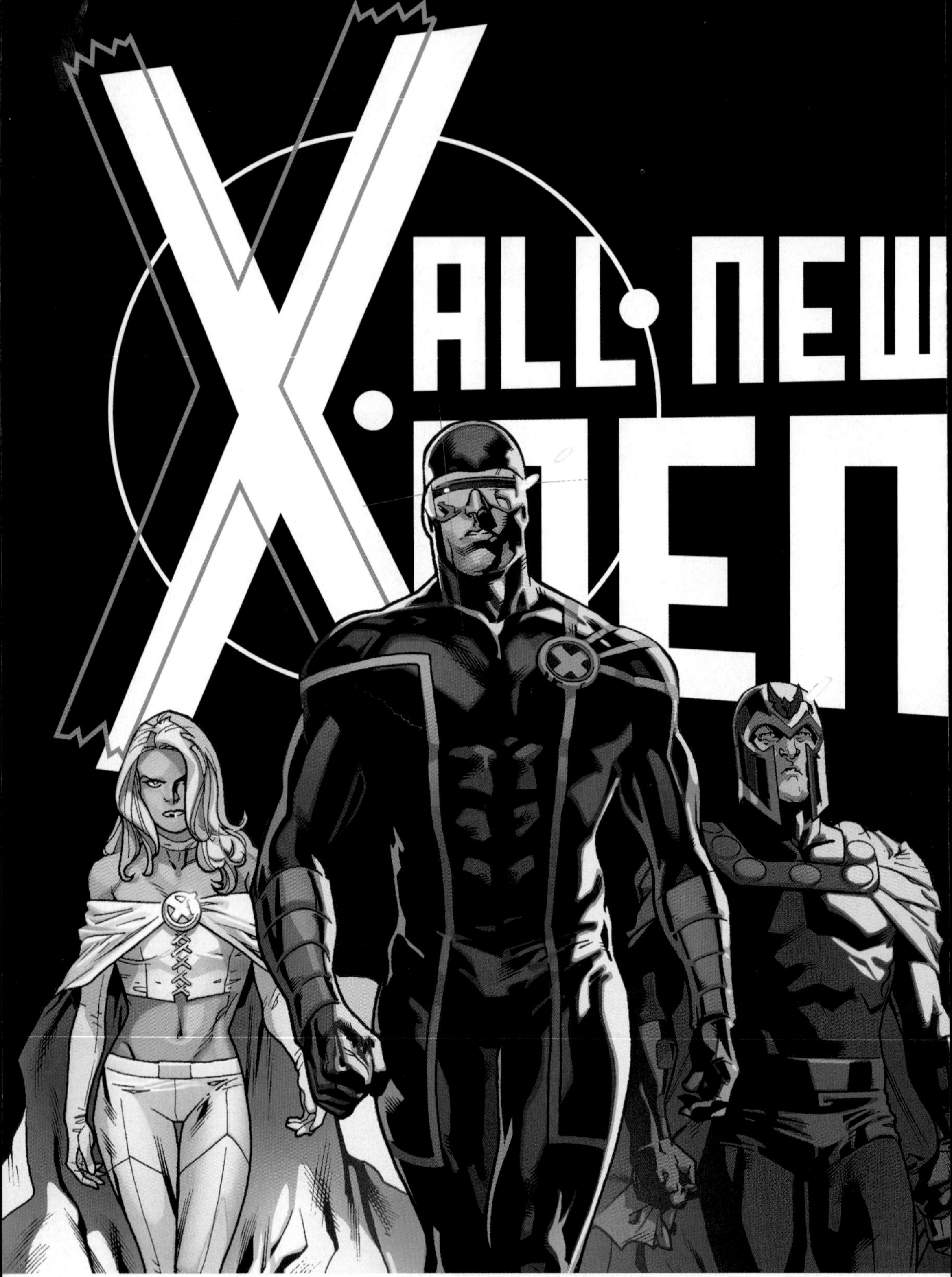
ALL·NEW

YESTERDAY'S
X-MEN

BEAST
HANK McCOY

MARVEL GIRL
JEAN GREY

CYCLOPS
SCOTT SUMMERS

ANGEL
WARREN WORTHINGTON III

ICEMAN
BOBBY DRAKE

orn with genetic mutations that give them abilities beyond those of normal humans, mutants are the next stage in evolution. As such, they are feared and hated by humanity. But a group of mutants known as the X-Men fight for peaceful coexistence between mutants and humankind.

This fight seemed lost when the Scarlet Witch depowered 99% of mutants, leaving X-Men leader Cyclops and his species on the brink of extinction. But when the Phoenix, a cosmic force of both destruction and creation, returned to Earth, Cyclops saw it as a sign of hope for the future of the mutants. In the end, Cyclops, possessed and corrupted by the Phoenix Force, struck down Professor Xavier, and it took the combined might of the Avengers and X-Men to defeat him. Just when all seemed lost, the power of the Phoenix Force was dispersed, sparking the rebirth of mutantkind.

As the rest of the X-Men settle back into life at the Jean Grey School for Higher Learning, Cyclops finds himself a fugitive and outcast with few allies.

BRIAN MICHAEL
BENDIS
WRITER

STUART
IMMONEN
PENCILER

WADE VON
GRAWBADGER
INKER

MARTE
GRACIA
COLORIST

VC'S CORY
PETIT
LETTERER

JORDAN D.
WHITE
ASSISTANT EDITOR

NICK
LOWE
EDITOR

COLLECTION EDITOR: **JENNIFER GRÜNWALD**
ASSISTANT EDITORS: **ALEX STARBUCK** & **NELSON RIBEIRO**
EDITOR, SPECIAL PROJECTS: **MARK D. BEAZLEY**
SENIOR EDITOR, SPECIAL PROJECTS: **JEFF YOUNGQUIST**
SVP OF PRINT & DIGITAL PUBLISHING SALES: **DAVID GABRIEL**
BOOK DESIGNER: **RODOLFO MURAGUCHI**

EDITOR IN CHIEF: **AXEL ALONSO**
CHIEF CREATIVE OFFICER: **JOE QUESADA**
PUBLISHER: **DAN BUCKLEY**
EXECUTIVE PRODUCER: **ALAN FINE**

ALL-NEW X-MEN VOL. 1: YESTERDAY'S X-MEN. Contains material originally published in magazine form as ALL-NEW X-MEN #1-5. First printing 2013. Hardcover ISBN# 978-0-7851-6820-1. Softcover ISBN# 978-0-7851-6637-5. Published by MARVEL WORLDWIDE, INC., a subsidiary of MARVEL ENTERTAINMENT, LLC. OFFICE OF PUBLICATION: 135 West 50th Street, New York, NY 10020. Copyright © 2012 and 2013 Marvel Characters, Inc. All rights reserved. All characters featured in this issue and the distinctive names and likenesses thereof, and all related indicia are trademarks of Marvel Characters, Inc. No similarity between any of the names, characters, persons, and/or institutions in this magazine with those of any living or dead person or institution is intended, and any such similarity which may exist is purely coincidental. **Printed in the U.S.A.** ALAN FINE, EVP - Office of the President, Marvel Worldwide, Inc. and EVP & CMO Marvel Characters B.V.; DAN BUCKLEY, Publisher & President - Print, Animation & Digital Divisions; JOE QUESADA, Chief Creative Officer; TOM BREVOORT, SVP of Publishing; DAVID BOGART, SVP of Operations & Procurement, Publishing; RUWAN JAYATILLEKE, SVP & Associate Publisher, Publishing; C.B. CEBULSKI, SVP of Creator & Content Development; DAVID GABRIEL, SVP of Print & Digital Publishing Sales; JIM O'KEEFE, VP of Operations & Logistics; DAN CARR, Executive Director of Publishing Technology; SUSAN CRESPI, Editorial Operations Manager; ALEX MORALES, Publishing Operations Manager; STAN LEE, Chairman Emeritus. For information regarding advertising in Marvel Comics or on Marvel.com, please contact Niza Disla, Director of Marvel Partnerships, at ndisla@marvel.com. For Marvel subscription inquiries, please call 800-217-9158. **Manufactured between 1/21/2013 and 3/4/2013 (hardcover), and 1/21/2013 and 11/4/2013 (softcover), by R.R. DONNELLEY, INC., SALEM, VA, USA.**

10 9 8 7 6 5 4 3 2 1

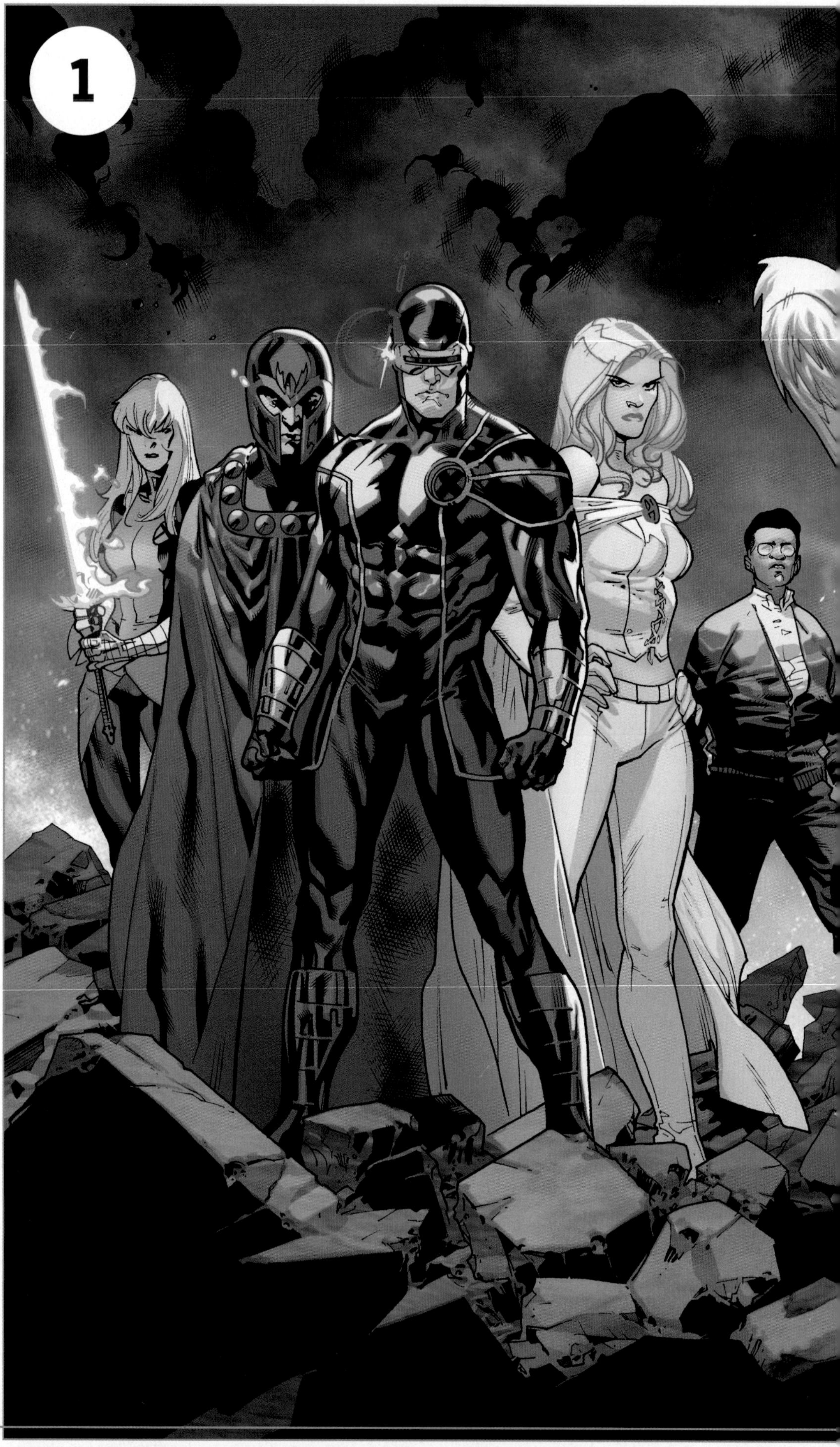

1

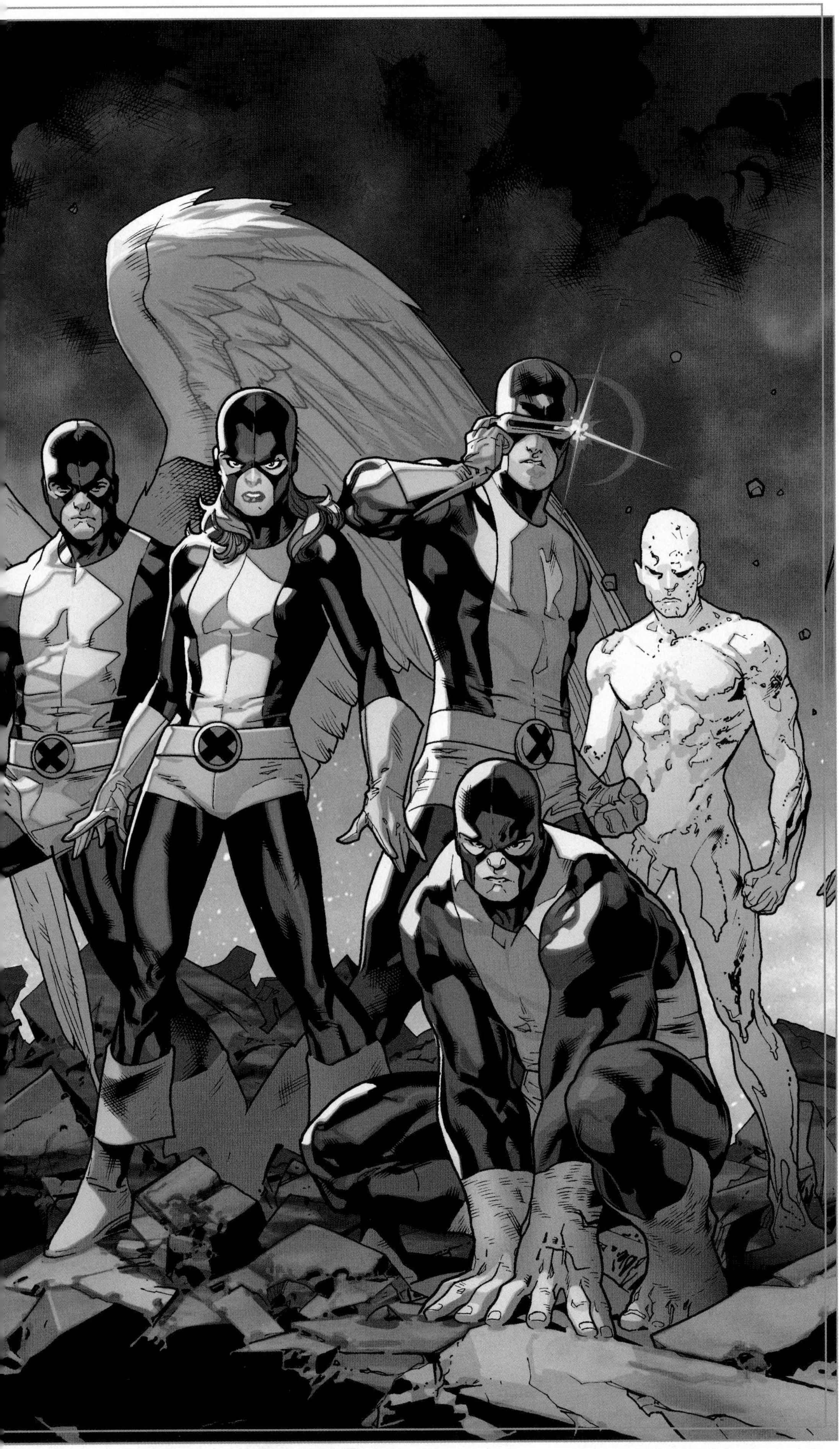

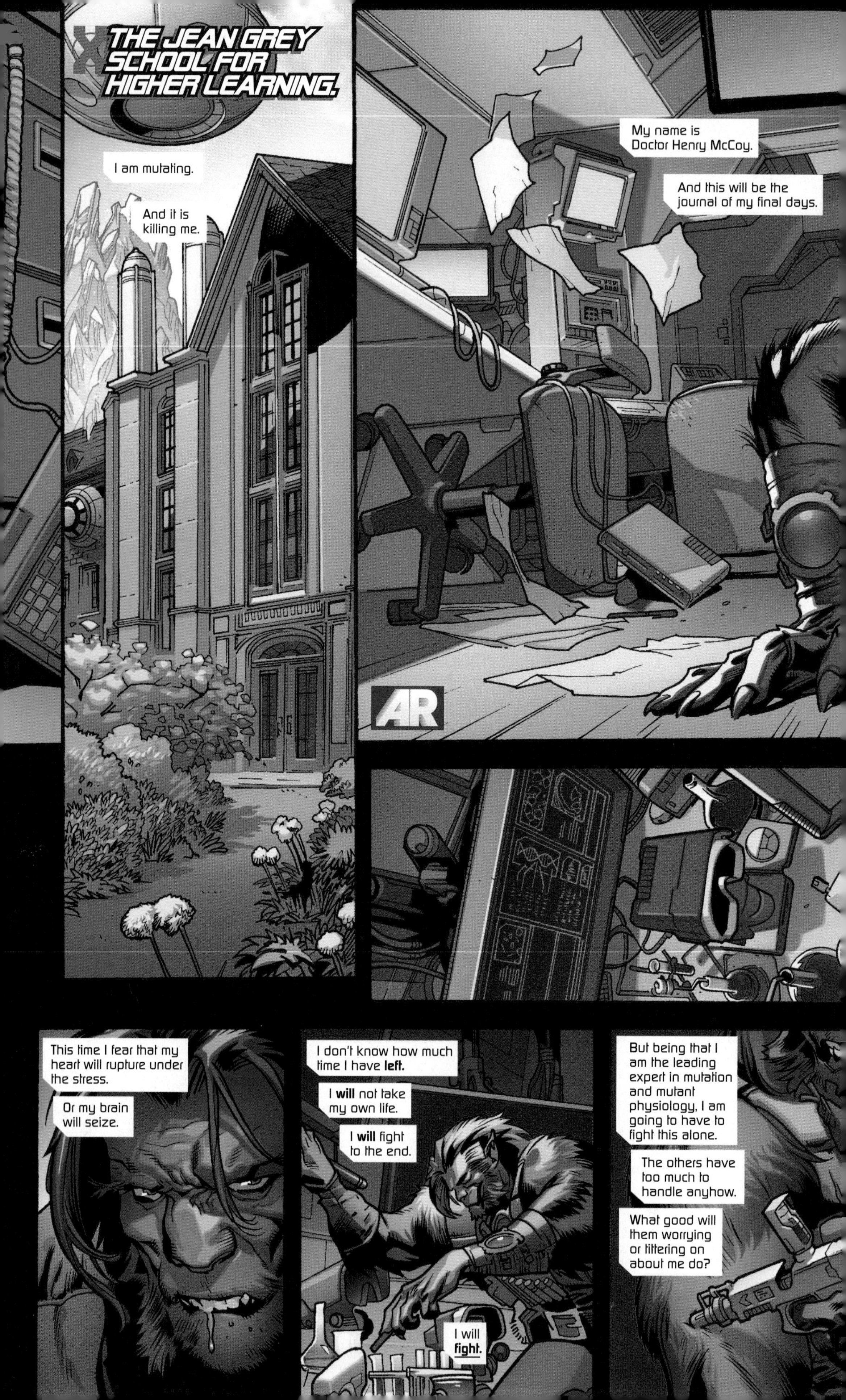
THE JEAN GREY SCHOOL FOR HIGHER LEARNING.
I am mutating.
And it is killing me.
My name is Doctor Henry McCoy.
And this will be the journal of my final days.
AR
This time I fear that my heart will rupture under the stress.
Or my brain will seize.
I don't know how much time I have **left.**
I **will** not take my own life.
I **will** fight to the end.
I will **fight.**
But being that I am the leading expert in mutation and mutant physiology, I am going to have to fight this alone.
The others have too much to handle anyhow.
What good will them worrying or tittering on about me do?

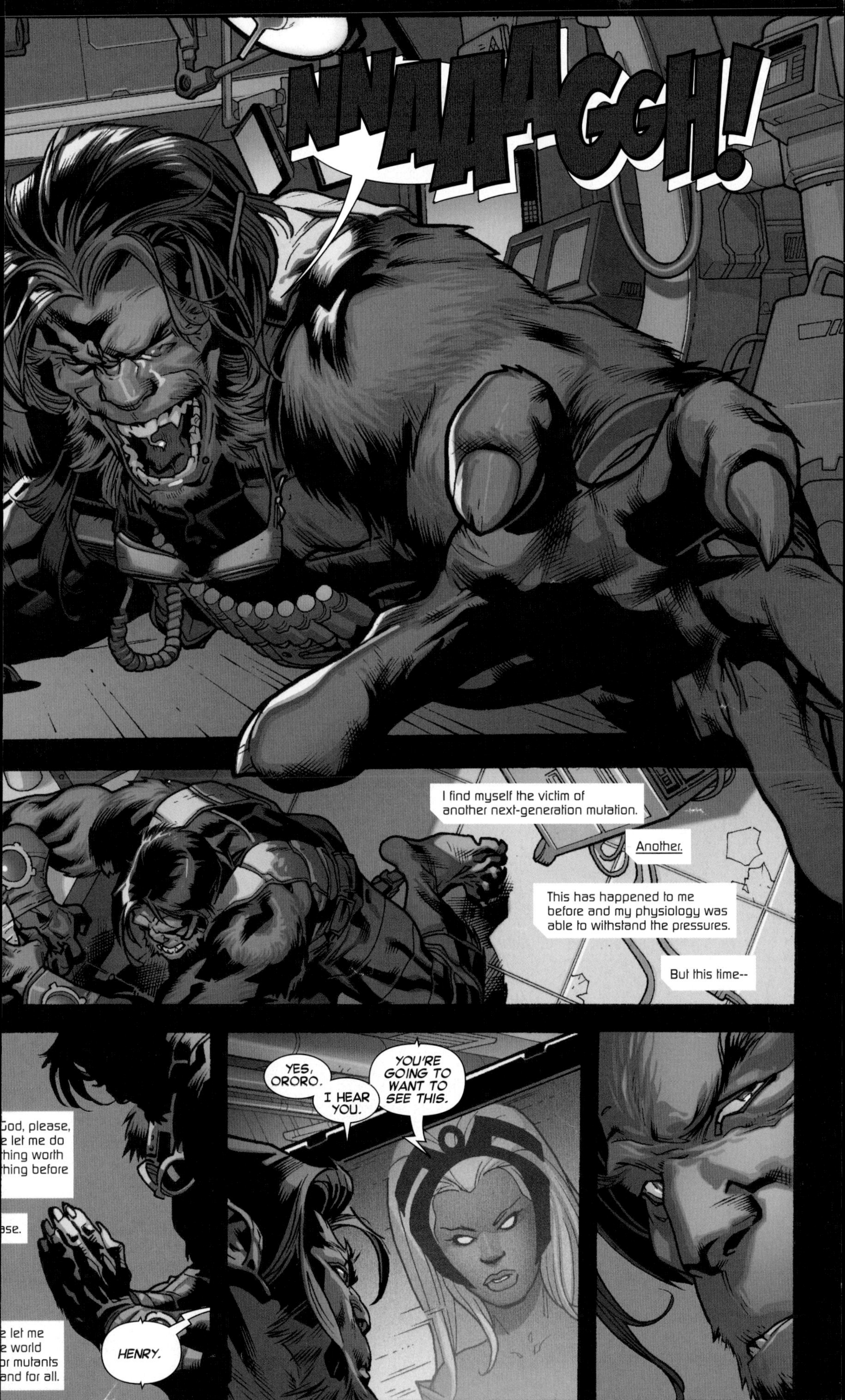

NNAAAGGH!
I find myself the victim of another next-generation mutation.
Another.
This has happened to me before and my physiology was able to withstand the pressures.
But this time--
God, please, e let me do thing worth thing before
ase.
e let me e world or mutants and for all.
HENRY.
YES, ORORO.
I HEAR YOU.
YOU'RE GOING TO WANT TO SEE THIS.

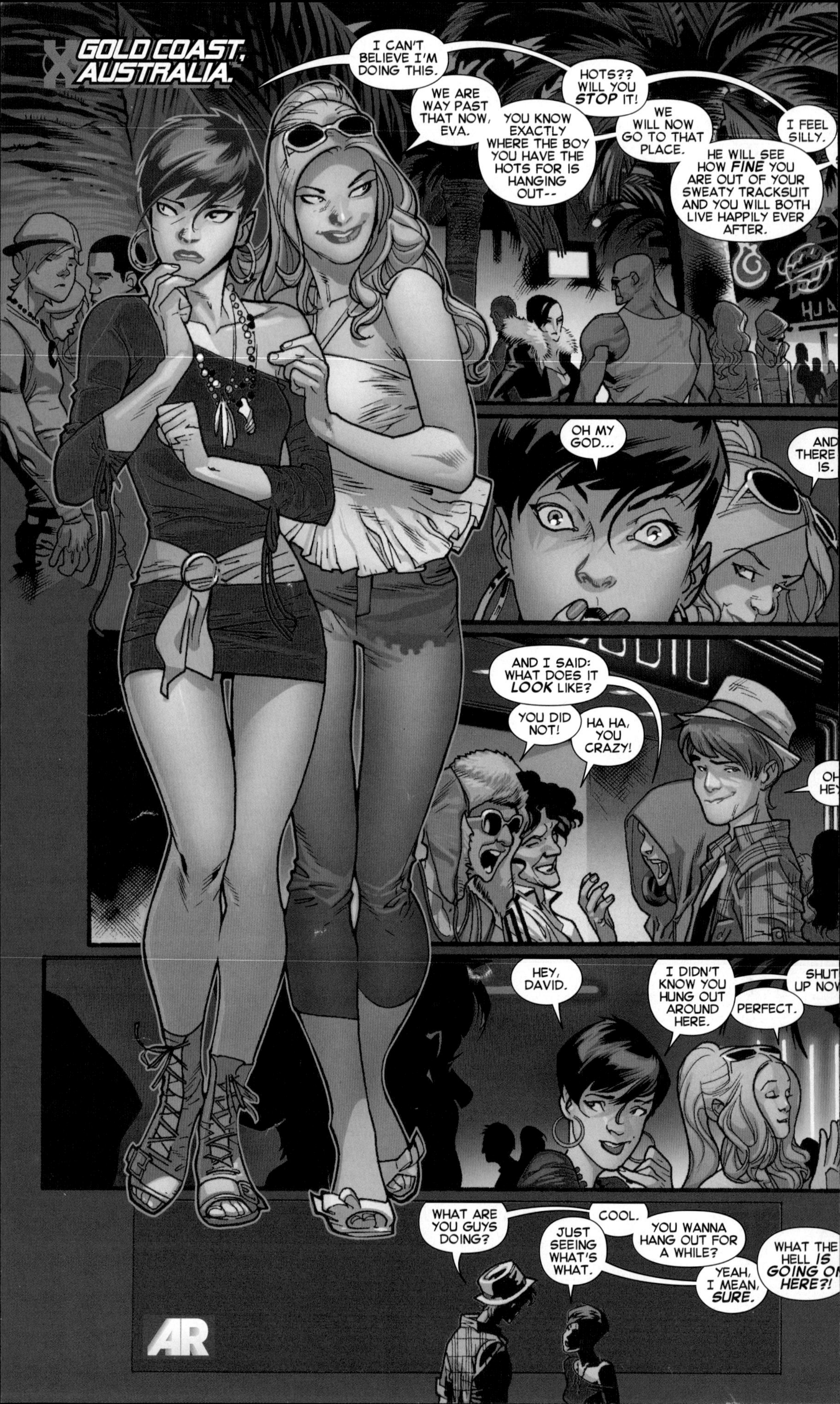
GOLD COAST, AUSTRALIA.
I CAN'T BELIEVE I'M DOING THIS.
WE ARE WAY PAST THAT NOW, EVA.
YOU KNOW EXACTLY WHERE THE BOY YOU HAVE THE HOTS FOR IS HANGING OUT--
HOTS?? WILL YOU STOP IT!
WE WILL NOW GO TO THAT PLACE.
I FEEL SILLY.
HE WILL SEE HOW FINE YOU ARE OUT OF YOUR SWEATY TRACKSUIT AND YOU WILL BOTH LIVE HAPPILY EVER AFTER.
OH MY GOD...
AND THERE IS.
AND I SAID: WHAT DOES IT LOOK LIKE?
YOU DID NOT!
HA HA, YOU CRAZY!
HEY, DAVID.
I DIDN'T KNOW YOU HUNG OUT AROUND HERE.
PERFECT.
WHAT ARE YOU GUYS DOING?
COOL.
JUST SEEING WHAT'S WHAT.
YOU WANNA HANG OUT FOR A WHILE?
YEAH, I MEAN, SURE.
AR

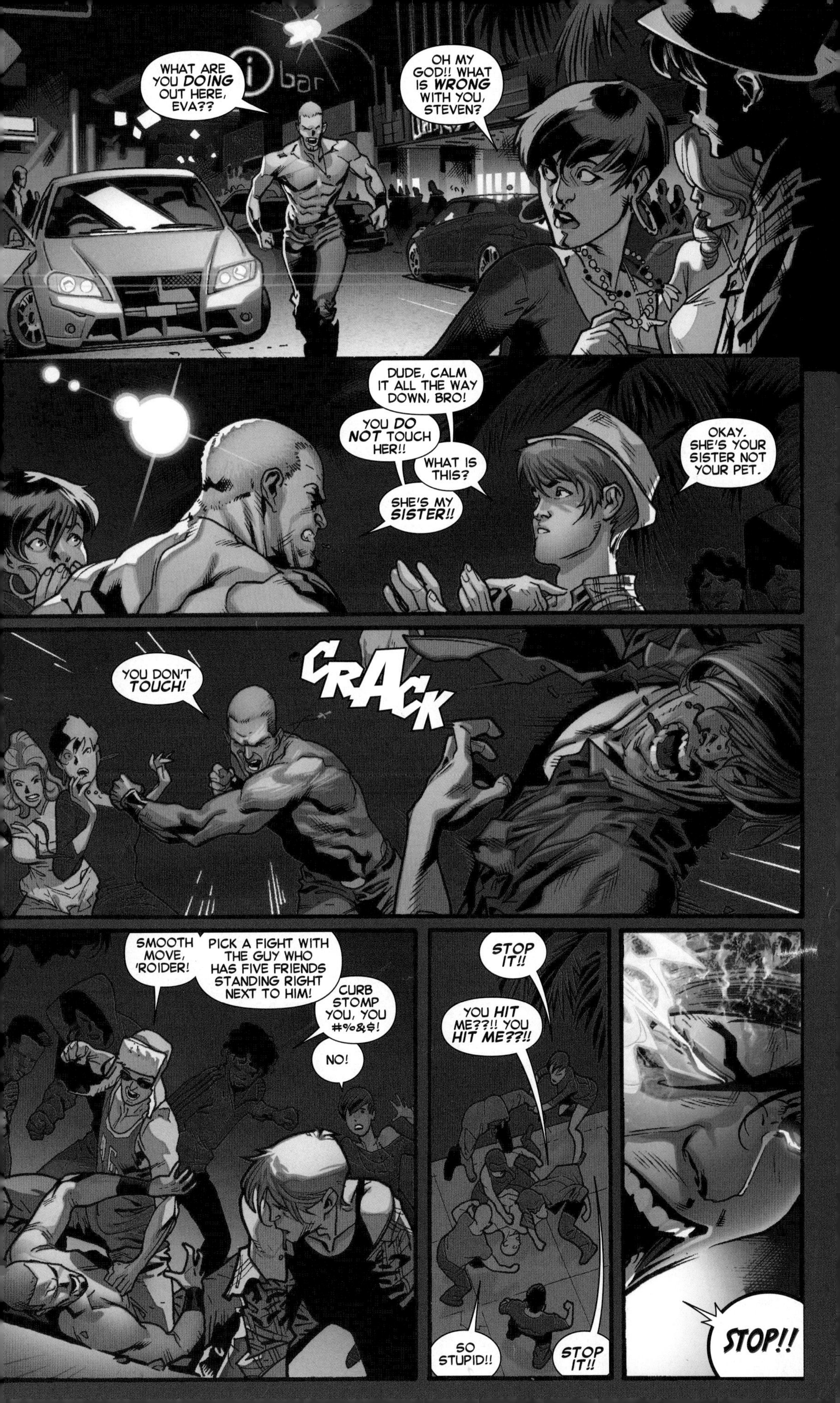

WHAT ARE YOU DOING OUT HERE, EVA??
OH MY GOD!! WHAT IS WRONG WITH YOU, STEVEN?
DUDE, CALM IT ALL THE WAY DOWN, BRO!
YOU DO NOT TOUCH HER!!
WHAT IS THIS?
SHE'S MY SISTER!!
OKAY. SHE'S YOUR SISTER NOT YOUR PET.
YOU DON'T TOUCH!
CRACK
SMOOTH MOVE, 'ROIDER!
PICK A FIGHT WITH THE GUY WHO HAS FIVE FRIENDS STANDING RIGHT NEXT TO HIM!
CURB STOMP YOU, YOU #%&$!
NO!
STOP IT!!
YOU HIT ME??!! YOU HIT ME??!!
SO STUPID!!
STOP IT!!
STOP!!

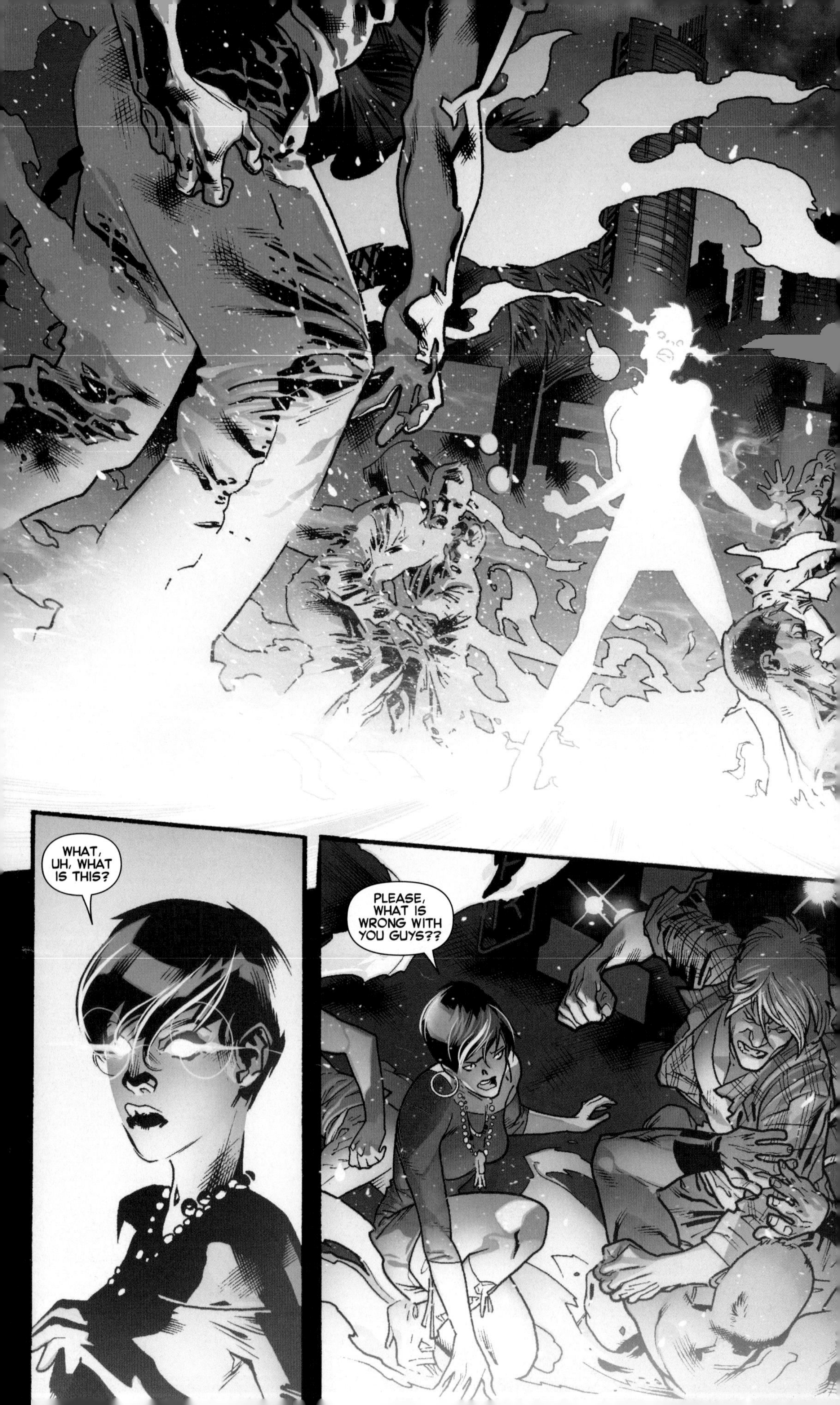
WHAT, UH, WHAT IS THIS?
PLEASE, WHAT IS WRONG WITH YOU GUYS??

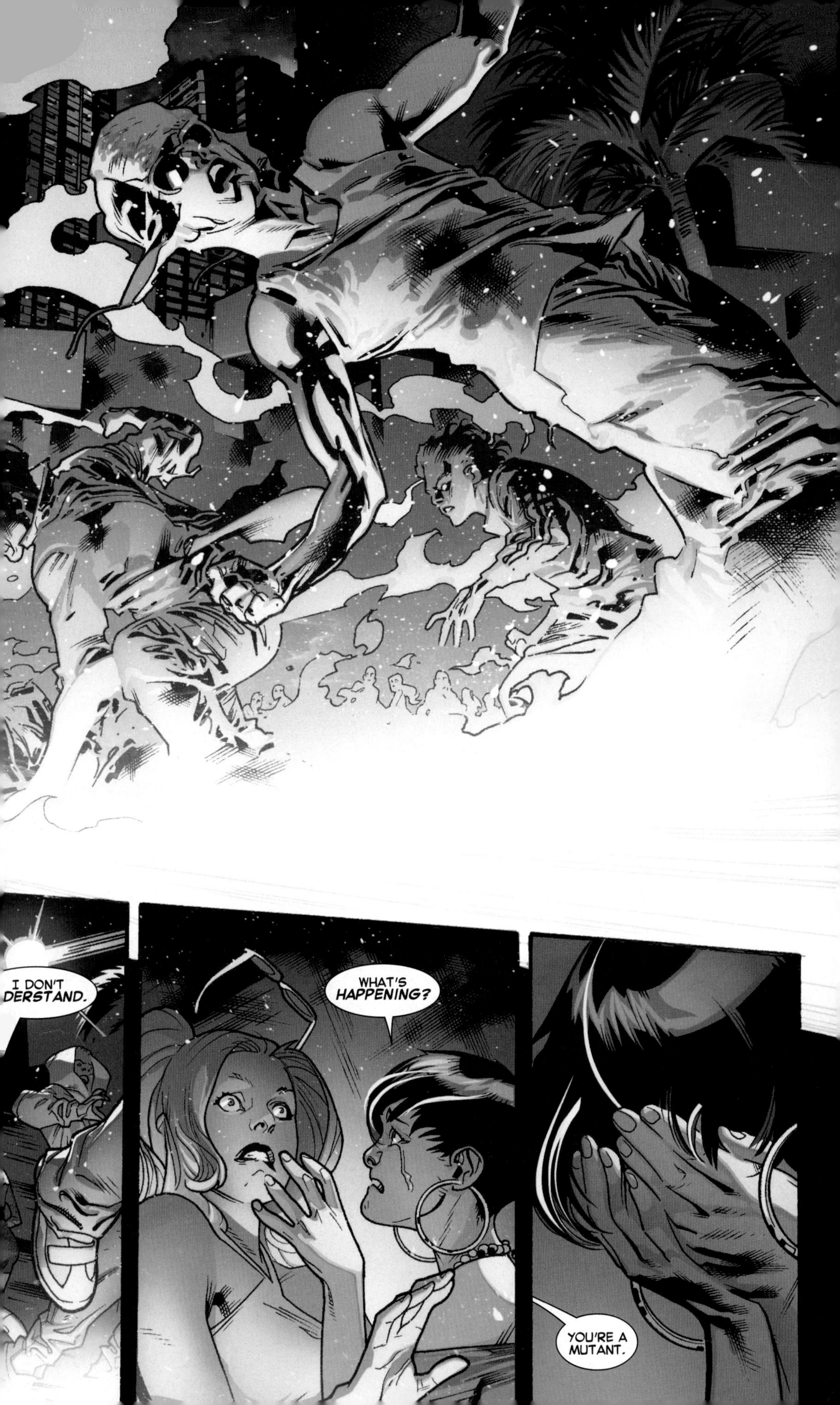

I DON'T
DERSTAND.
WHAT'S
HAPPENING?
YOU'RE A
MUTANT.

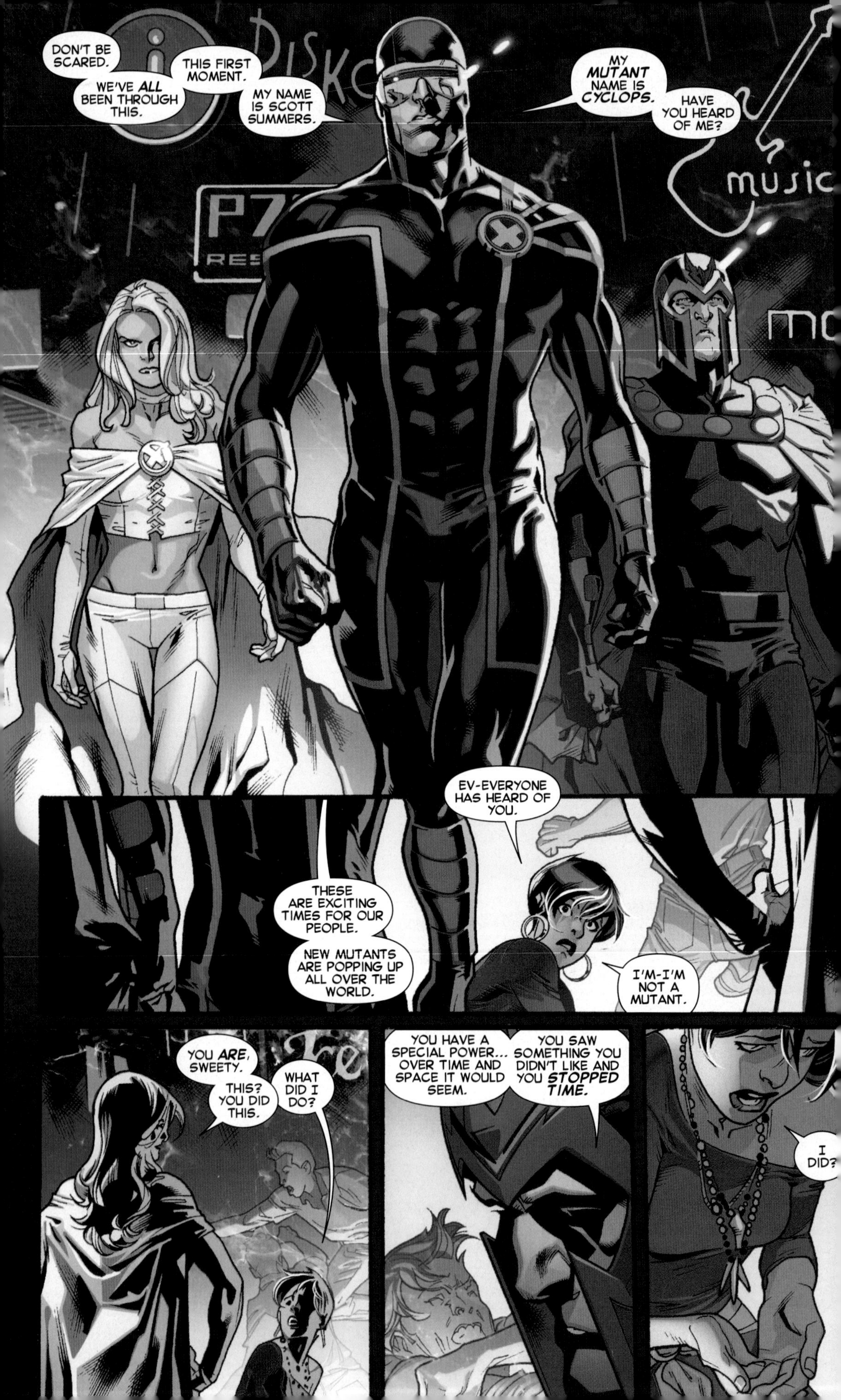
DON'T BE SCARED.
WE'VE ALL BEEN THROUGH THIS.
THIS FIRST MOMENT.
MY NAME IS SCOTT SUMMERS.
MY MUTANT NAME IS CYCLOPS.
HAVE YOU HEARD OF ME?
EV-EVERYONE HAS HEARD OF YOU.
THESE ARE EXCITING TIMES FOR OUR PEOPLE.
NEW MUTANTS ARE POPPING UP ALL OVER THE WORLD.
I'M-I'M NOT A MUTANT.
YOU ARE, SWEETY.
THIS? YOU DID THIS.
WHAT DID I DO?
YOU HAVE A SPECIAL POWER... OVER TIME AND SPACE IT WOULD SEEM.
YOU SAW SOMETHING YOU DIDN'T LIKE AND YOU STOPPED TIME.
I DID?

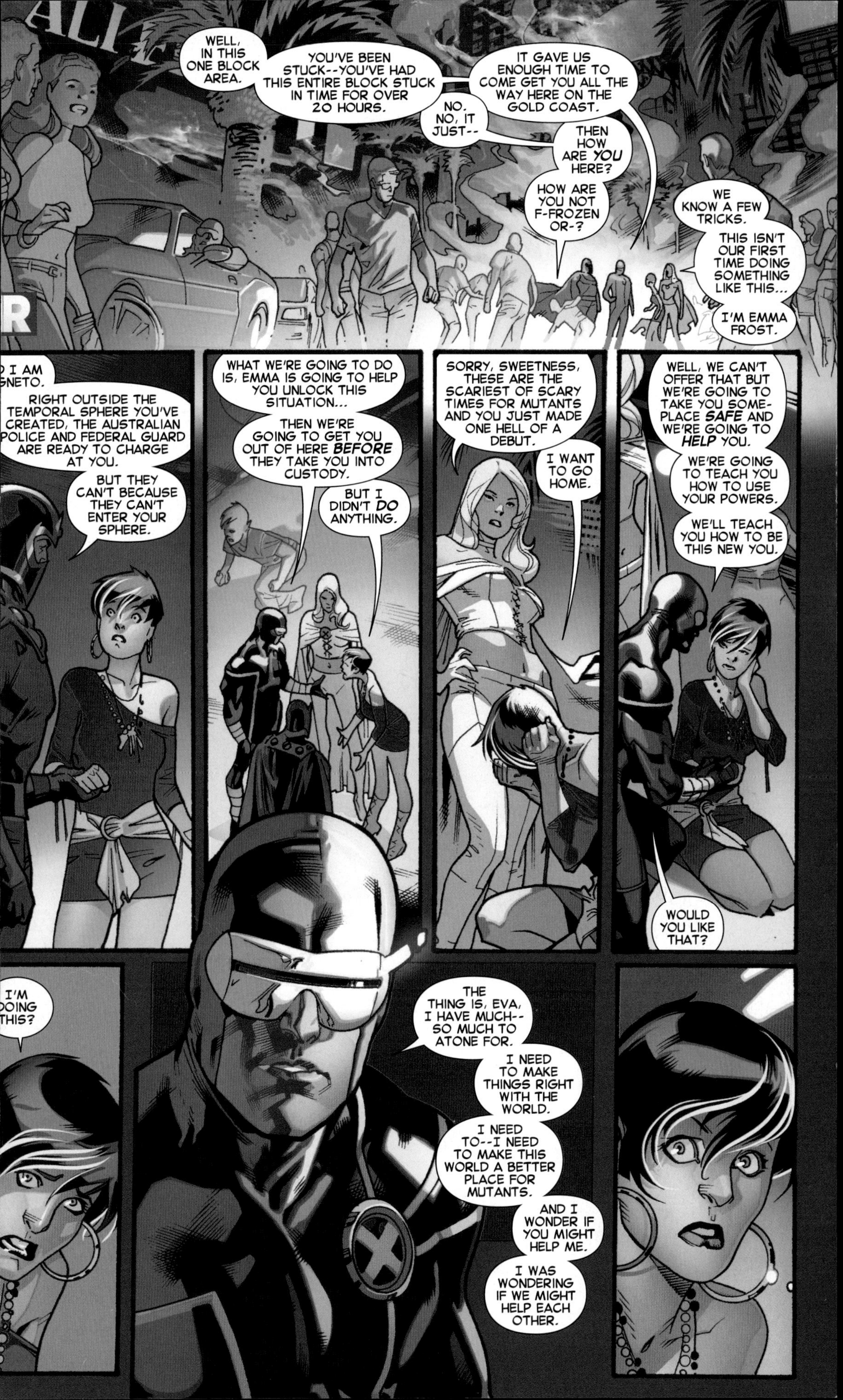

WELL, IN THIS ONE BLOCK AREA.
YOU'VE BEEN STUCK--YOU'VE HAD THIS ENTIRE BLOCK STUCK IN TIME FOR OVER 20 HOURS.
IT GAVE US ENOUGH TIME TO COME GET YOU ALL THE WAY HERE ON THE GOLD COAST.
NO. NO, IT JUST--
THEN HOW ARE YOU HERE?
HOW ARE YOU NOT F-FROZEN OR-?
WE KNOW A FEW TRICKS.
THIS ISN'T OUR FIRST TIME DOING SOMETHING LIKE THIS...
I'M EMMA FROST.
I AM GNETO.
RIGHT OUTSIDE THE TEMPORAL SPHERE YOU'VE CREATED, THE AUSTRALIAN POLICE AND FEDERAL GUARD ARE READY TO CHARGE AT YOU.
BUT THEY CAN'T BECAUSE THEY CAN'T ENTER YOUR SPHERE.
WHAT WE'RE GOING TO DO IS, EMMA IS GOING TO HELP YOU UNLOCK THIS SITUATION...
THEN WE'RE GOING TO GET YOU OUT OF HERE BEFORE THEY TAKE YOU INTO CUSTODY.
BUT I DIDN'T DO ANYTHING.
SORRY, SWEETNESS, THESE ARE THE SCARIEST OF SCARY TIMES FOR MUTANTS AND YOU JUST MADE ONE HELL OF A DEBUT.
I WANT TO GO HOME.
WELL, WE CAN'T OFFER THAT BUT WE'RE GOING TO TAKE YOU SOME-PLACE SAFE AND WE'RE GOING TO HELP YOU.
WE'RE GOING TO TEACH YOU HOW TO USE YOUR POWERS.
WE'LL TEACH YOU HOW TO BE THIS NEW YOU.
WOULD YOU LIKE THAT?
I'M DOING THIS?
THE THING IS, EVA, I HAVE MUCH--SO MUCH TO ATONE FOR.
I NEED TO MAKE THINGS RIGHT WITH THE WORLD.
I NEED TO--I NEED TO MAKE THIS WORLD A BETTER PLACE FOR MUTANTS.
AND I WONDER IF YOU MIGHT HELP ME.
I WAS WONDERING IF WE MIGHT HELP EACH OTHER.

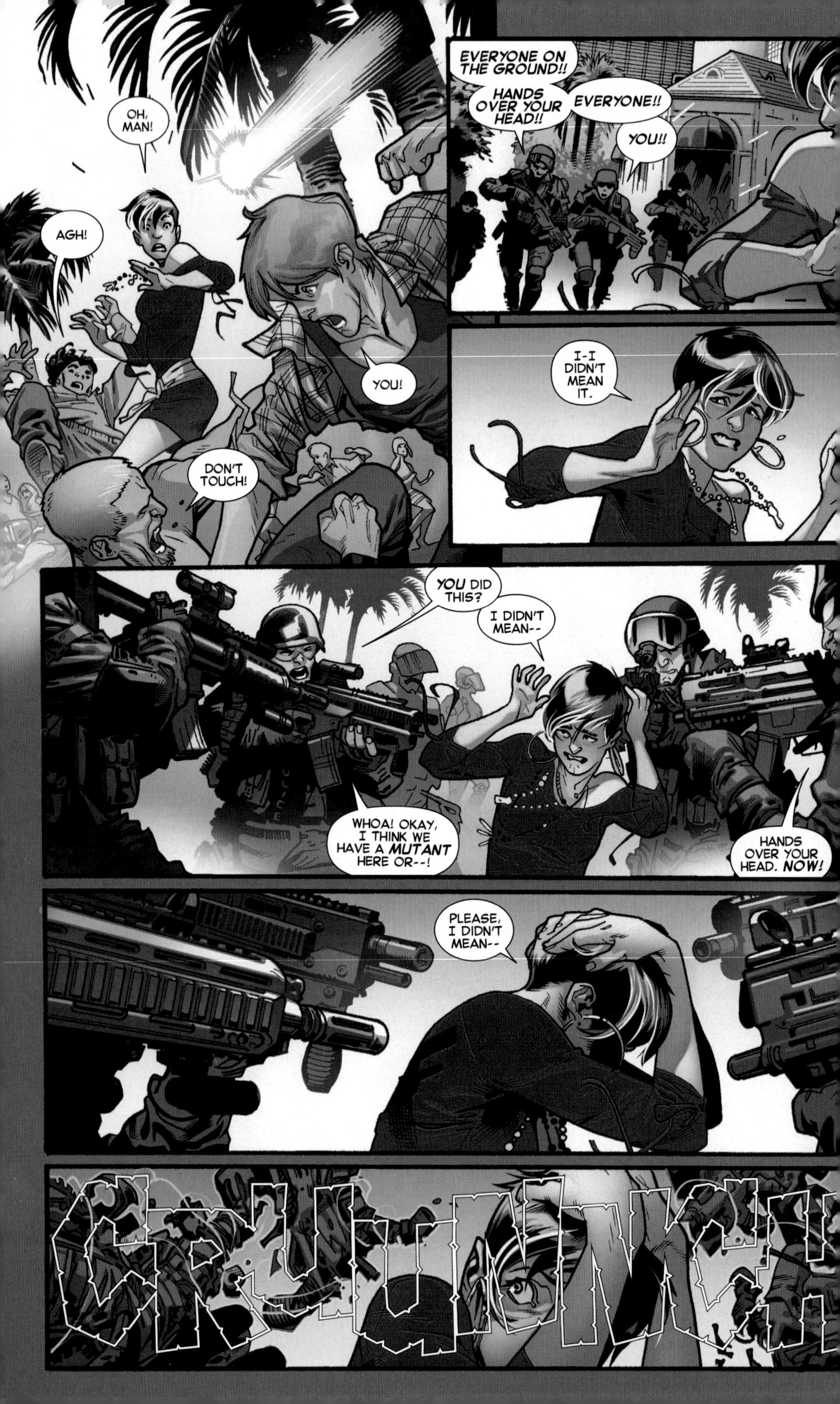
OH, MAN!
AGH!
YOU!
DON'T TOUCH!
EVERYONE ON THE GROUND!!
HANDS OVER YOUR HEAD!!
EVERYONE!!
YOU!!
I-I DIDN'T MEAN IT.
YOU DID THIS?
I DIDN'T MEAN--
WHOA! OKAY, I THINK WE HAVE A MUTANT HERE OR--!
HANDS OVER YOUR HEAD. NOW!
PLEASE, I DIDN'T MEAN--
CRUUNNCH

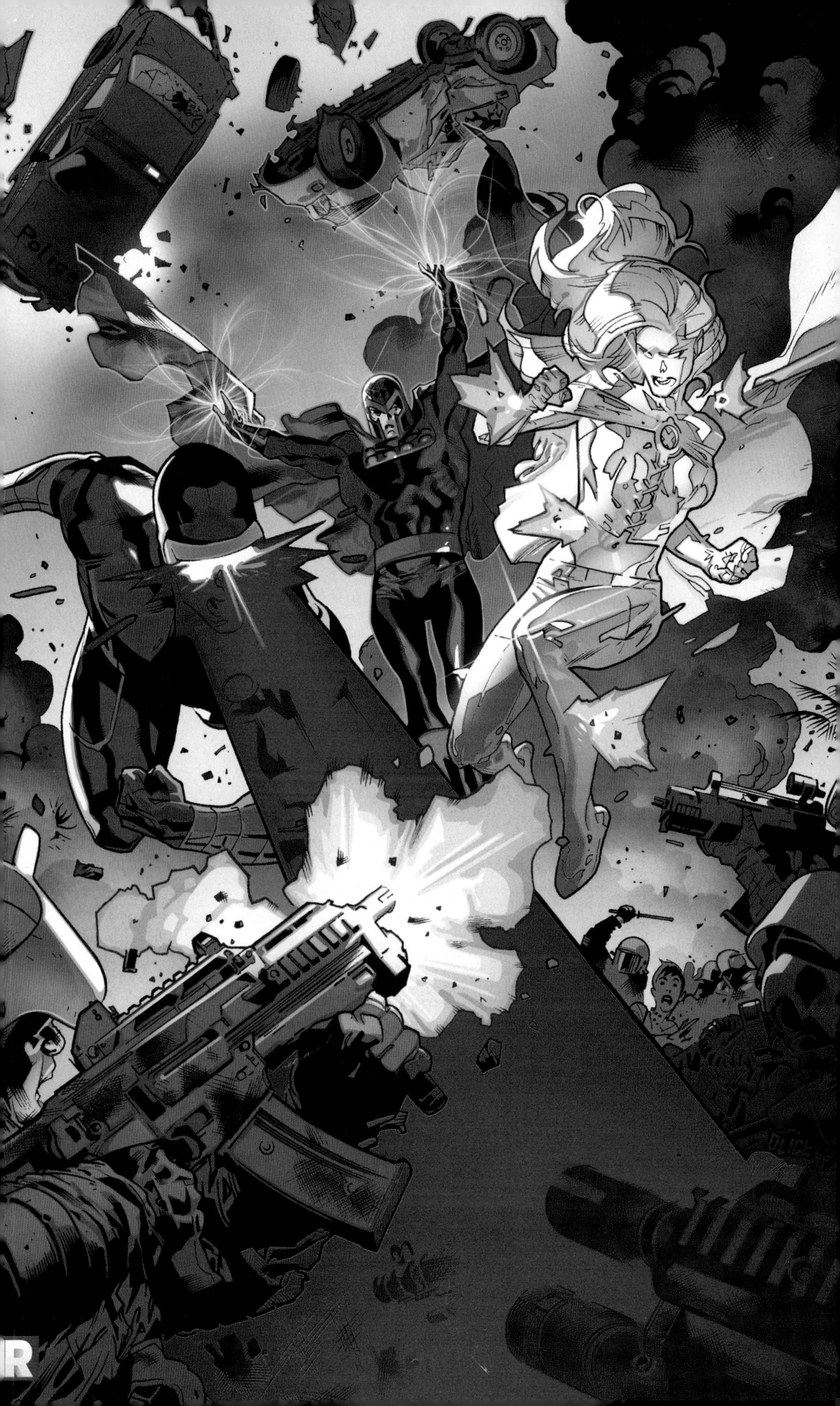
Police

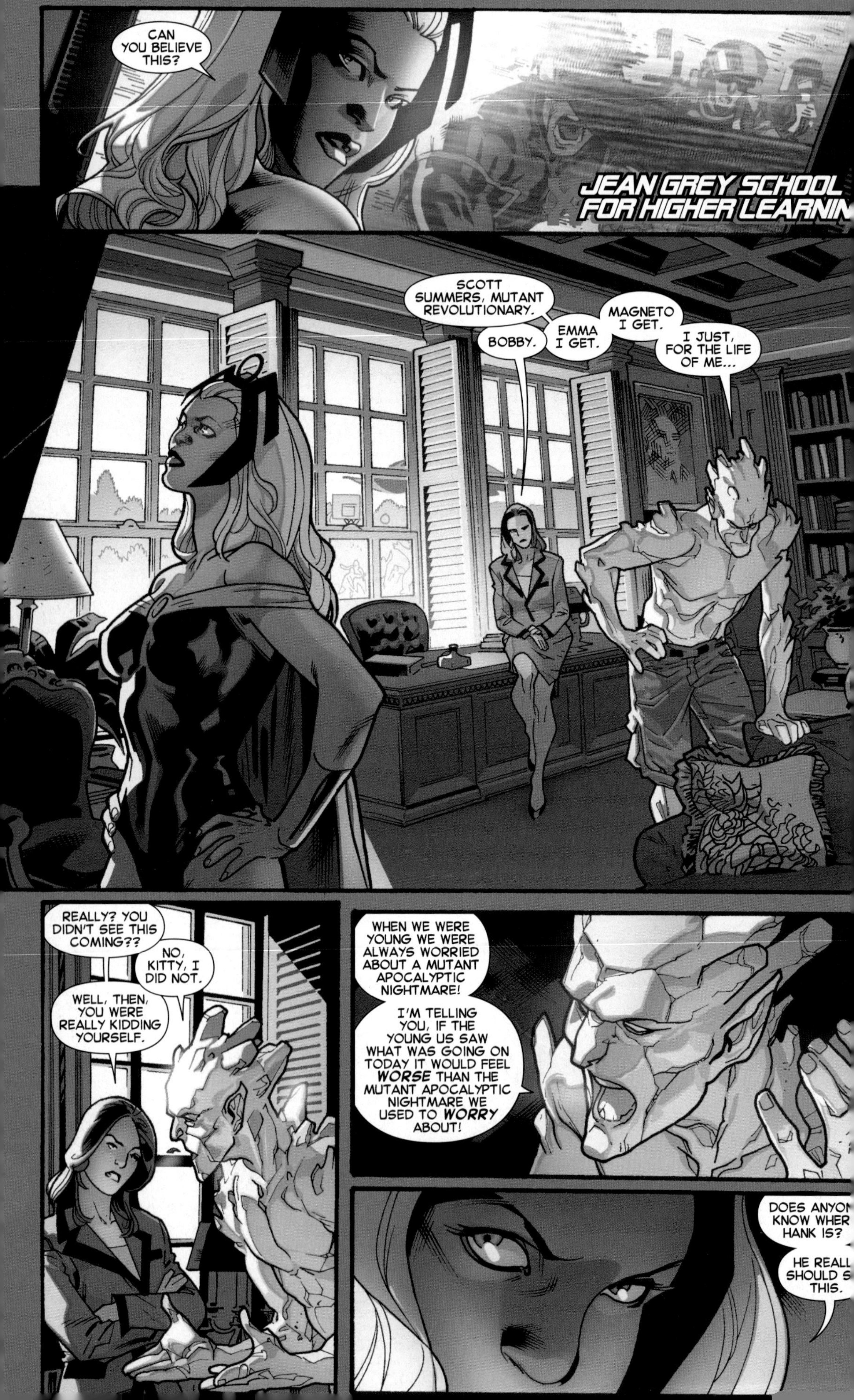
CAN YOU BELIEVE THIS?
JEAN GREY SCHOOL FOR HIGHER LEARNIN
SCOTT SUMMERS, MUTANT REVOLUTIONARY.
BOBBY.
EMMA I GET.
MAGNETO I GET.
I JUST, FOR THE LIFE OF ME...
REALLY? YOU DIDN'T SEE THIS COMING??
NO, KITTY, I DID NOT.
WELL, THEN, YOU WERE REALLY KIDDING YOURSELF.
WHEN WE WERE YOUNG WE WERE ALWAYS WORRIED ABOUT A MUTANT APOCALYPTIC NIGHTMARE!
I'M TELLING YOU, IF THE YOUNG US SAW WHAT WAS GOING ON TODAY IT WOULD FEEL WORSE THAN THE MUTANT APOCALYPTIC NIGHTMARE WE USED TO WORRY ABOUT!
DOES ANYON KNOW WHER HANK IS?
HE REALL SHOULD S THIS.

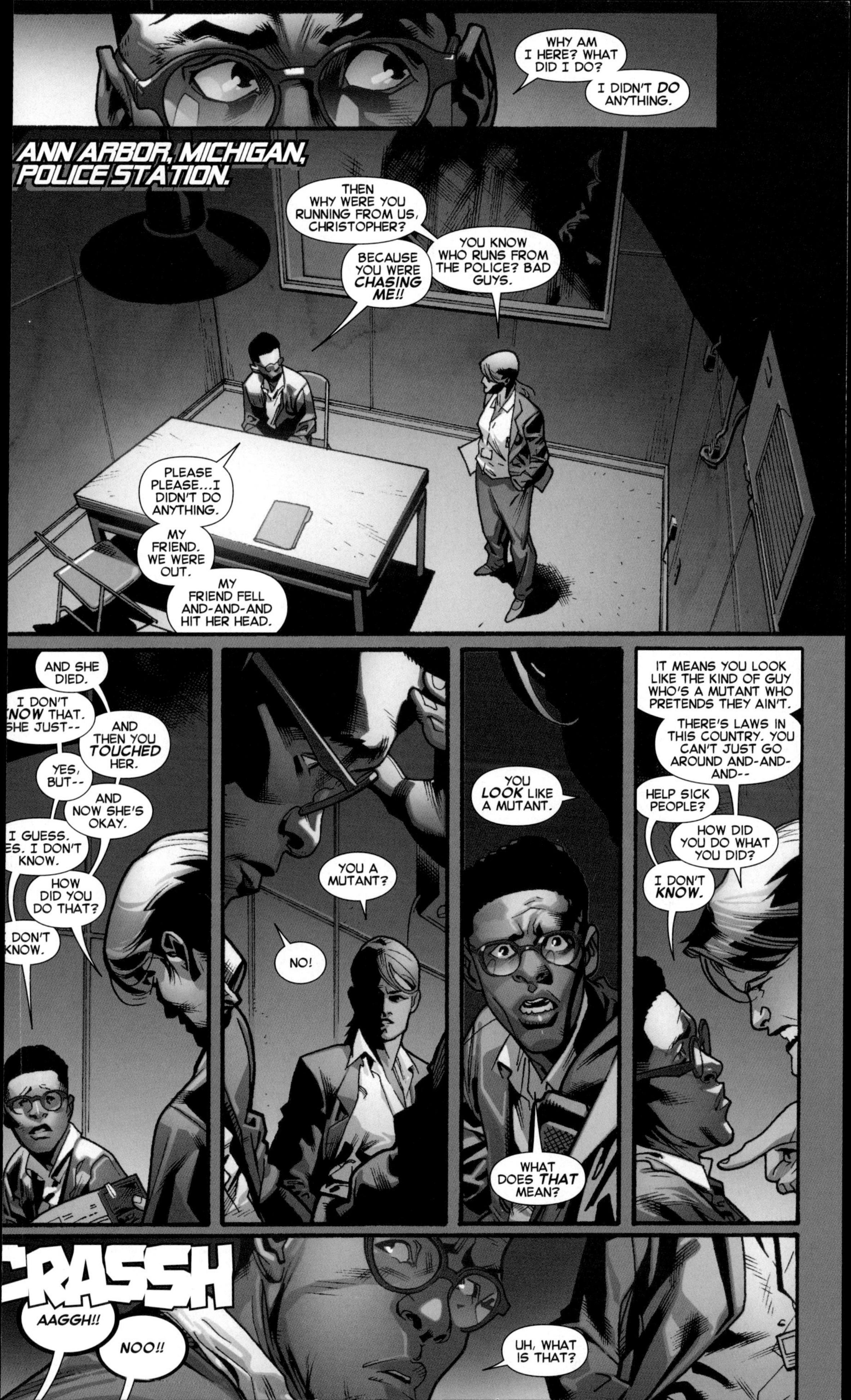
WHY AM I HERE? WHAT DID I DO?
I DIDN'T DO ANYTHING.
ANN ARBOR, MICHIGAN, POLICE STATION.
THEN WHY WERE YOU RUNNING FROM US, CHRISTOPHER?
BECAUSE YOU WERE CHASING ME!!
YOU KNOW WHO RUNS FROM THE POLICE? BAD GUYS.
PLEASE PLEASE...I DIDN'T DO ANYTHING.
MY FRIEND. WE WERE OUT.
MY FRIEND FELL AND-AND-AND HIT HER HEAD.
AND SHE DIED.
I DON'T KNOW THAT. SHE JUST--
AND THEN YOU TOUCHED HER.
YES, BUT--
AND NOW SHE'S OKAY.
I GUESS. YES. I DON'T KNOW.
HOW DID YOU DO THAT?
I DON'T KNOW.
YOU A MUTANT?
NO!
YOU LOOK LIKE A MUTANT.
WHAT DOES THAT MEAN?
IT MEANS YOU LOOK LIKE THE KIND OF GUY WHO'S A MUTANT WHO PRETENDS THEY AIN'T.
THERE'S LAWS IN THIS COUNTRY. YOU CAN'T JUST GO AROUND AND-AND-AND--
HELP SICK PEOPLE?
HOW DID YOU DO WHAT YOU DID?
I DON'T KNOW.
CRASSH
AAGGH!!
NOO!!
UH, WHAT IS THAT?

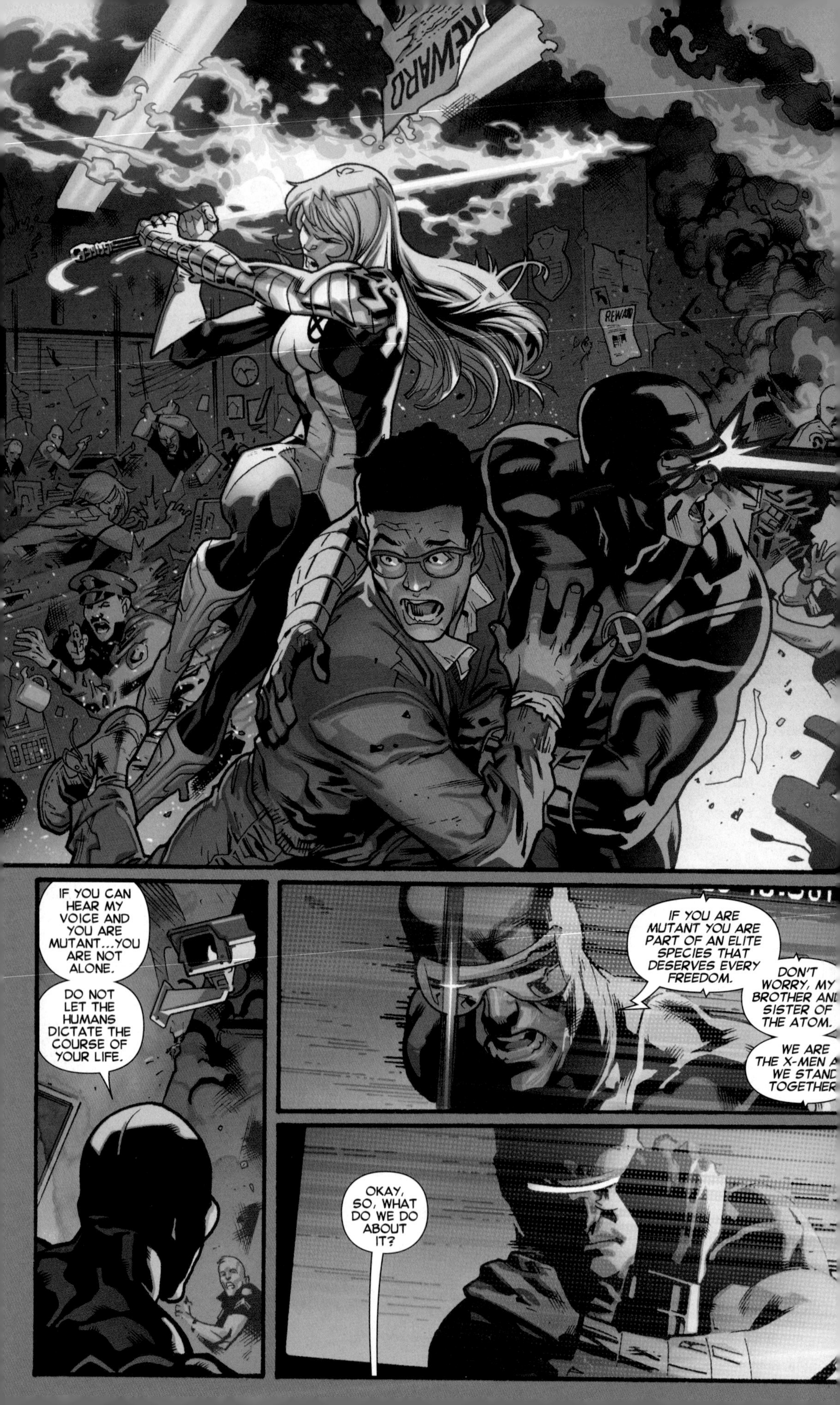

REWARD
REWARD
IF YOU CAN HEAR MY VOICE AND YOU ARE MUTANT...YOU ARE NOT ALONE.
DO NOT LET THE HUMANS DICTATE THE COURSE OF YOUR LIFE.
IF YOU ARE MUTANT YOU ARE PART OF AN ELITE SPECIES THAT DESERVES EVERY FREEDOM.
DON'T WORRY, MY BROTHER AND SISTER OF THE ATOM.
WE ARE THE X-MEN A WE STAND TOGETHER
OKAY, SO, WHAT DO WE DO ABOUT IT?

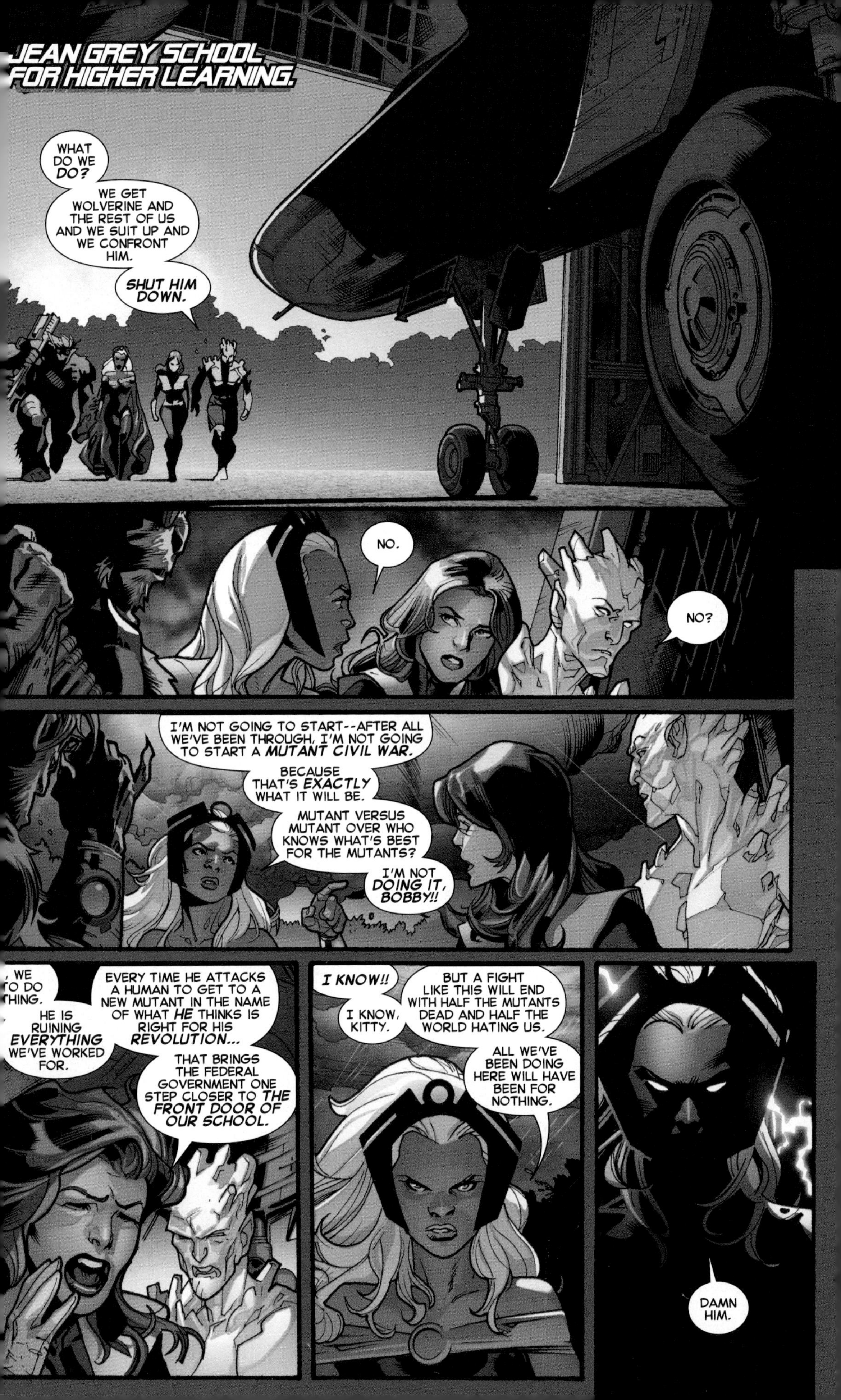

JEAN GREY SCHOOL FOR HIGHER LEARNING.
WHAT DO WE DO?
WE GET WOLVERINE AND THE REST OF US AND WE SUIT UP AND WE CONFRONT HIM.
SHUT HIM DOWN.
NO.
NO?
I'M NOT GOING TO START--AFTER ALL WE'VE BEEN THROUGH, I'M NOT GOING TO START A MUTANT CIVIL WAR.
BECAUSE THAT'S EXACTLY WHAT IT WILL BE.
MUTANT VERSUS MUTANT OVER WHO KNOWS WHAT'S BEST FOR THE MUTANTS?
I'M NOT DOING IT, BOBBY!!
, WE O DO HING.
HE IS RUINING EVERYTHING WE'VE WORKED FOR.
EVERY TIME HE ATTACKS A HUMAN TO GET TO A NEW MUTANT IN THE NAME OF WHAT HE THINKS IS RIGHT FOR HIS REVOLUTION...
THAT BRINGS THE FEDERAL GOVERNMENT ONE STEP CLOSER TO THE FRONT DOOR OF OUR SCHOOL.
I KNOW!!
I KNOW, KITTY.
BUT A FIGHT LIKE THIS WILL END WITH HALF THE MUTANTS DEAD AND HALF THE WORLD HATING US.
ALL WE'VE BEEN DOING HERE WILL HAVE BEEN FOR NOTHING.
DAMN HIM.

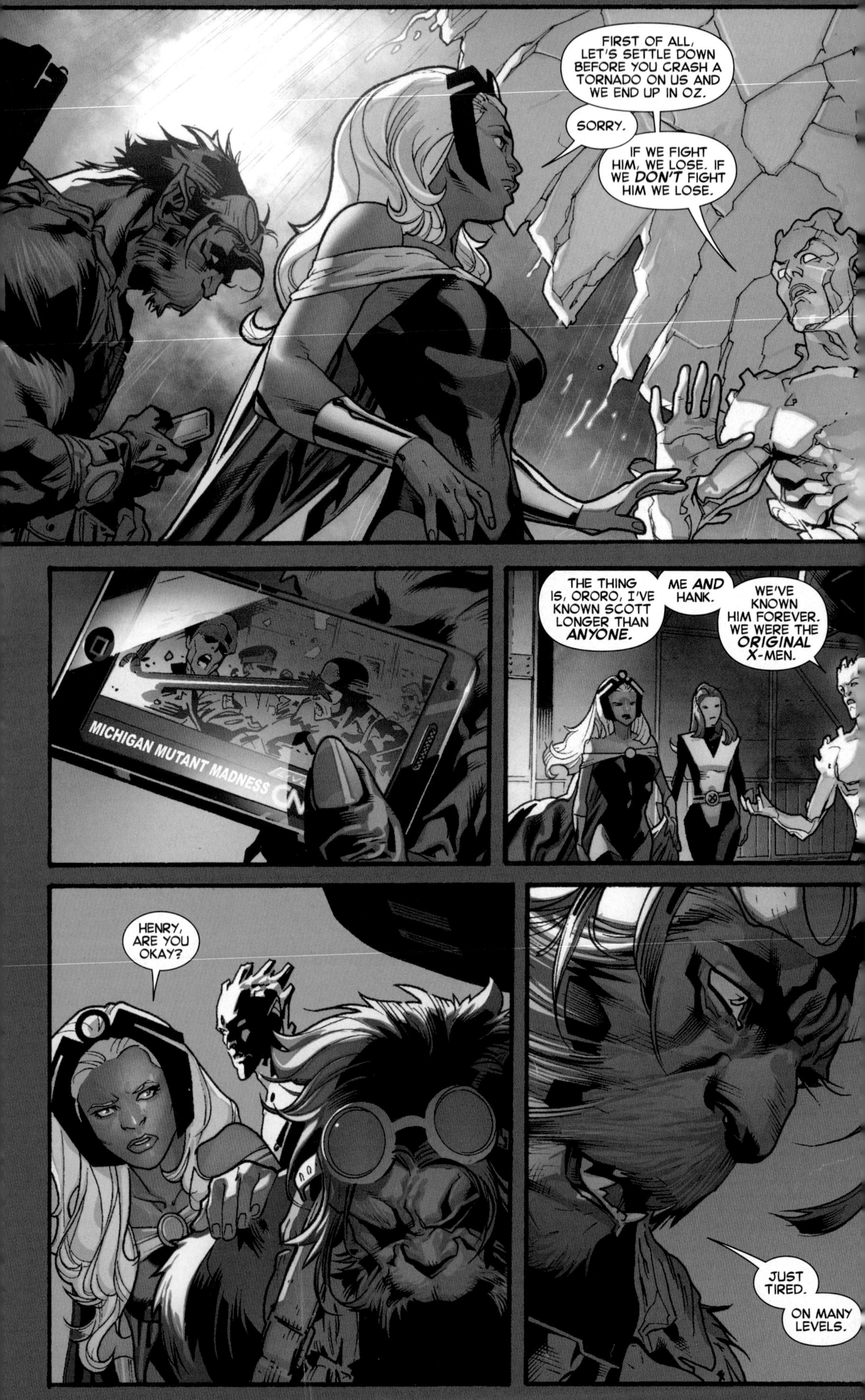
FIRST OF ALL, LET'S SETTLE DOWN BEFORE YOU CRASH A TORNADO ON US AND WE END UP IN OZ.
SORRY.
IF WE FIGHT HIM, WE LOSE. IF WE DON'T FIGHT HIM WE LOSE.
MICHIGAN MUTANT MADNESS
THE THING IS, ORORO, I'VE KNOWN SCOTT LONGER THAN ANYONE.
ME AND HANK.
WE'VE KNOWN HIM FOREVER. WE WERE THE ORIGINAL X-MEN.
HENRY, ARE YOU OKAY?
JUST TIRED.
ON MANY LEVELS.

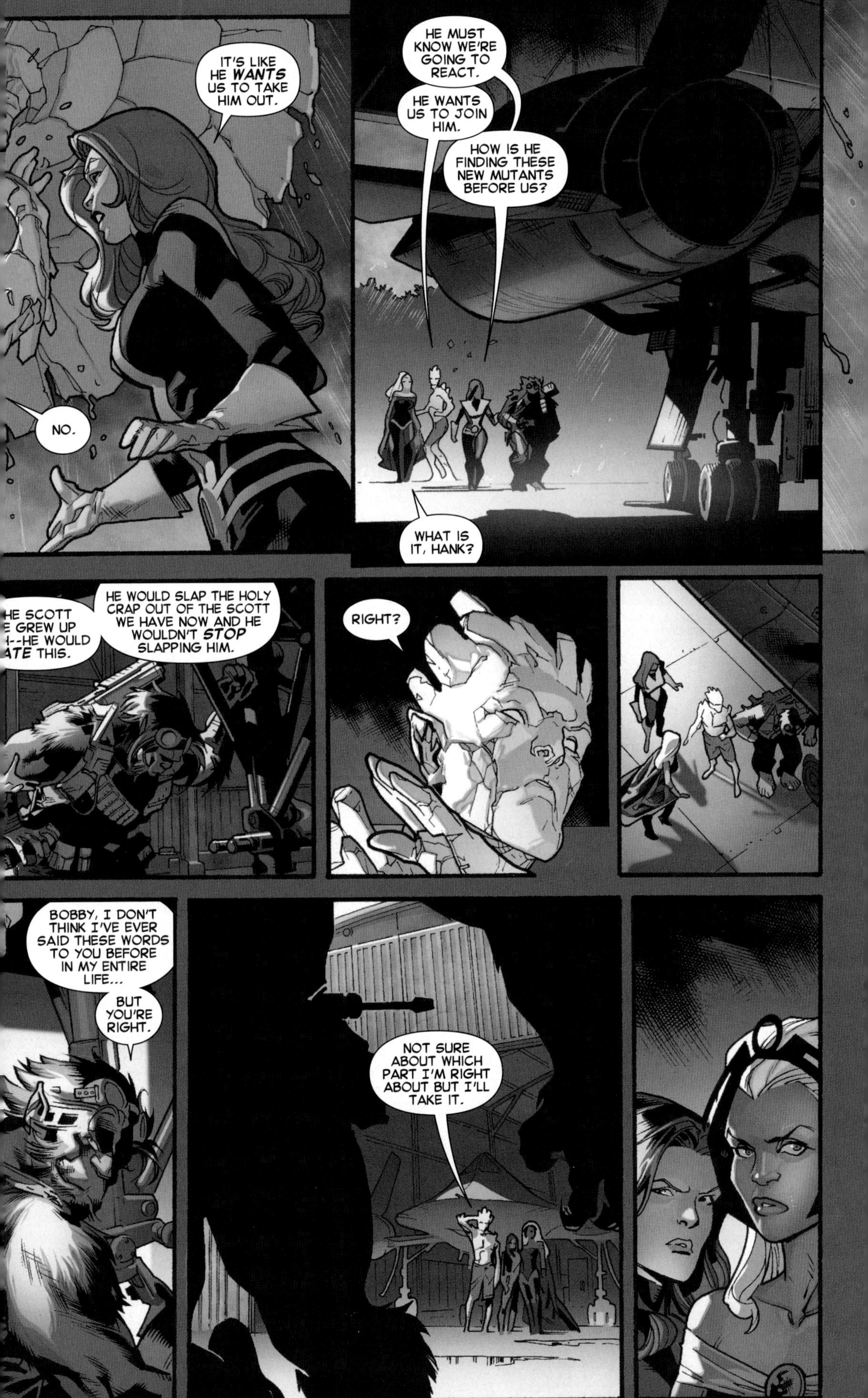
IT'S LIKE HE WANTS US TO TAKE HIM OUT.
NO.
HE MUST KNOW WE'RE GOING TO REACT.
HE WANTS US TO JOIN HIM.
HOW IS HE FINDING THESE NEW MUTANTS BEFORE US?
WHAT IS IT, HANK?
HE SCOTT E GREW UP H--HE WOULD ATE THIS.
HE WOULD SLAP THE HOLY CRAP OUT OF THE SCOTT WE HAVE NOW AND HE WOULDN'T STOP SLAPPING HIM.
RIGHT?
BOBBY, I DON'T THINK I'VE EVER SAID THESE WORDS TO YOU BEFORE IN MY ENTIRE LIFE...
BUT YOU'RE RIGHT.
NOT SURE ABOUT WHICH PART I'M RIGHT ABOUT BUT I'LL TAKE IT.

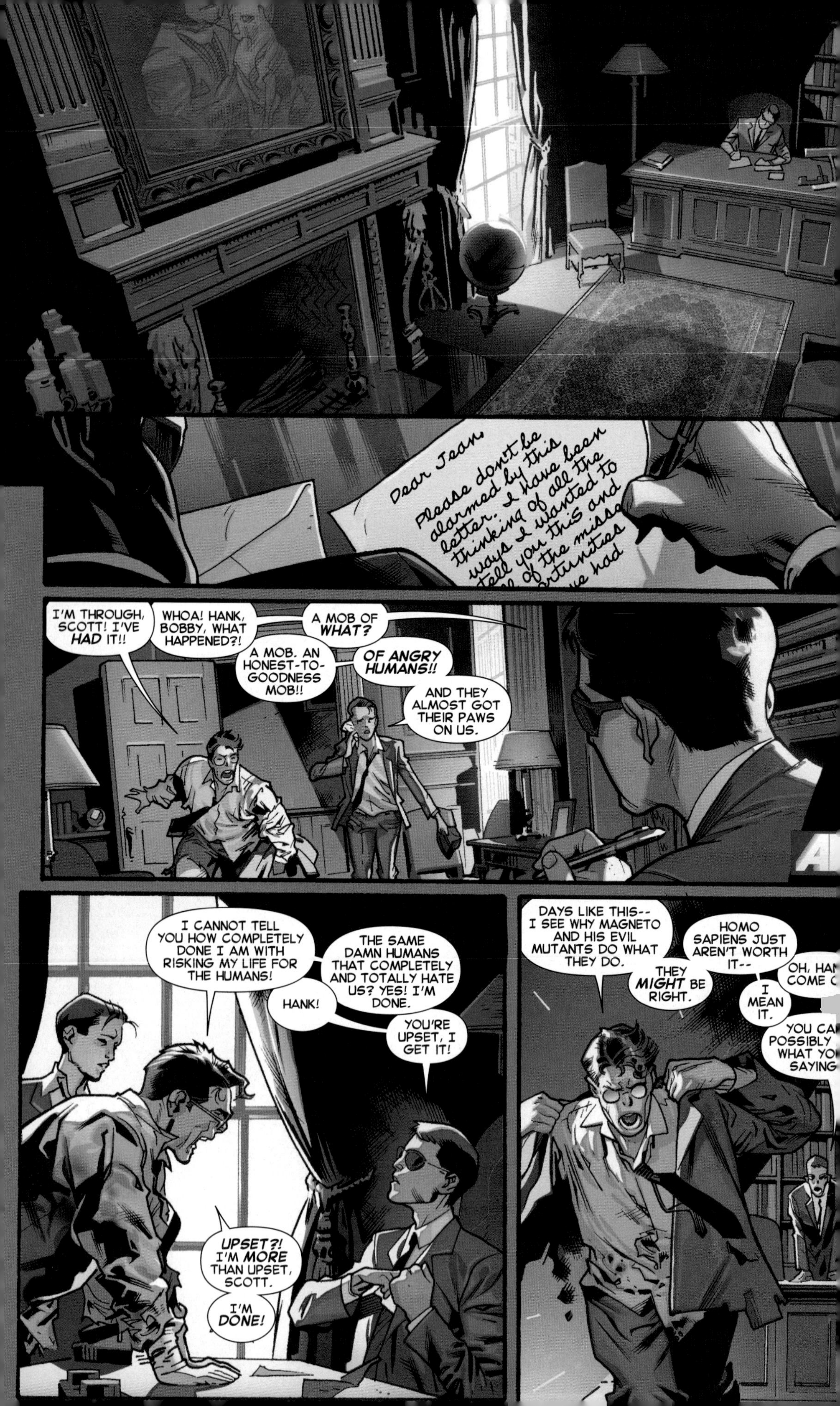

Dear Jean,
Please don't be alarmed by this letter. I have been thinking of all the ways I wanted to tell you this and
I'M THROUGH, SCOTT! I'VE *HAD* IT!!
WHOA! HANK, BOBBY, WHAT HAPPENED?!
A MOB. AN HONEST-TO-GOODNESS MOB!!
A MOB OF *WHAT?*
OF ANGRY HUMANS!!
AND THEY ALMOST GOT THEIR PAWS ON US.
I CANNOT TELL YOU HOW COMPLETELY DONE I AM WITH RISKING MY LIFE FOR THE HUMANS!
THE SAME DAMN HUMANS THAT COMPLETELY AND TOTALLY HATE US? YES! I'M DONE.
HANK!
YOU'RE UPSET, I GET IT!
UPSET?! I'M *MORE* THAN UPSET, SCOTT.
I'M *DONE!*
DAYS LIKE THIS-- I SEE WHY MAGNETO AND HIS EVIL MUTANTS DO WHAT THEY DO.
THEY *MIGHT* BE RIGHT.
HOMO SAPIENS JUST AREN'T WORTH IT--
OH, HAN
COME C
I MEAN IT.
YOU CA
POSSIBLY
WHAT YO
SAYING

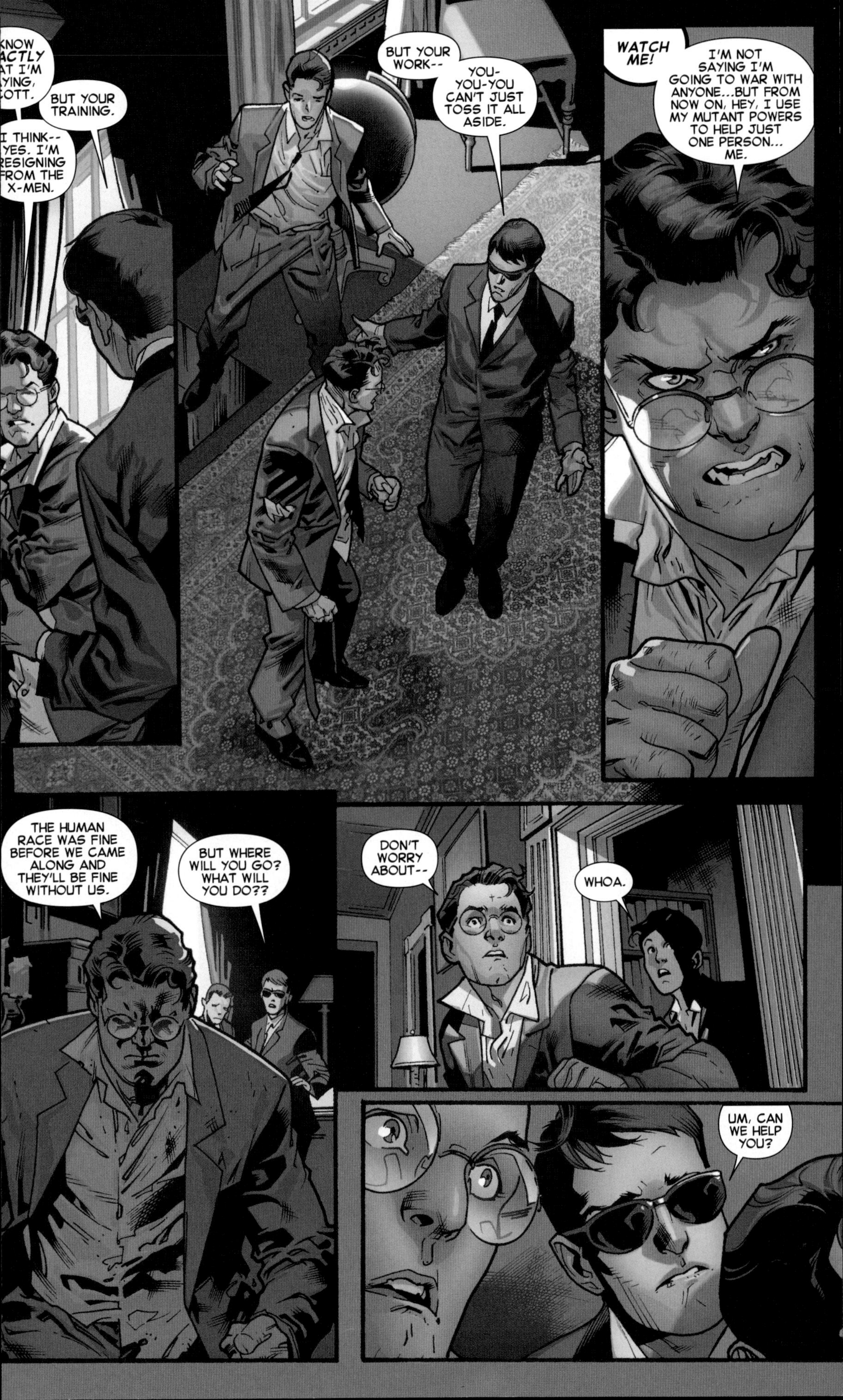
KNOW ACTLY AT I'M YING, OTT.
BUT YOUR TRAINING.
I THINK-- YES. I'M RESIGNING FROM THE X-MEN.
BUT YOUR WORK--
YOU- YOU-YOU CAN'T JUST TOSS IT ALL ASIDE.
WATCH ME!
I'M NOT SAYING I'M GOING TO WAR WITH ANYONE...BUT FROM NOW ON, HEY, I USE MY MUTANT POWERS TO HELP JUST ONE PERSON... ME.
THE HUMAN RACE WAS FINE BEFORE WE CAME ALONG AND THEY'LL BE FINE WITHOUT US.
BUT WHERE WILL YOU GO? WHAT WILL YOU DO??
DON'T WORRY ABOUT--
WHOA.
UM, CAN WE HELP YOU?

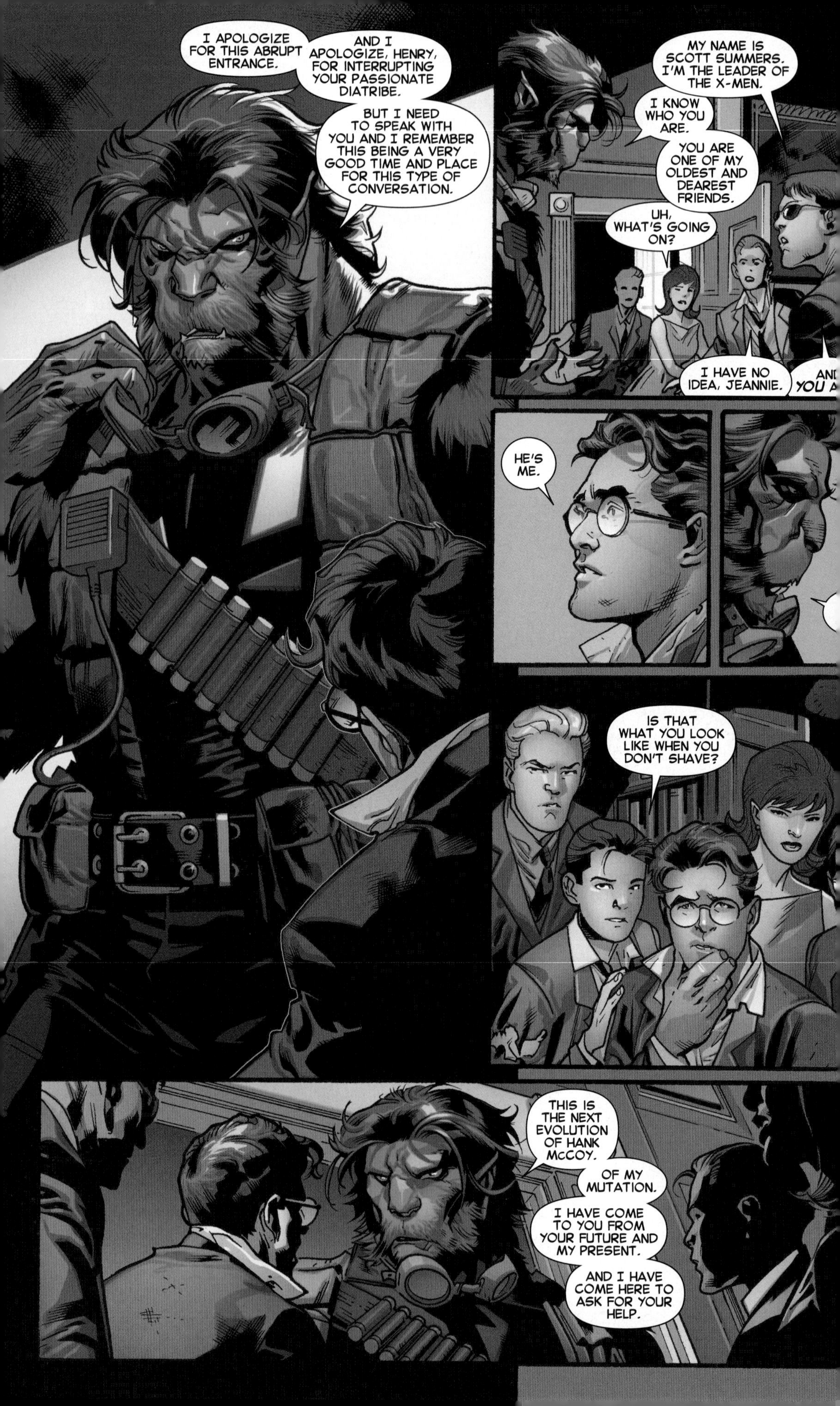
I APOLOGIZE FOR THIS ABRUPT ENTRANCE.
AND I APOLOGIZE, HENRY, FOR INTERRUPTING YOUR PASSIONATE DIATRIBE.
BUT I NEED TO SPEAK WITH YOU AND I REMEMBER THIS BEING A VERY GOOD TIME AND PLACE FOR THIS TYPE OF CONVERSATION.
MY NAME IS SCOTT SUMMERS. I'M THE LEADER OF THE X-MEN.
I KNOW WHO YOU ARE.
YOU ARE ONE OF MY OLDEST AND DEAREST FRIENDS.
UH, WHAT'S GOING ON?
I HAVE NO IDEA, JEANNIE.
HE'S ME.
IS THAT WHAT YOU LOOK LIKE WHEN YOU DON'T SHAVE?
THIS IS THE NEXT EVOLUTION OF HANK McCOY.
OF MY MUTATION.
I HAVE COME TO YOU FROM YOUR FUTURE AND MY PRESENT.
AND I HAVE COME HERE TO ASK FOR YOUR HELP.

I'M...GOING TO CALL THE PROFESSOR...

I ACTUALLY WOULD ADVISE AGAINST THAT.

HE WOULD NEVER APPROVE OF DOING WHAT I'M ABOUT TO ASK YOU TO DO.

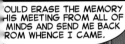

...OULD ERASE THE MEMORY ...HIS MEETING FROM ALL OF ...MINDS AND SEND ME BACK ...ROM WHENCE I CAME.

HANK, WHAT IS-- IS THIS TRUE?

FOR YOU/US TO BREAK THE PROTOCOLS OF THE SPACE-TIME CONTINUUM...

YES. THINGS ARE NOT GOING WELL FOR US.

NO.

IS IT OUR KIDS?

IT'S YOU, SCOTT.

I NEED YOU TO COME TO MY PRESENT DAY AND I NEED YOU TO TALK TO YOURSELF.

I NEED YOU TO STOP YOURSELF FROM COMMITTING MUTANT GENOCIDE.

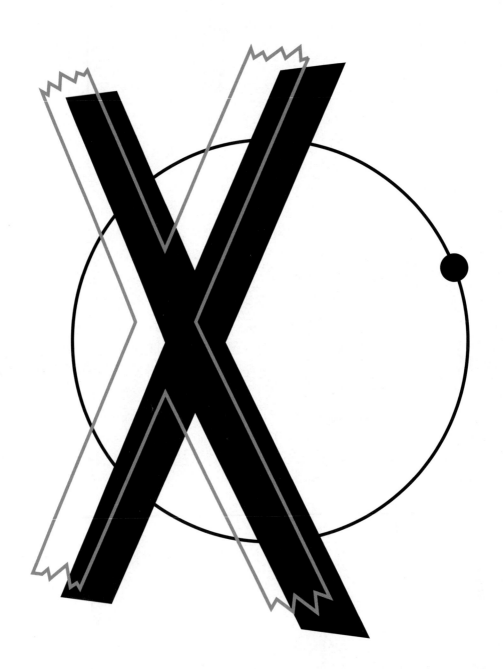

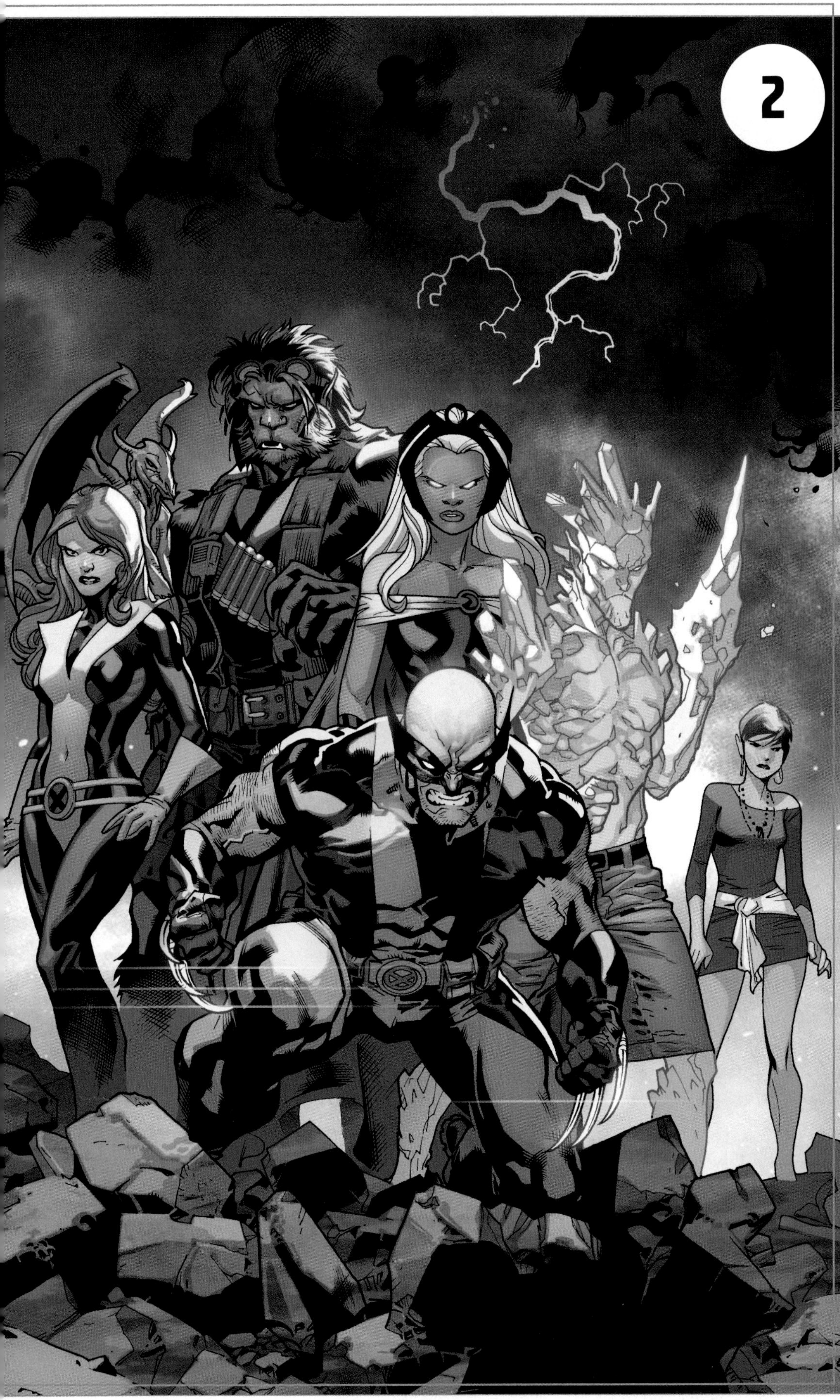
2

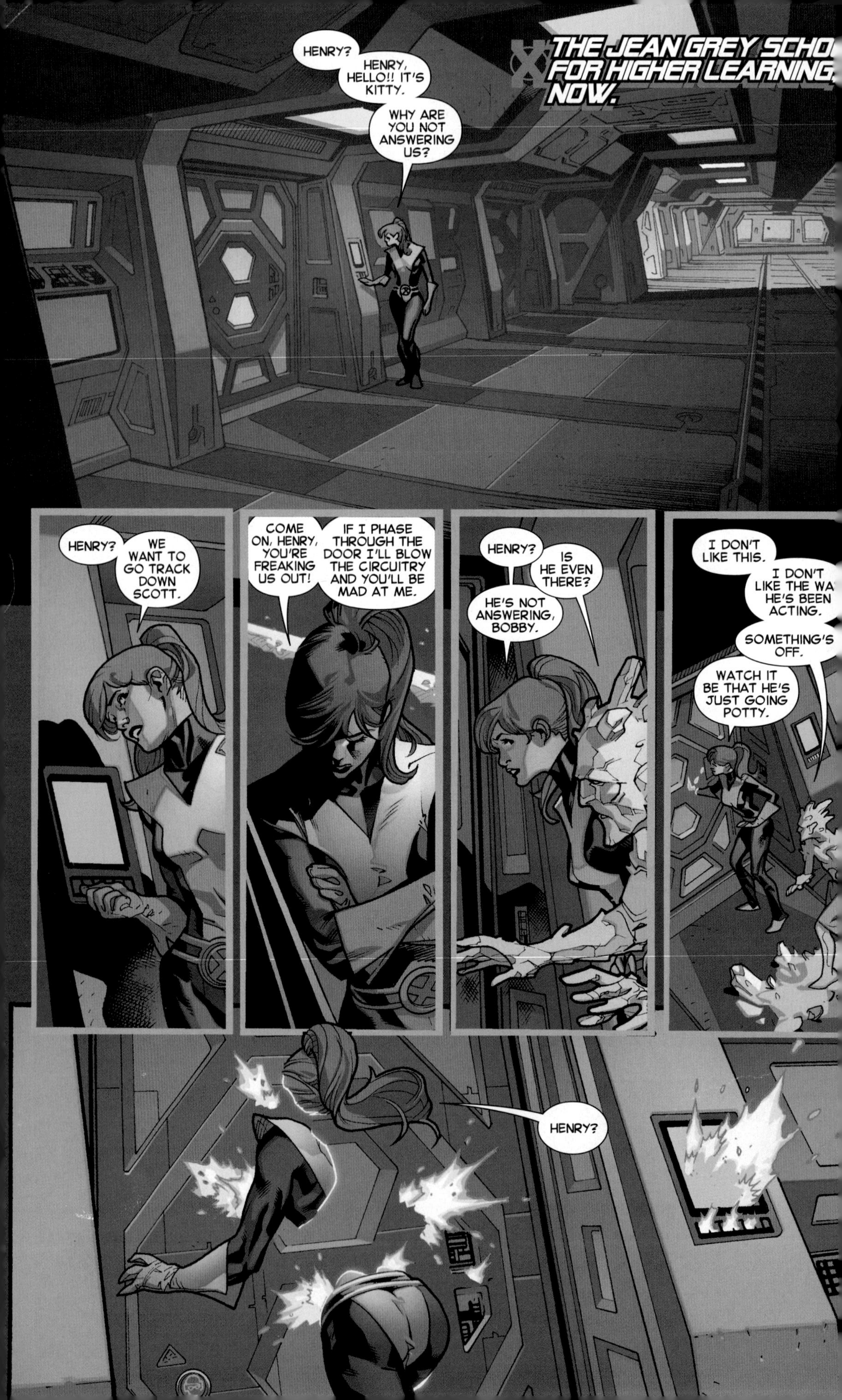
HENRY?
HENRY, HELLO!! IT'S KITTY.
WHY ARE YOU NOT ANSWERING US?
THE JEAN GREY SCHO
FOR HIGHER LEARNING,
NOW.
HENRY?
WE WANT TO GO TRACK DOWN SCOTT.
COME ON, HENRY, YOU'RE FREAKING US OUT!
IF I PHASE THROUGH THE DOOR I'LL BLOW THE CIRCUITRY AND YOU'LL BE MAD AT ME.
HENRY?
IS HE EVEN THERE?
HE'S NOT ANSWERING, BOBBY.
I DON'T LIKE THIS.
I DON'T LIKE THE WA
HE'S BEEN ACTING.
SOMETHING'S OFF.
WATCH IT BE THAT HE'S JUST GOING POTTY.
HENRY?

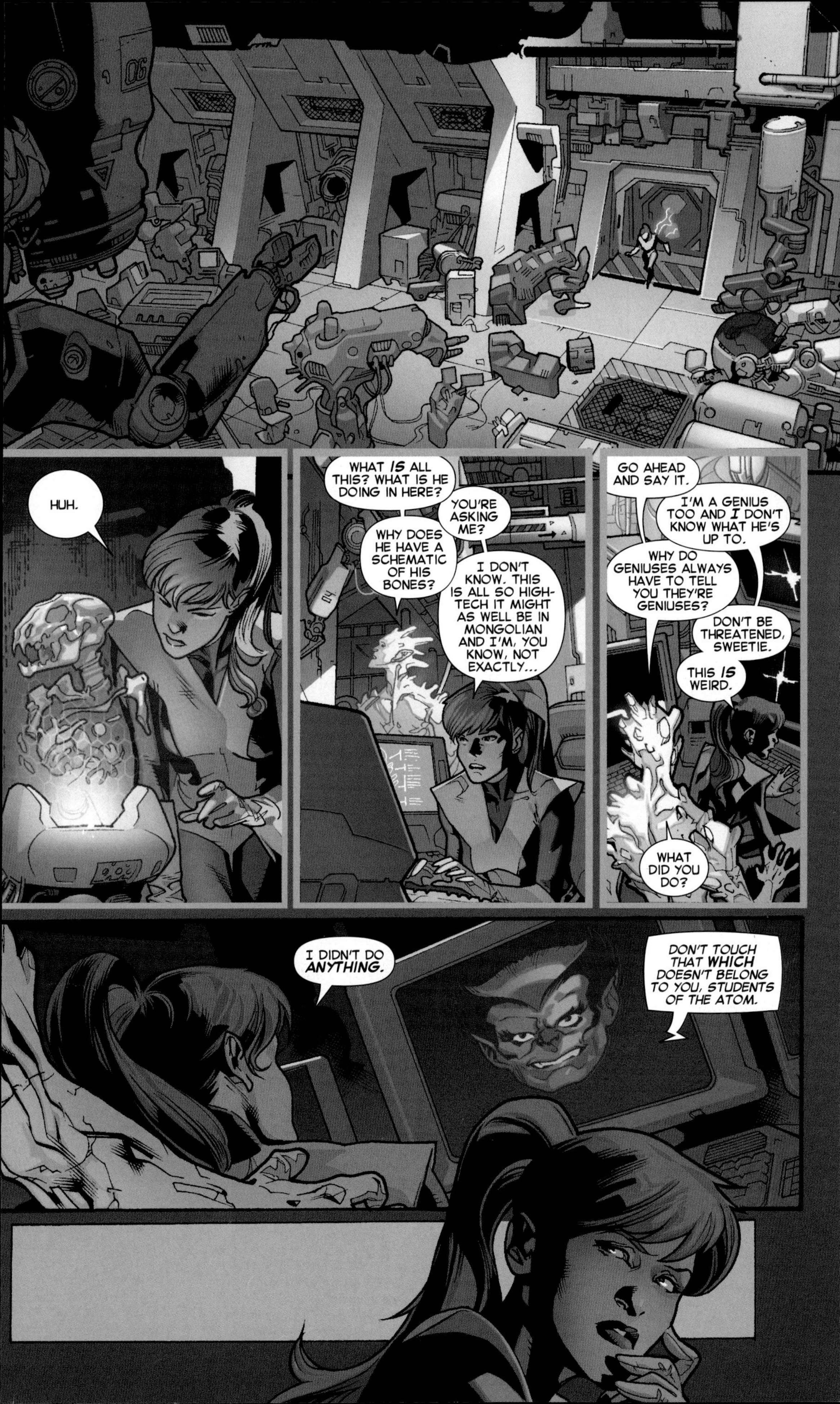
HUH.
WHAT IS ALL THIS? WHAT IS HE DOING IN HERE?
WHY DOES HE HAVE A SCHEMATIC OF HIS BONES?
YOU'RE ASKING ME?
I DON'T KNOW. THIS IS ALL SO HIGH-TECH IT MIGHT AS WELL BE IN MONGOLIAN AND I'M, YOU KNOW, NOT EXACTLY...
GO AHEAD AND SAY IT.
I'M A GENIUS TOO AND I DON'T KNOW WHAT HE'S UP TO.
WHY DO GENIUSES ALWAYS HAVE TO TELL YOU THEY'RE GENIUSES?
DON'T BE THREATENED, SWEETIE.
THIS IS WEIRD.
WHAT DID YOU DO?
I DIDN'T DO ANYTHING.
DON'T TOUCH THAT WHICH DOESN'T BELONG TO YOU, STUDENTS OF THE ATOM.

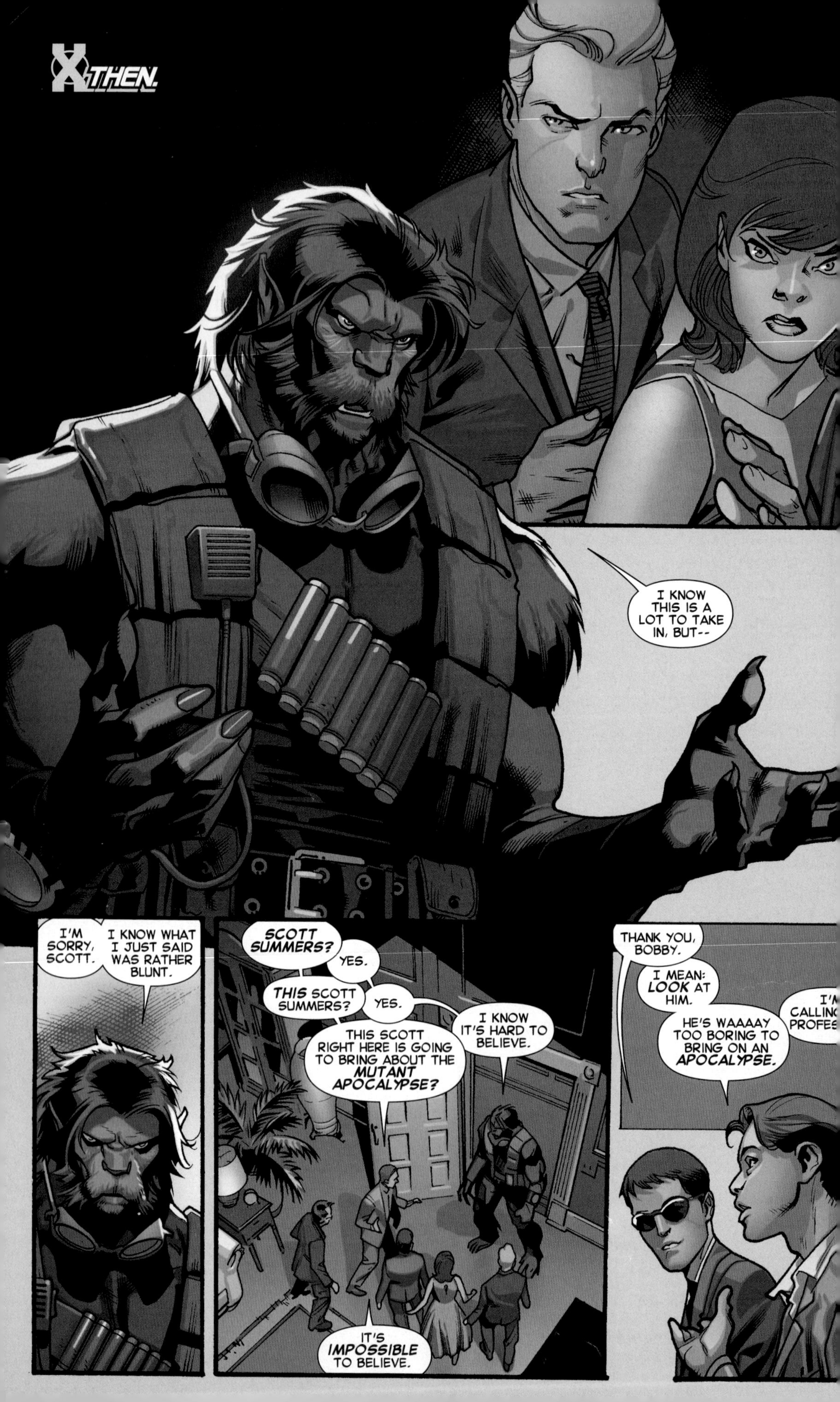

THEN.
I KNOW THIS IS A LOT TO TAKE IN, BUT--
I'M SORRY, SCOTT.
I KNOW WHAT I JUST SAID WAS RATHER BLUNT.
SCOTT SUMMERS?
YES.
THIS SCOTT SUMMERS?
YES.
THIS SCOTT RIGHT HERE IS GOING TO BRING ABOUT THE MUTANT APOCALYPSE?
I KNOW IT'S HARD TO BELIEVE.
IT'S IMPOSSIBLE TO BELIEVE.
THANK YOU, BOBBY.
I MEAN: LOOK AT HIM.
HE'S WAAAAY TOO BORING TO BRING ON AN APOCALYPSE.

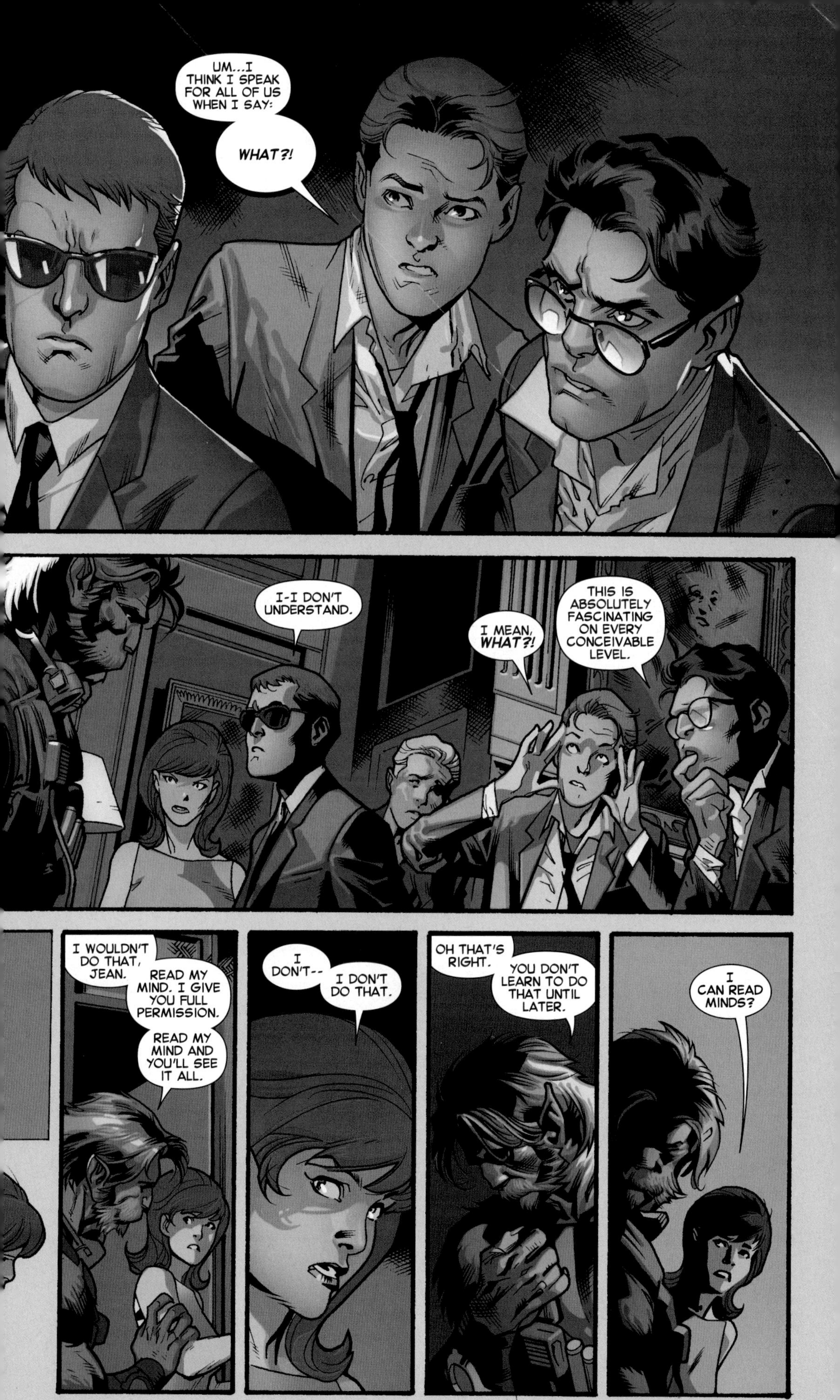
UM...I THINK I SPEAK FOR ALL OF US WHEN I SAY:
WHAT?!
I-I DON'T UNDERSTAND.
I MEAN, WHAT?!
THIS IS ABSOLUTELY FASCINATING ON EVERY CONCEIVABLE LEVEL.
I WOULDN'T DO THAT, JEAN.
READ MY MIND. I GIVE YOU FULL PERMISSION.
READ MY MIND AND YOU'LL SEE IT ALL.
I DON'T--
I DON'T DO THAT.
OH THAT'S RIGHT.
YOU DON'T LEARN TO DO THAT UNTIL LATER.
I CAN READ MINDS?

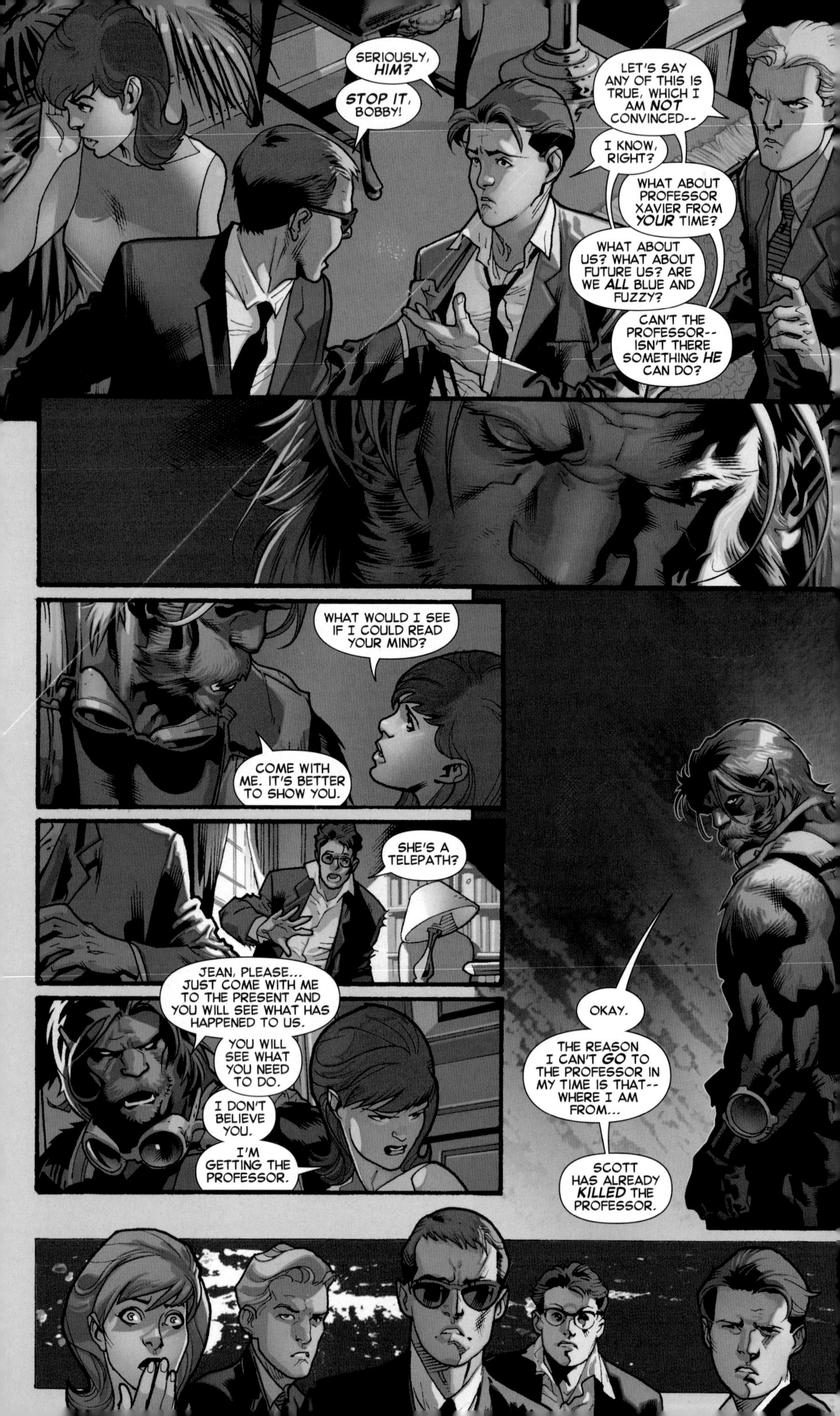
SERIOUSLY, HIM?
STOP IT, BOBBY!
LET'S SAY ANY OF THIS IS TRUE, WHICH I AM NOT CONVINCED--
I KNOW, RIGHT?
WHAT ABOUT PROFESSOR XAVIER FROM YOUR TIME?
WHAT ABOUT US? WHAT ABOUT FUTURE US? ARE WE ALL BLUE AND FUZZY?
CAN'T THE PROFESSOR-- ISN'T THERE SOMETHING HE CAN DO?
WHAT WOULD I SEE IF I COULD READ YOUR MIND?
COME WITH ME. IT'S BETTER TO SHOW YOU.
SHE'S A TELEPATH?
JEAN, PLEASE... JUST COME WITH ME TO THE PRESENT AND YOU WILL SEE WHAT HAS HAPPENED TO US.
YOU WILL SEE WHAT YOU NEED TO DO.
I DON'T BELIEVE YOU.
I'M GETTING THE PROFESSOR.
OKAY.
THE REASON I CAN'T GO TO THE PROFESSOR IN MY TIME IS THAT-- WHERE I AM FROM...
SCOTT HAS ALREADY KILLED THE PROFESSOR.

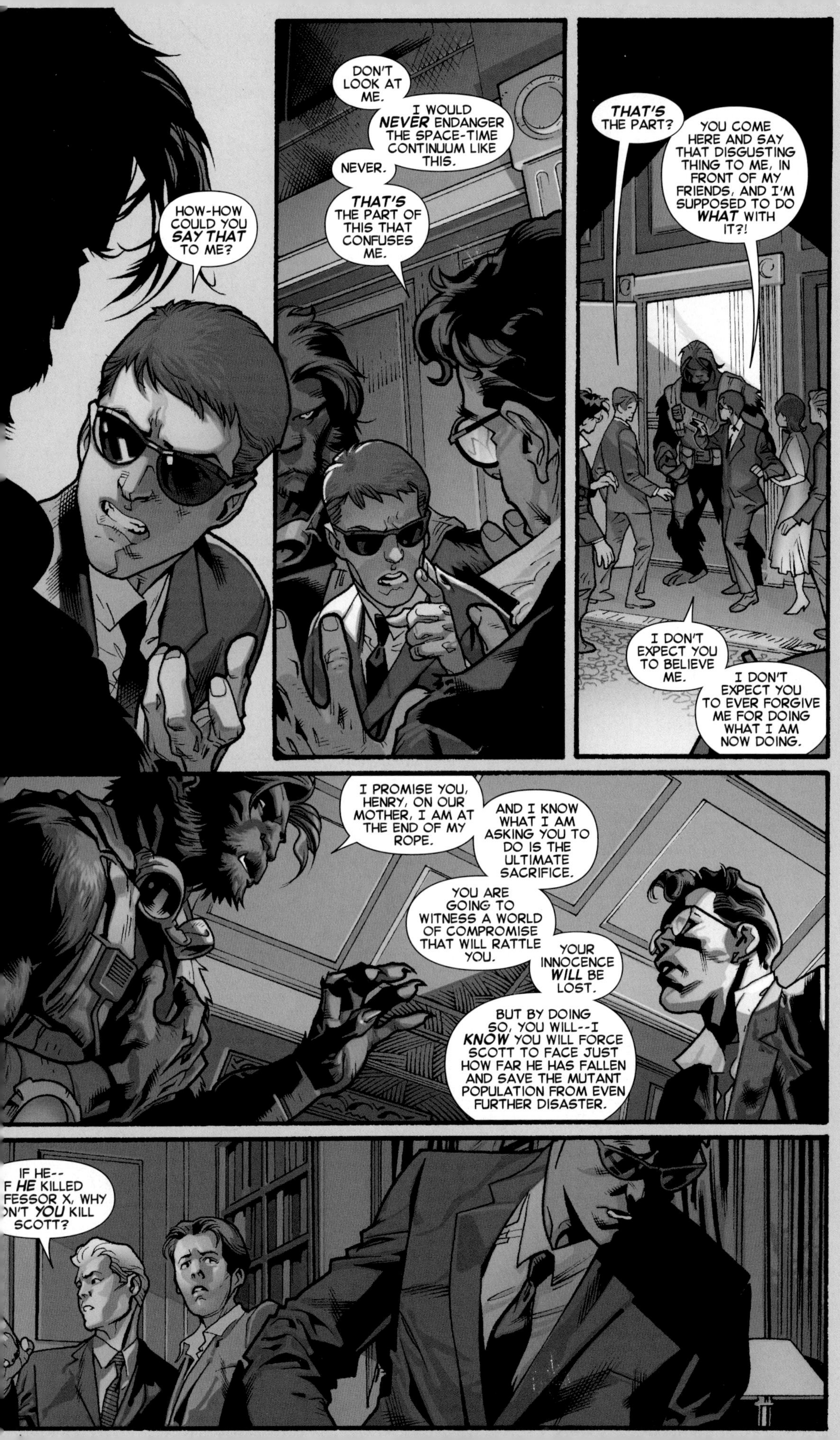
HOW-HOW COULD YOU SAY THAT TO ME?
DON'T LOOK AT ME.
I WOULD NEVER ENDANGER THE SPACE-TIME CONTINUUM LIKE THIS.
NEVER.
THAT'S THE PART OF THIS THAT CONFUSES ME.
THAT'S THE PART?
YOU COME HERE AND SAY THAT DISGUSTING THING TO ME, IN FRONT OF MY FRIENDS, AND I'M SUPPOSED TO DO WHAT WITH IT?!
I DON'T EXPECT YOU TO BELIEVE ME.
I DON'T EXPECT YOU TO EVER FORGIVE ME FOR DOING WHAT I AM NOW DOING.
I PROMISE YOU, HENRY, ON OUR MOTHER, I AM AT THE END OF MY ROPE.
AND I KNOW WHAT I AM ASKING YOU TO DO IS THE ULTIMATE SACRIFICE.
YOU ARE GOING TO WITNESS A WORLD OF COMPROMISE THAT WILL RATTLE YOU.
YOUR INNOCENCE WILL BE LOST.
BUT BY DOING SO, YOU WILL--I KNOW YOU WILL FORCE SCOTT TO FACE JUST HOW FAR HE HAS FALLEN AND SAVE THE MUTANT POPULATION FROM EVEN FURTHER DISASTER.
IF HE-- F HE KILLED FESSOR X, WHY N'T YOU KILL SCOTT?

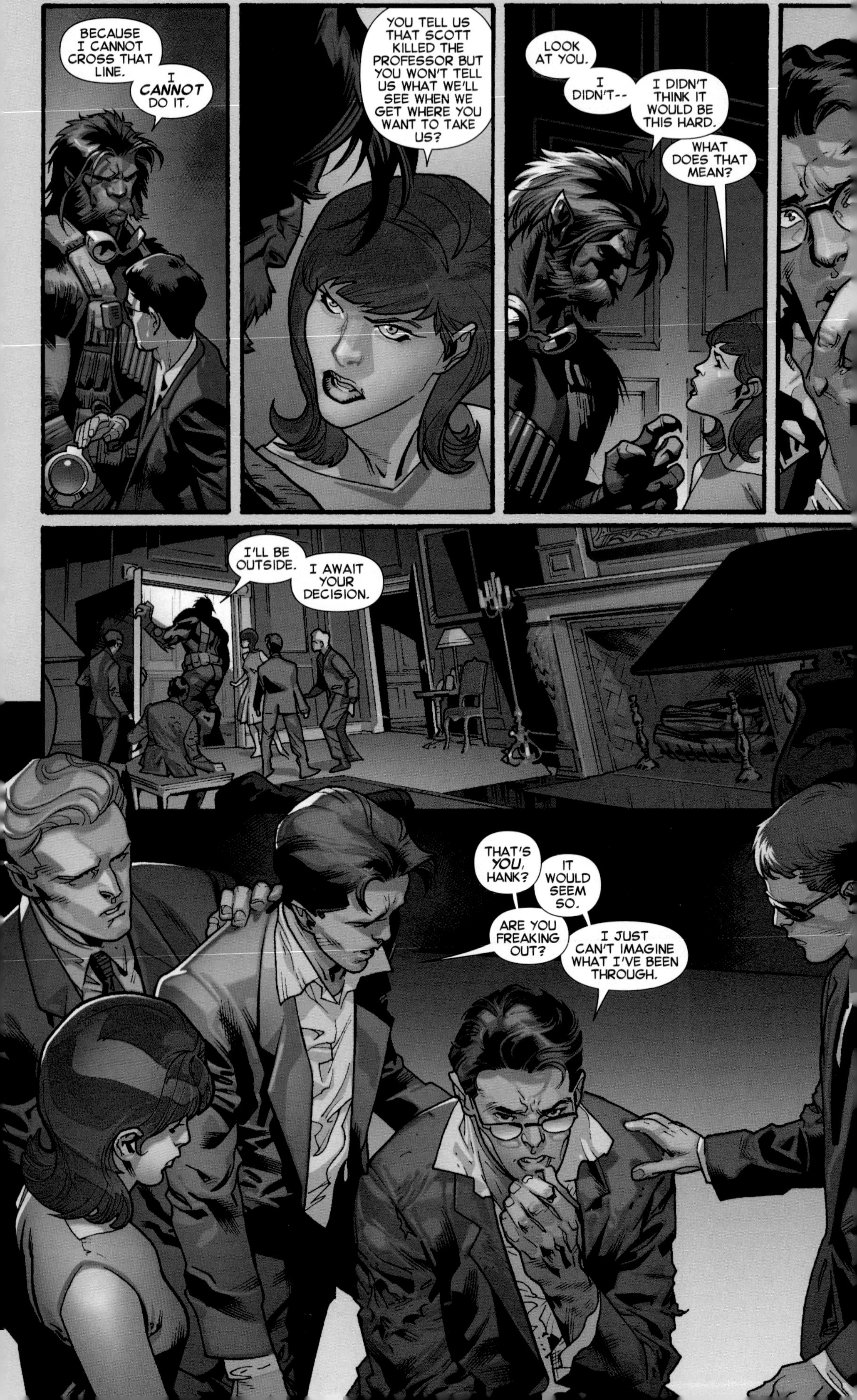
BECAUSE I CANNOT CROSS THAT LINE.
I *CANNOT* DO IT.
YOU TELL US THAT SCOTT KILLED THE PROFESSOR BUT YOU WON'T TELL US WHAT WE'LL SEE WHEN WE GET WHERE YOU WANT TO TAKE US?
LOOK AT YOU.
I DIDN'T--
I DIDN'T THINK IT WOULD BE THIS HARD.
WHAT DOES THAT MEAN?
I'LL BE OUTSIDE.
I AWAIT YOUR DECISION.
THAT'S *YOU*, HANK?
IT WOULD SEEM SO.
ARE YOU FREAKING OUT?
I JUST CAN'T IMAGINE WHAT I'VE BEEN THROUGH.

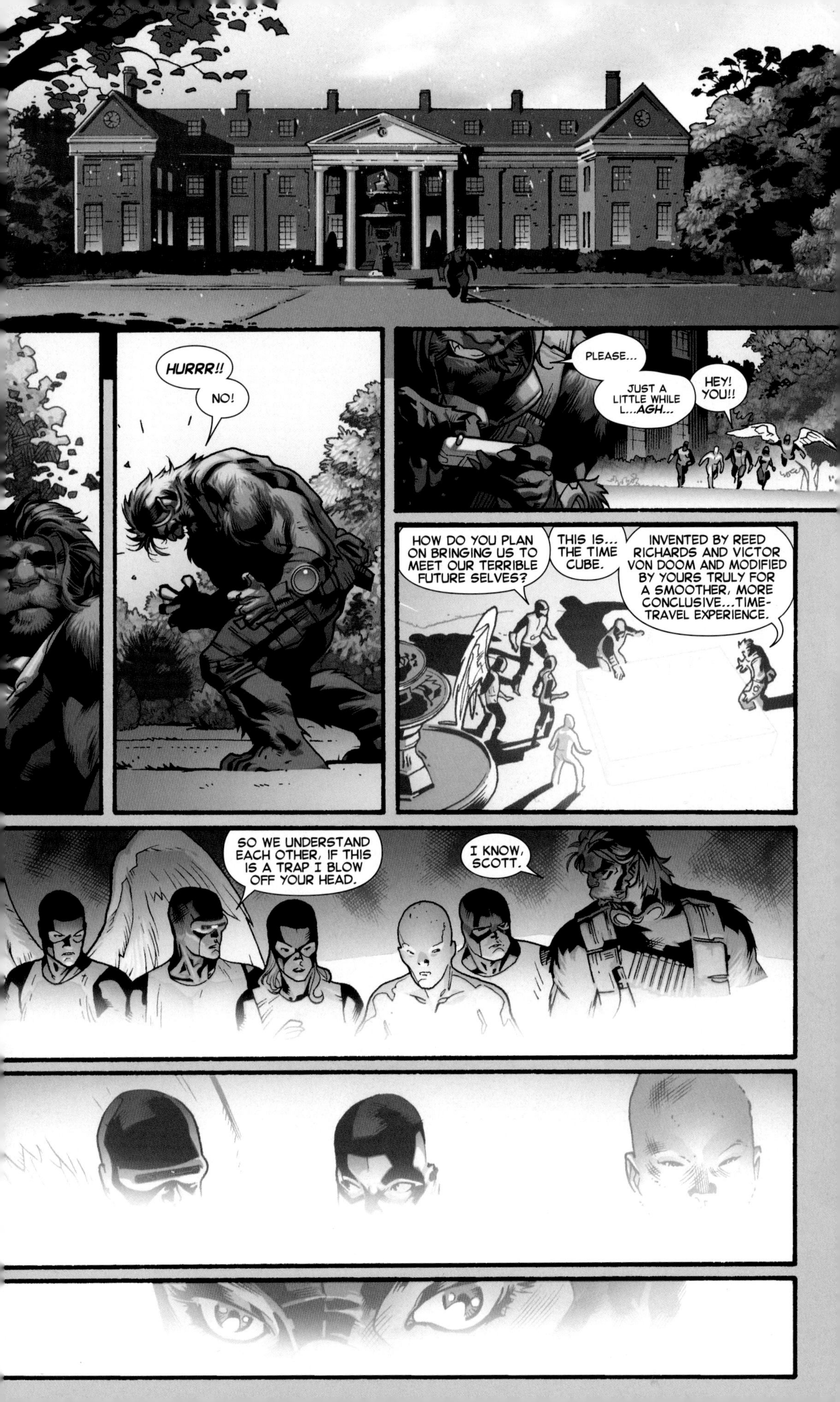
HURRR!!
NO!
PLEASE...
JUST A LITTLE WHILE L...AGH...
HEY! YOU!!
HOW DO YOU PLAN ON BRINGING US TO MEET OUR TERRIBLE FUTURE SELVES?
THIS IS... THE TIME CUBE.
INVENTED BY REED RICHARDS AND VICTOR VON DOOM AND MODIFIED BY YOURS TRULY FOR A SMOOTHER, MORE CONCLUSIVE...TIME-TRAVEL EXPERIENCE.
SO WE UNDERSTAND EACH OTHER, IF THIS IS A TRAP I BLOW OFF YOUR HEAD.
I KNOW, SCOTT.

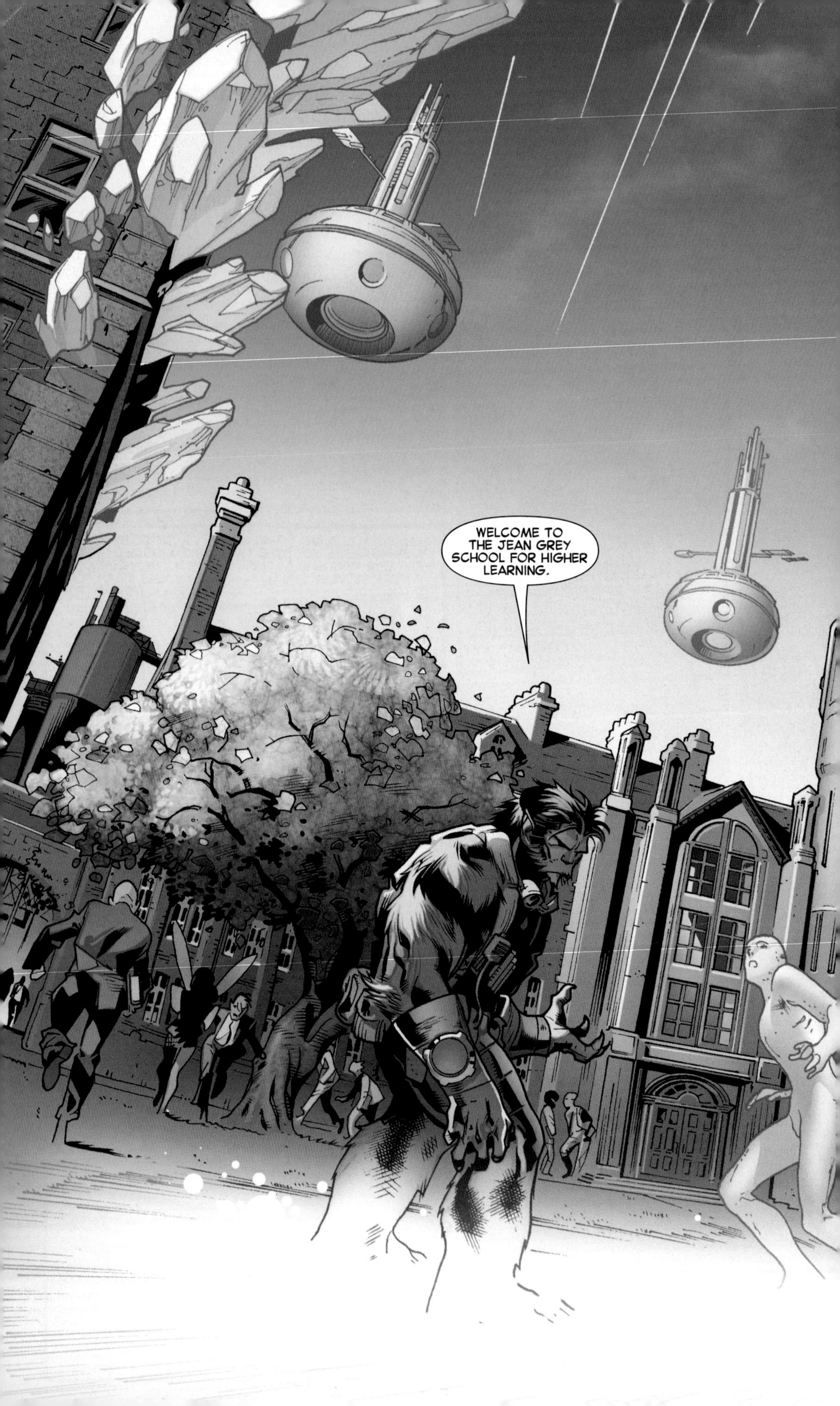
WELCOME TO THE JEAN GREY SCHOOL FOR HIGHER LEARNING.

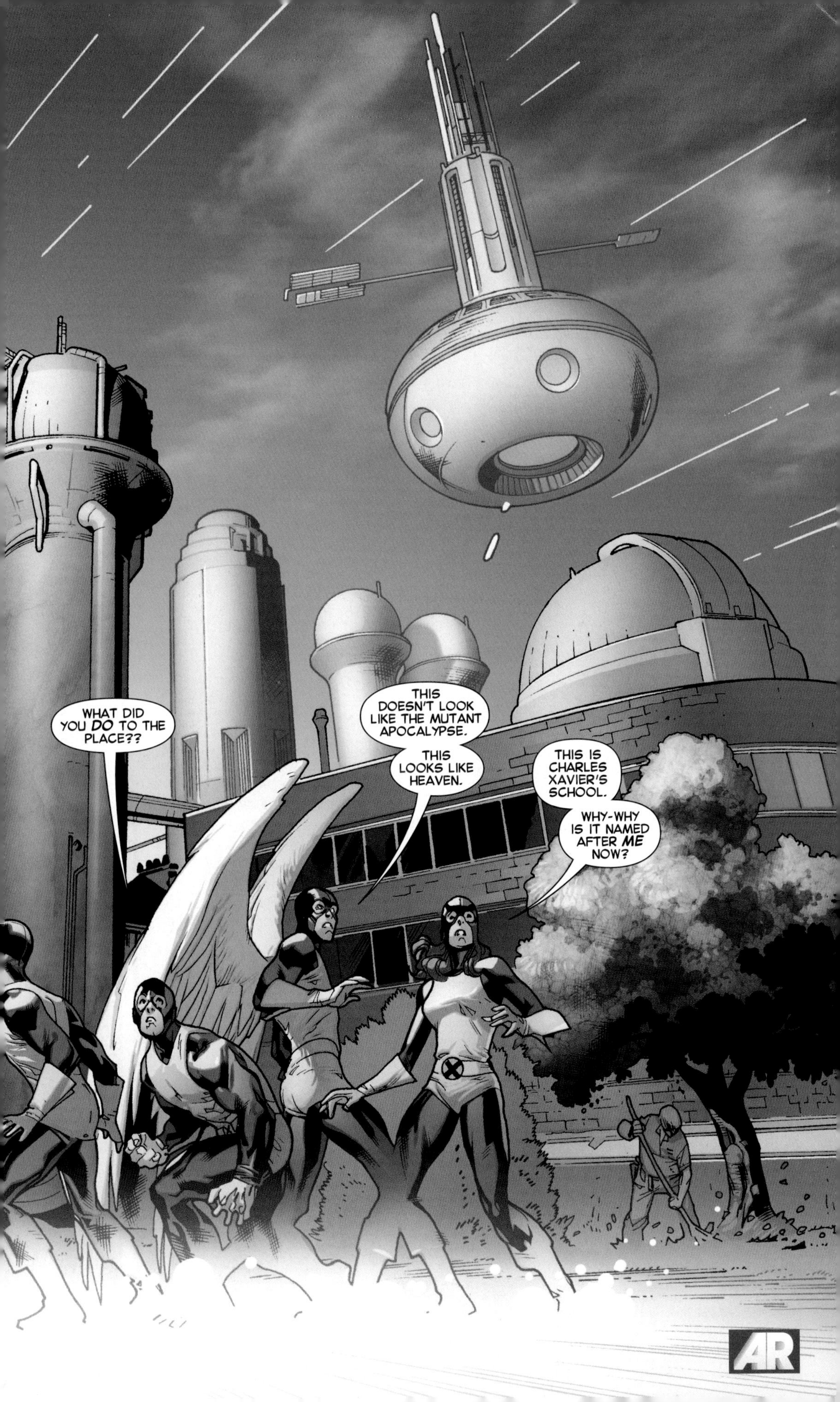
WHAT DID YOU *DO* TO THE PLACE??
THIS DOESN'T LOOK LIKE THE MUTANT APOCALYPSE.
THIS LOOKS LIKE HEAVEN.
THIS IS CHARLES XAVIER'S SCHOOL.
WHY-WHY IS IT NAMED AFTER *ME* NOW?

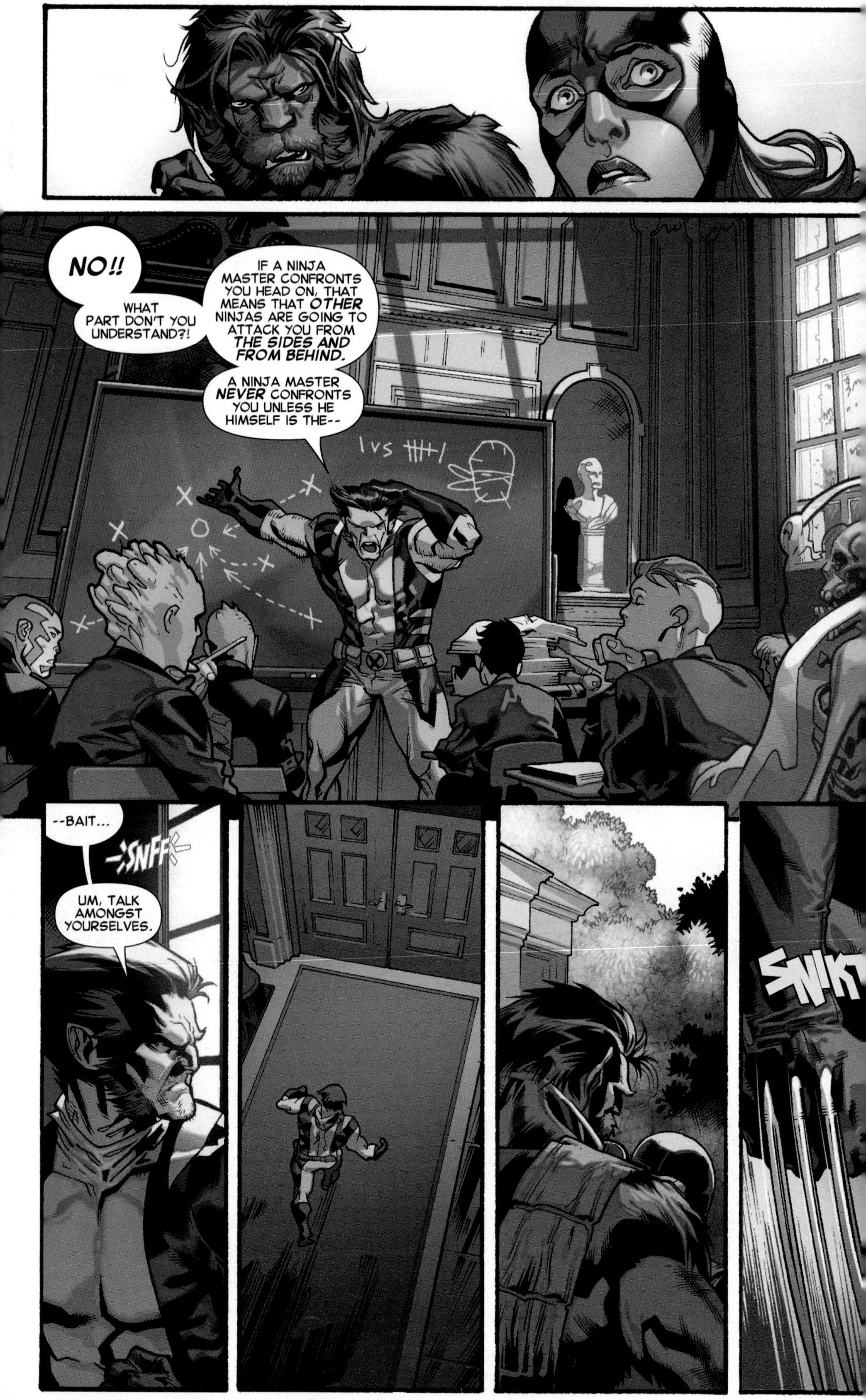

NO!!
WHAT PART DON'T YOU UNDERSTAND?!
IF A NINJA MASTER CONFRONTS YOU HEAD ON, THAT MEANS THAT OTHER NINJAS ARE GOING TO ATTACK YOU FROM THE SIDES AND FROM BEHIND.
A NINJA MASTER NEVER CONFRONTS YOU UNLESS HE HIMSELF IS THE--
1 VS 6
--BAIT...
SNFF
UM, TALK AMONGST YOURSELVES.
SNIKT

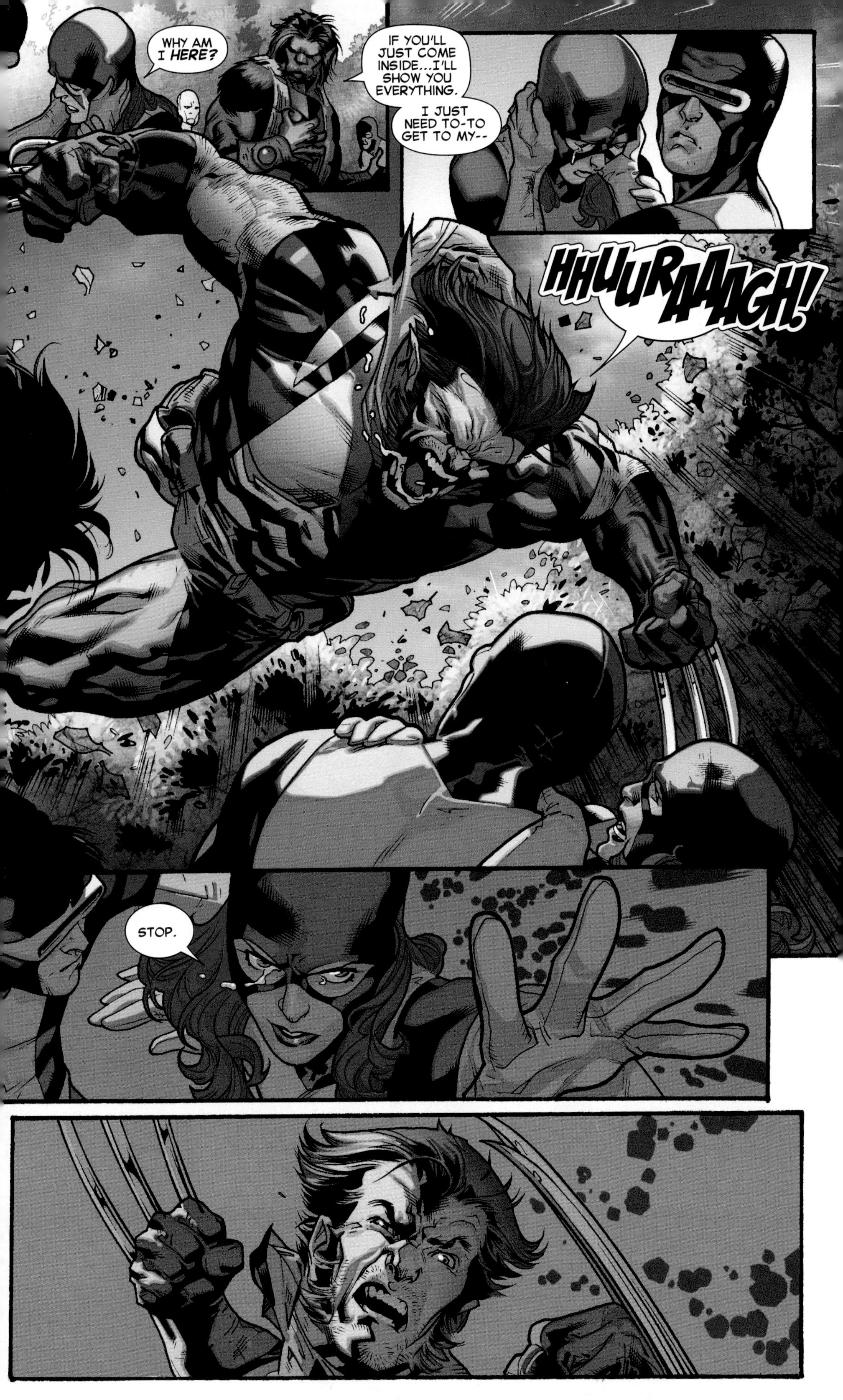
WHY AM I HERE?
IF YOU'LL JUST COME INSIDE...I'LL SHOW YOU EVERYTHING.
I JUST NEED TO-TO GET TO MY--
HHUURAAAGH!
STOP.

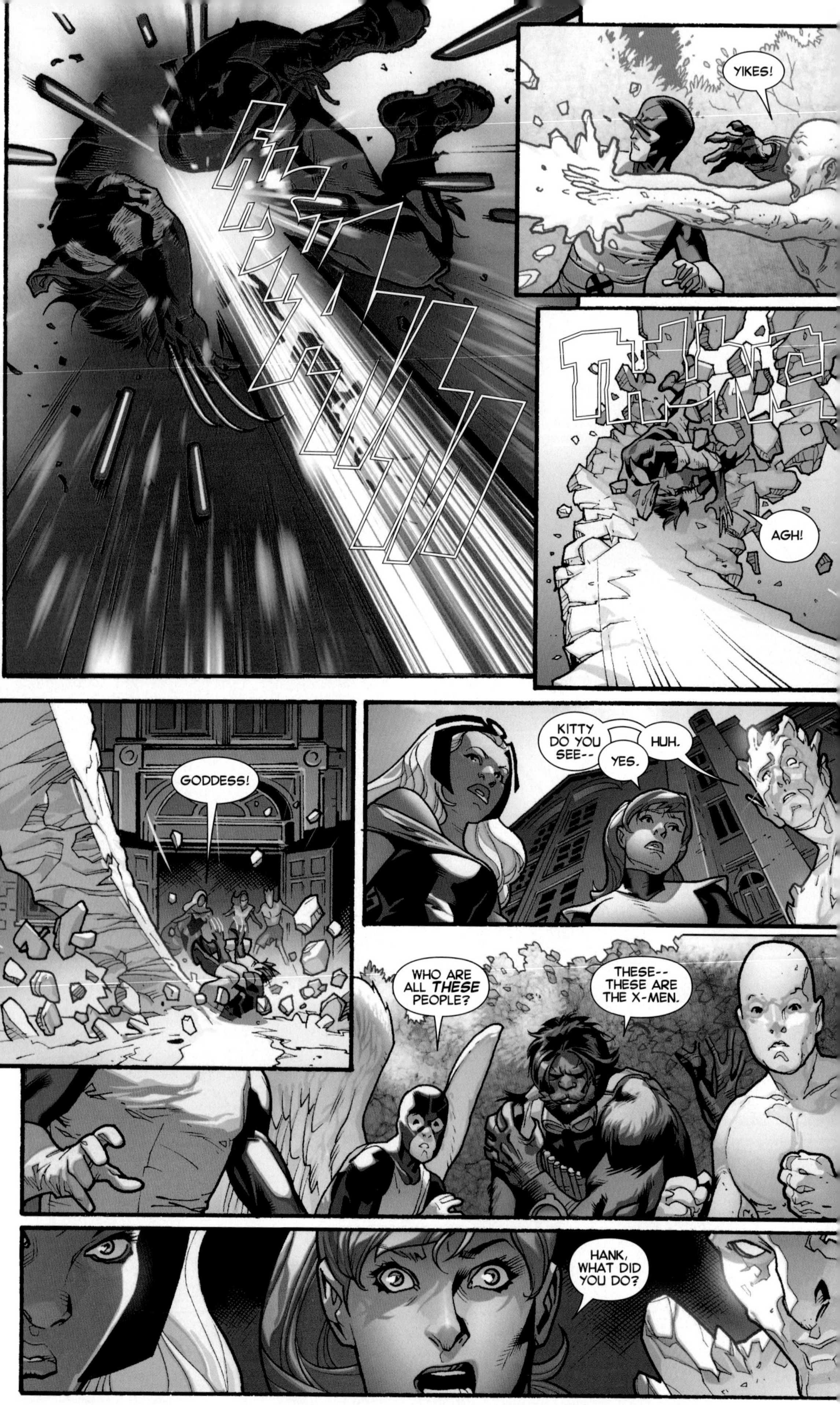
YIKES!
AGH!
GODDESS!
KITTY DO YOU SEE--
YES.
HUH.
WHO ARE ALL THESE PEOPLE?
THESE-- THESE ARE THE X-MEN.
HANK, WHAT DID YOU DO?

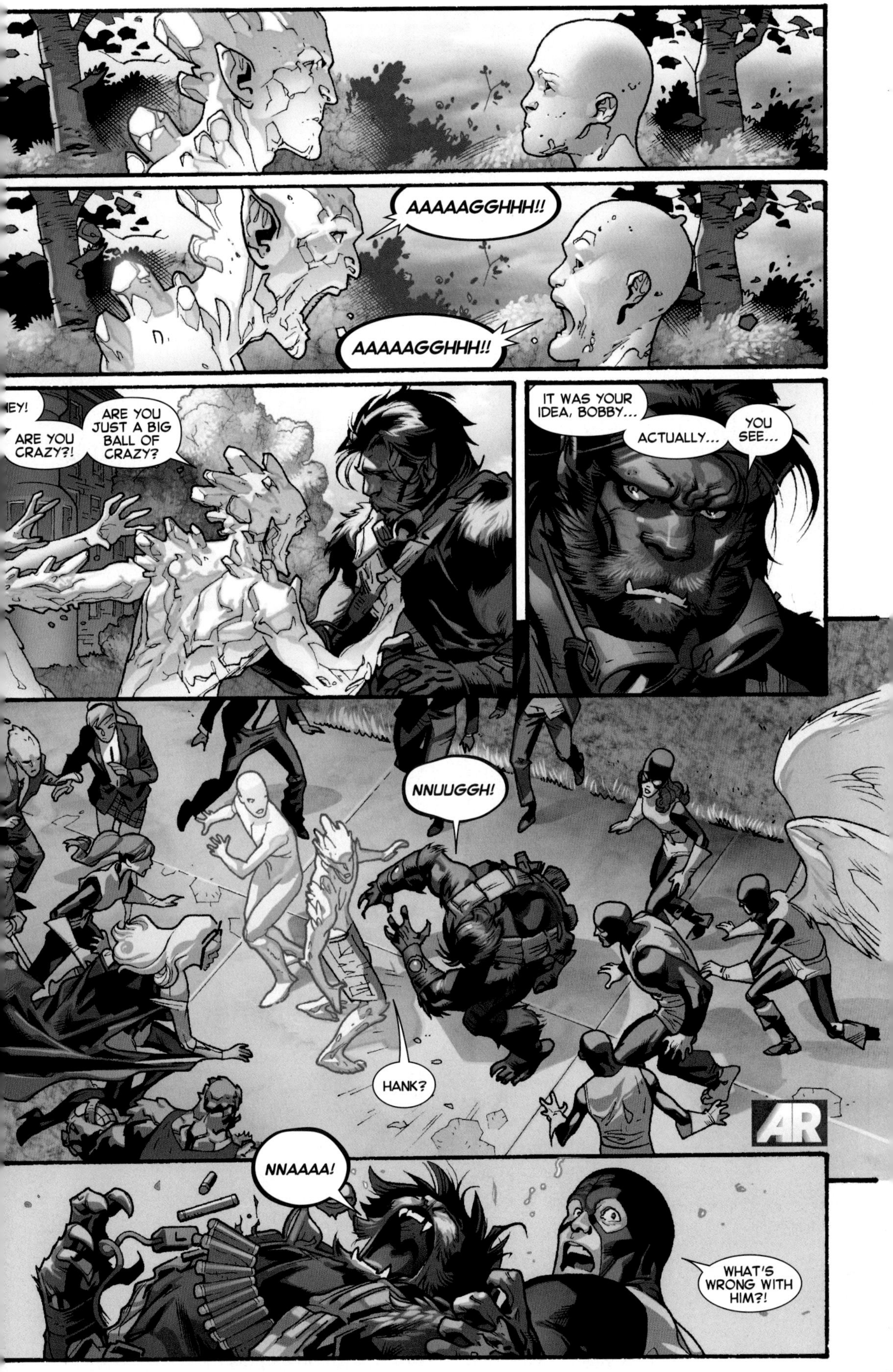

AAAAAGGHHH!!
AAAAAGGHHH!!
HEY!
ARE YOU CRAZY?!
ARE YOU JUST A BIG BALL OF CRAZY?
IT WAS YOUR IDEA, BOBBY...
ACTUALLY...
YOU SEE...
NNUUGGH!
HANK?
NNAAAA!
WHAT'S WRONG WITH HIM?!

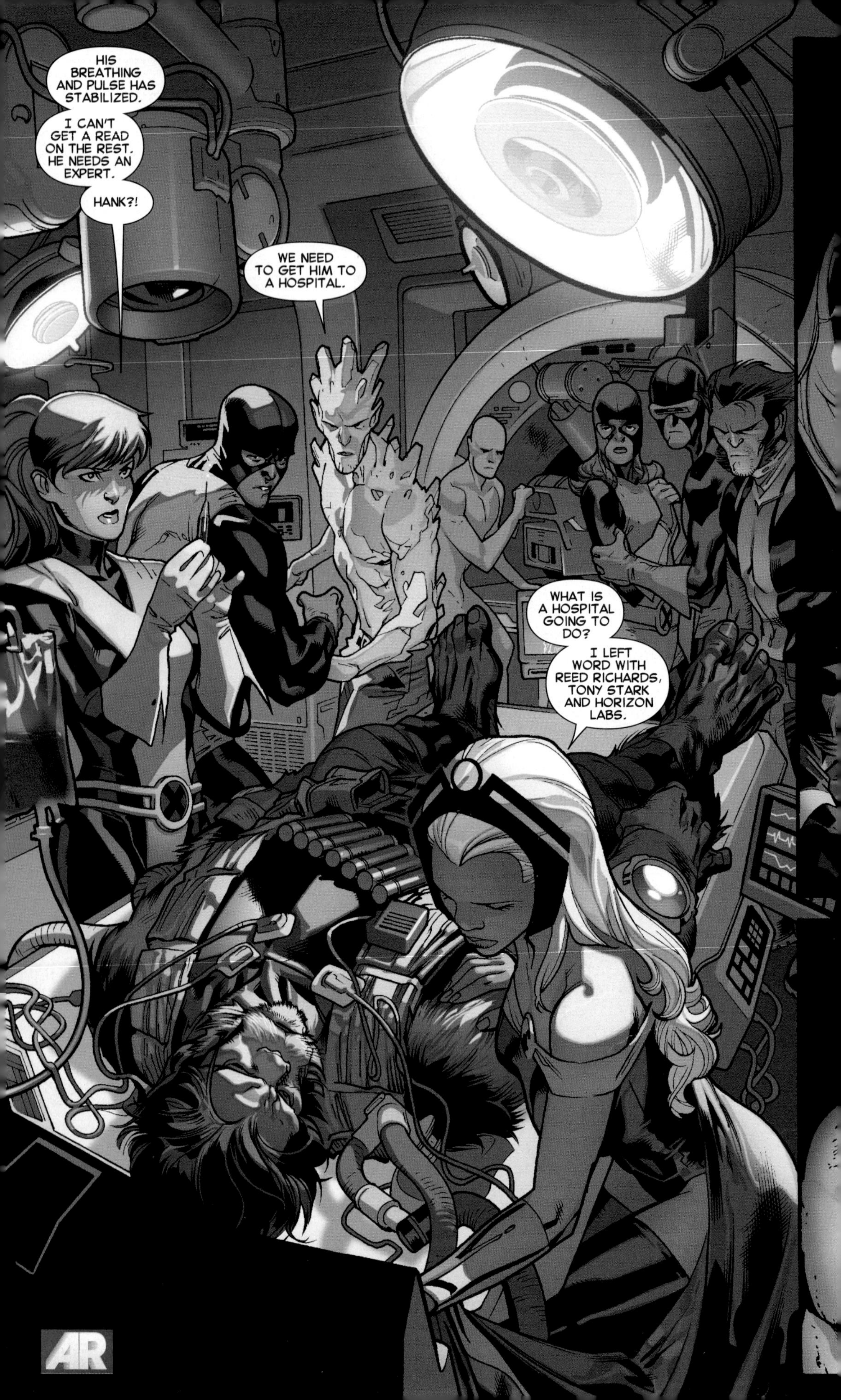
HIS BREATHING AND PULSE HAS STABILIZED.
I CAN'T GET A READ ON THE REST. HE NEEDS AN EXPERT.
HANK?!
WE NEED TO GET HIM TO A HOSPITAL.
WHAT IS A HOSPITAL GOING TO DO?
I LEFT WORD WITH REED RICHARDS, TONY STARK AND HORIZON LABS.

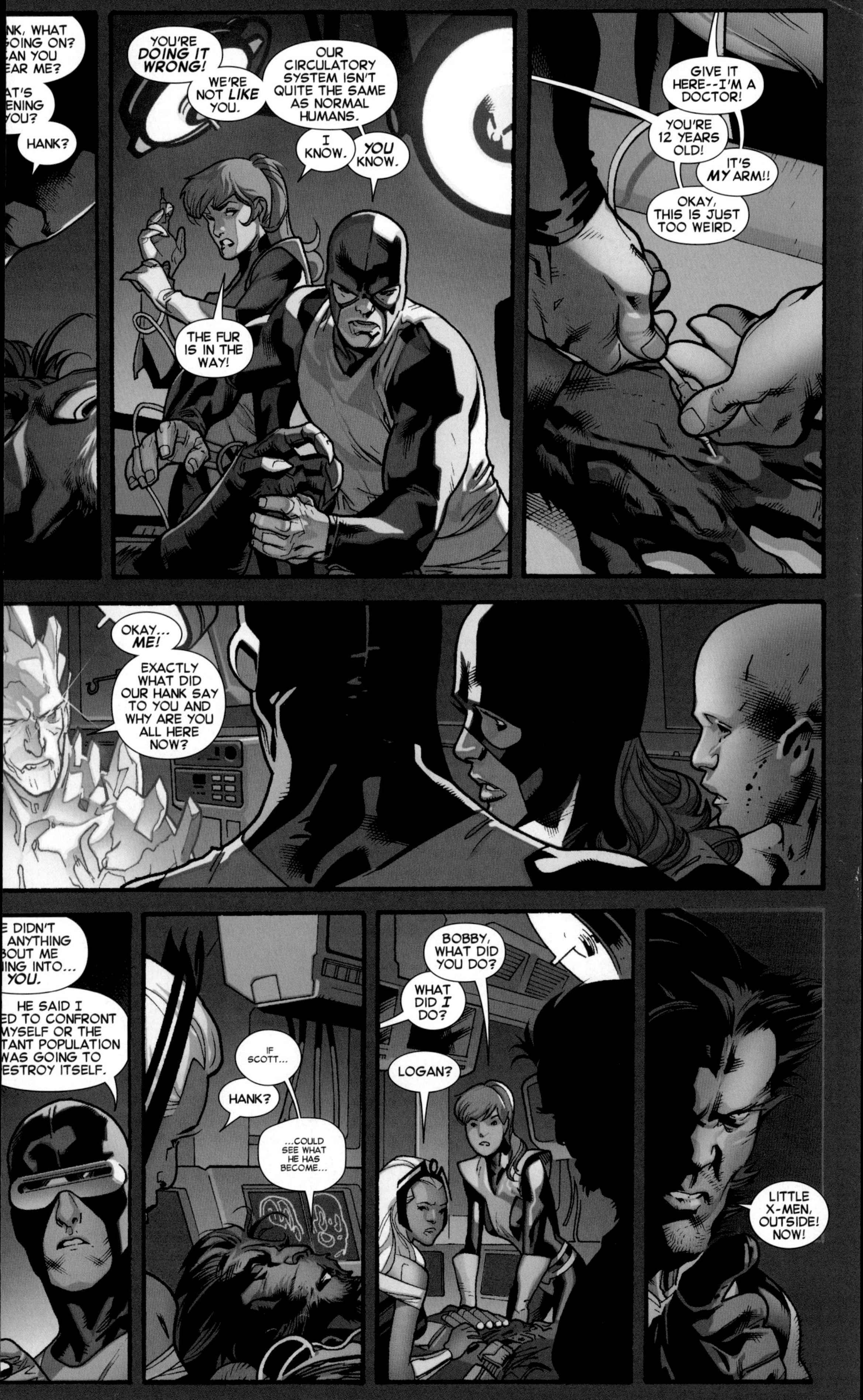
NK, WHAT GOING ON? EAN YOU EAR ME?
AT'S ENING YOU?
HANK?
YOU'RE DOING IT WRONG!
WE'RE NOT LIKE YOU.
OUR CIRCULATORY SYSTEM ISN'T QUITE THE SAME AS NORMAL HUMANS.
I KNOW.
YOU KNOW.
THE FUR IS IN THE WAY!
GIVE IT HERE--I'M A DOCTOR!
YOU'RE 12 YEARS OLD!
IT'S MY ARM!!
OKAY, THIS IS JUST TOO WEIRD.
OKAY... ME!
EXACTLY WHAT DID OUR HANK SAY TO YOU AND WHY ARE YOU ALL HERE NOW?
E DIDN'T ANYTHING BOUT ME ING INTO... YOU.
HE SAID I ED TO CONFRONT MYSELF OR THE TANT POPULATION WAS GOING TO ESTROY ITSELF.
IF SCOTT...
HANK?
...COULD SEE WHAT HE HAS BECOME...
BOBBY, WHAT DID YOU DO?
WHAT DID I DO?
LOGAN?
LITTLE X-MEN, OUTSIDE! NOW!

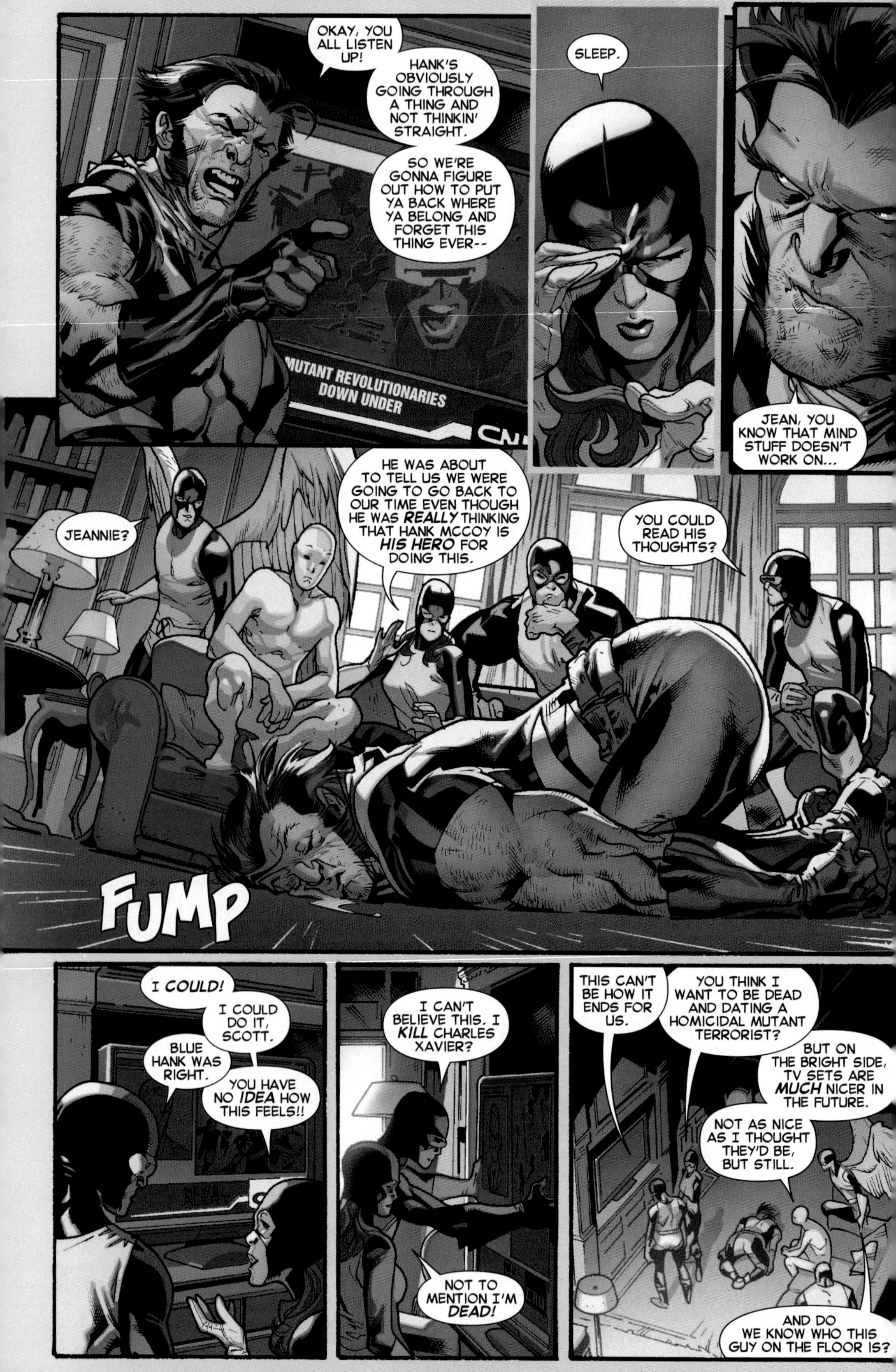

OKAY, YOU ALL LISTEN UP!
HANK'S OBVIOUSLY GOING THROUGH A THING AND NOT THINKIN' STRAIGHT.
SO WE'RE GONNA FIGURE OUT HOW TO PUT YA BACK WHERE YA BELONG AND FORGET THIS THING EVER--
MUTANT REVOLUTIONARIES DOWN UNDER
SLEEP.
JEAN, YOU KNOW THAT MIND STUFF DOESN'T WORK ON...
JEANNIE?
HE WAS ABOUT TO TELL US WE WERE GOING TO GO BACK TO OUR TIME EVEN THOUGH HE WAS REALLY THINKING THAT HANK MCCOY IS HIS HERO FOR DOING THIS.
YOU COULD READ HIS THOUGHTS?
FUMP
I COULD!
I COULD DO IT, SCOTT.
BLUE HANK WAS RIGHT.
YOU HAVE NO IDEA HOW THIS FEELS!!
I CAN'T BELIEVE THIS. I KILL CHARLES XAVIER?
NOT TO MENTION I'M DEAD!
THIS CAN'T BE HOW IT ENDS FOR US.
YOU THINK I WANT TO BE DEAD AND DATING A HOMICIDAL MUTANT TERRORIST?
BUT ON THE BRIGHT SIDE, TV SETS ARE MUCH NICER IN THE FUTURE.
NOT AS NICE AS I THOUGHT THEY'D BE, BUT STILL.
AND DO WE KNOW WHO THIS GUY ON THE FLOOR IS?

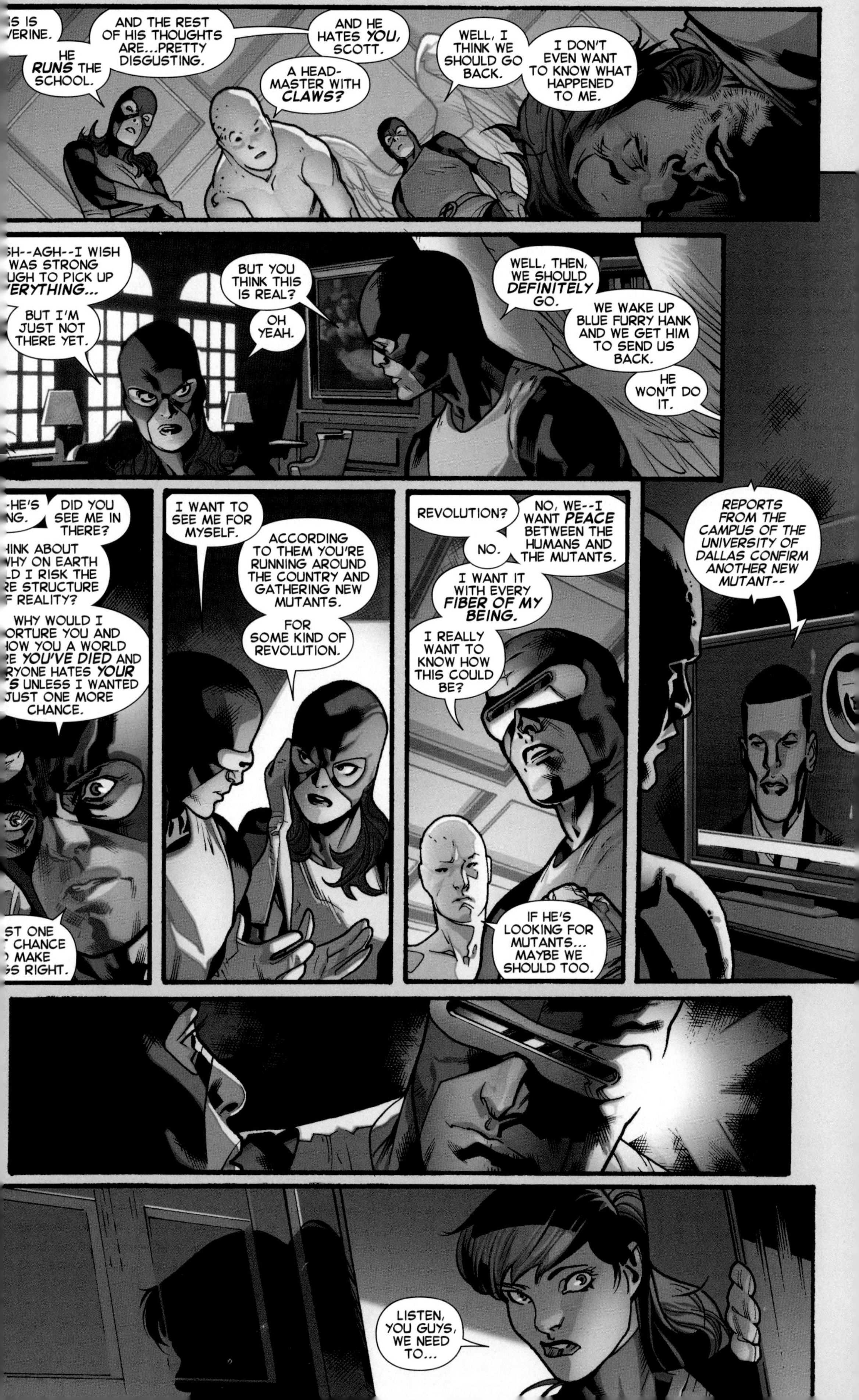

IS IS
VERINE.
HE RUNS THE SCHOOL.
AND THE REST OF HIS THOUGHTS ARE...PRETTY DISGUSTING.
A HEAD-MASTER WITH CLAWS?
AND HE HATES YOU, SCOTT.
WELL, I THINK WE SHOULD GO BACK.
I DON'T EVEN WANT TO KNOW WHAT HAPPENED TO ME.
GH--AGH--I WISH WAS STRONG UGH TO PICK UP VERYTHING...
BUT I'M JUST NOT THERE YET.
BUT YOU THINK THIS IS REAL?
OH YEAH.
WELL, THEN, WE SHOULD DEFINITELY GO.
WE WAKE UP BLUE FURRY HANK AND WE GET HIM TO SEND US BACK.
HE WON'T DO IT.
-HE'S NG.
DID YOU SEE ME IN THERE?
HINK ABOUT WHY ON EARTH LD I RISK THE RE STRUCTURE F REALITY?
WHY WOULD I ORTURE YOU AND HOW YOU A WORLD RE YOU'VE DIED AND RYONE HATES YOUR S UNLESS I WANTED JUST ONE MORE CHANCE.
ST ONE CHANCE MAKE GS RIGHT.
I WANT TO SEE ME FOR MYSELF.
ACCORDING TO THEM YOU'RE RUNNING AROUND THE COUNTRY AND GATHERING NEW MUTANTS.
FOR SOME KIND OF REVOLUTION.
REVOLUTION?
NO.
NO, WE--I WANT PEACE BETWEEN THE HUMANS AND THE MUTANTS.
I WANT IT WITH EVERY FIBER OF MY BEING.
I REALLY WANT TO KNOW HOW THIS COULD BE?
IF HE'S LOOKING FOR MUTANTS... MAYBE WE SHOULD TOO.
REPORTS FROM THE CAMPUS OF THE UNIVERSITY OF DALLAS CONFIRM ANOTHER NEW MUTANT--
LISTEN, YOU GUYS, WE NEED TO...

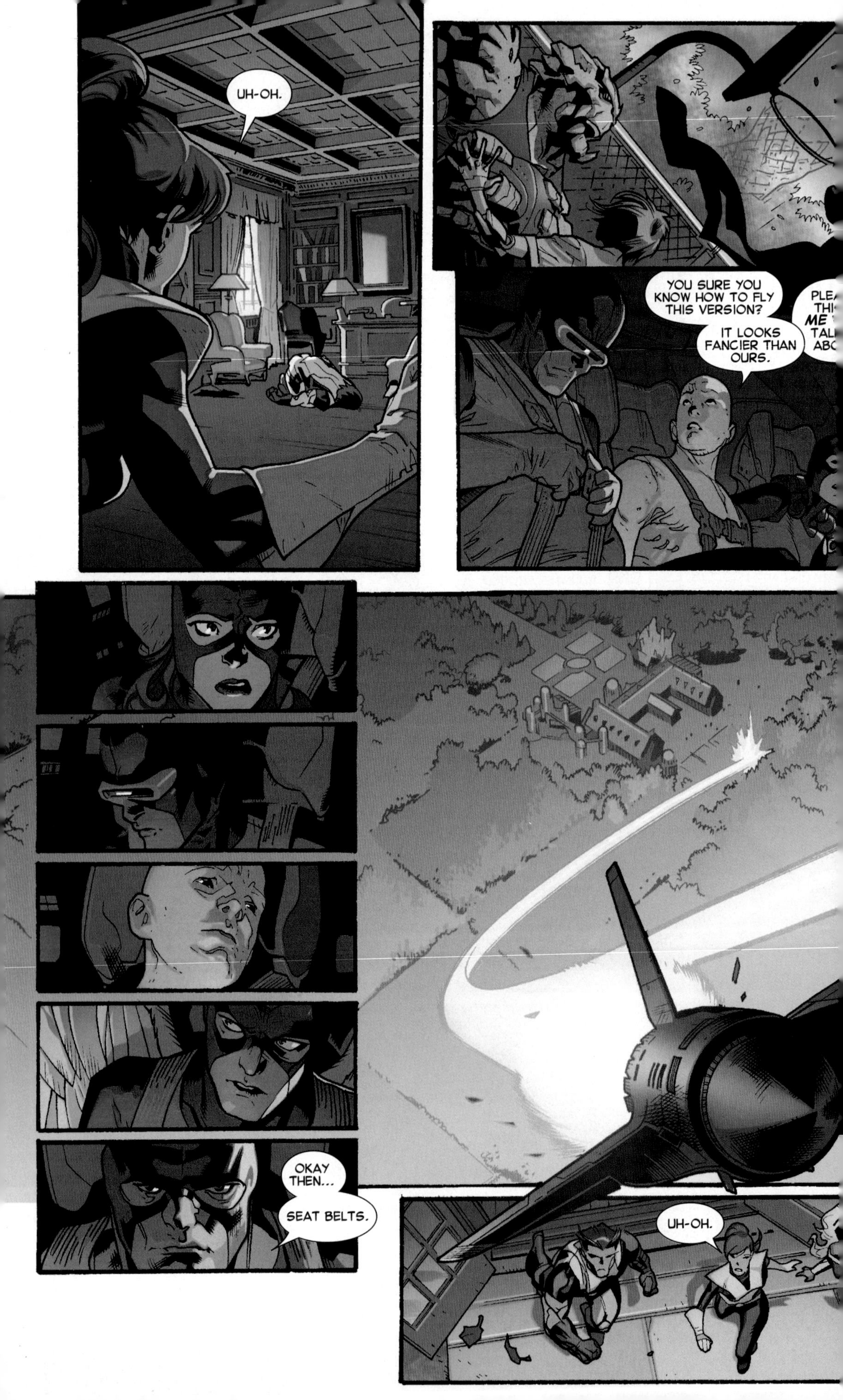
UH-OH.
YOU SURE YOU KNOW HOW TO FLY THIS VERSION?
IT LOOKS FANCIER THAN OURS.
OKAY THEN...
SEAT BELTS.
UH-OH.

FAROOOmmm

I REALLY
I SHOULD
BACK AND
TO HELP
YSELF.

EY
T LET
HANK.

AND THEY
HAVE AN
EXPERT ON
THE WAY.

AND THIS
IS WHAT YOU
WANTED YOU
TO DO.

LAST
CHANCE,
GUYS.

WE CAN TURN
AROUND NOW AND
NOT CRACK THE
SPACE-TIME
CONTINUUM.

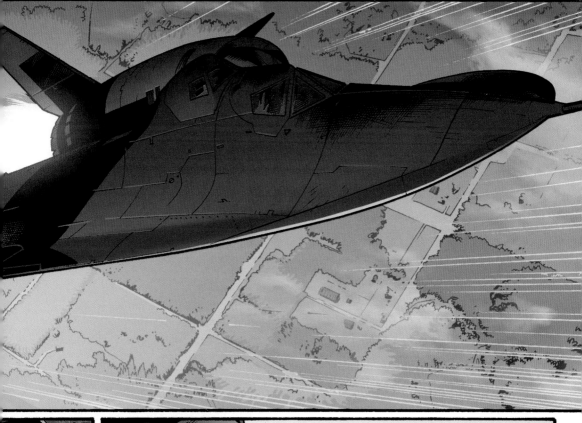

IT WAS
HER.

IT WAS
REALLY
HER.

JEANNIE...

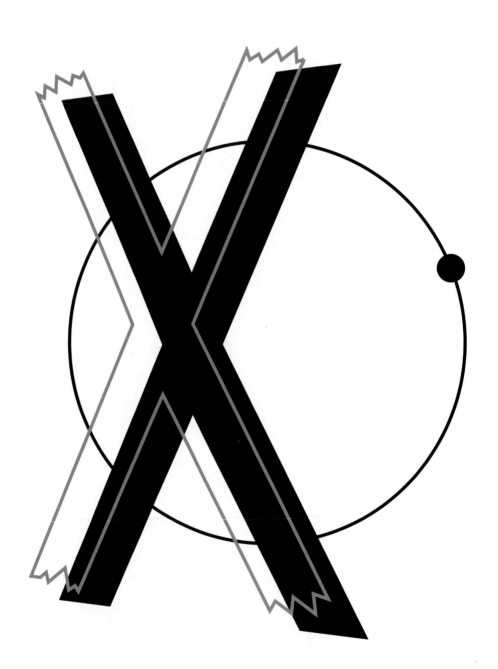

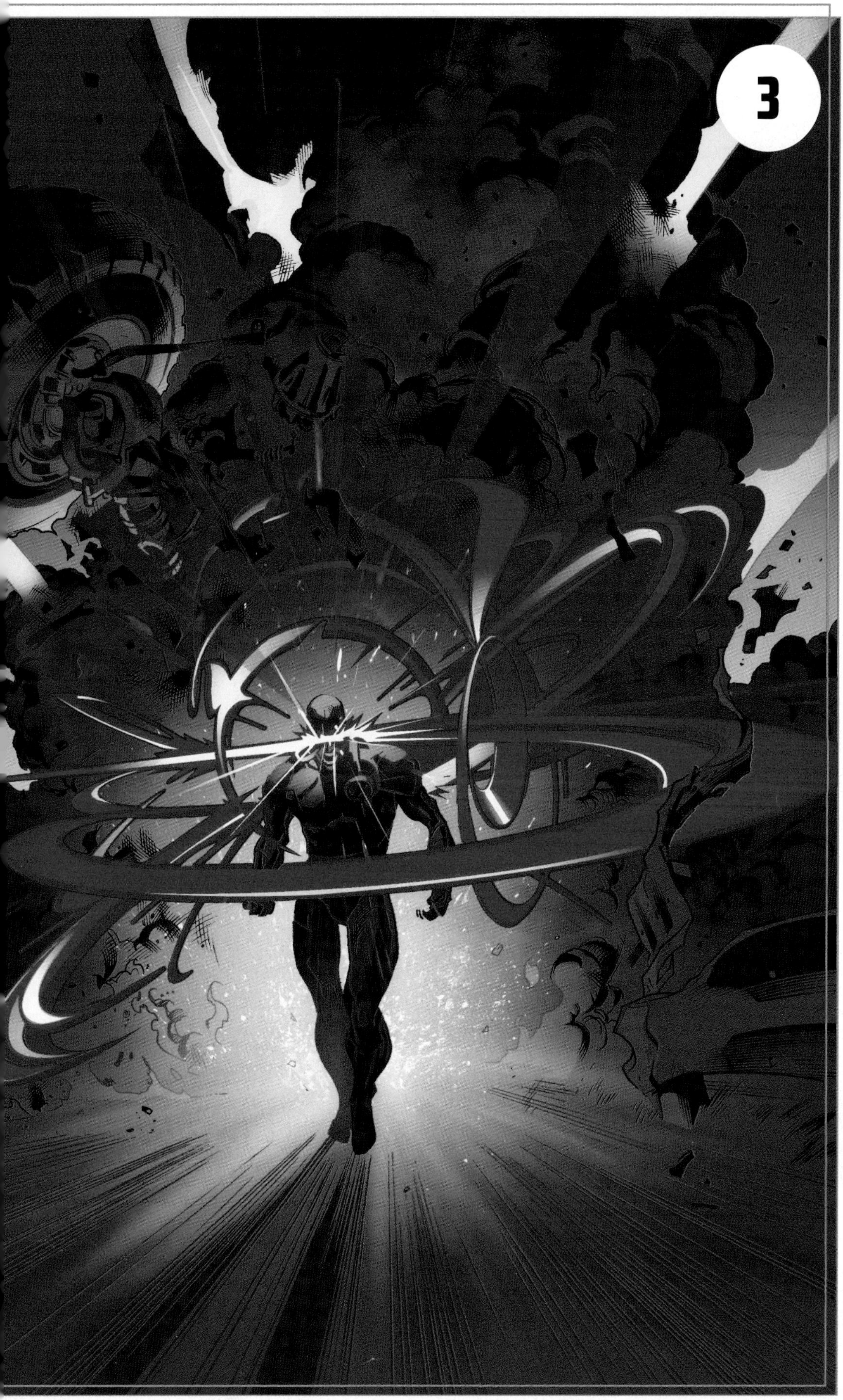
3

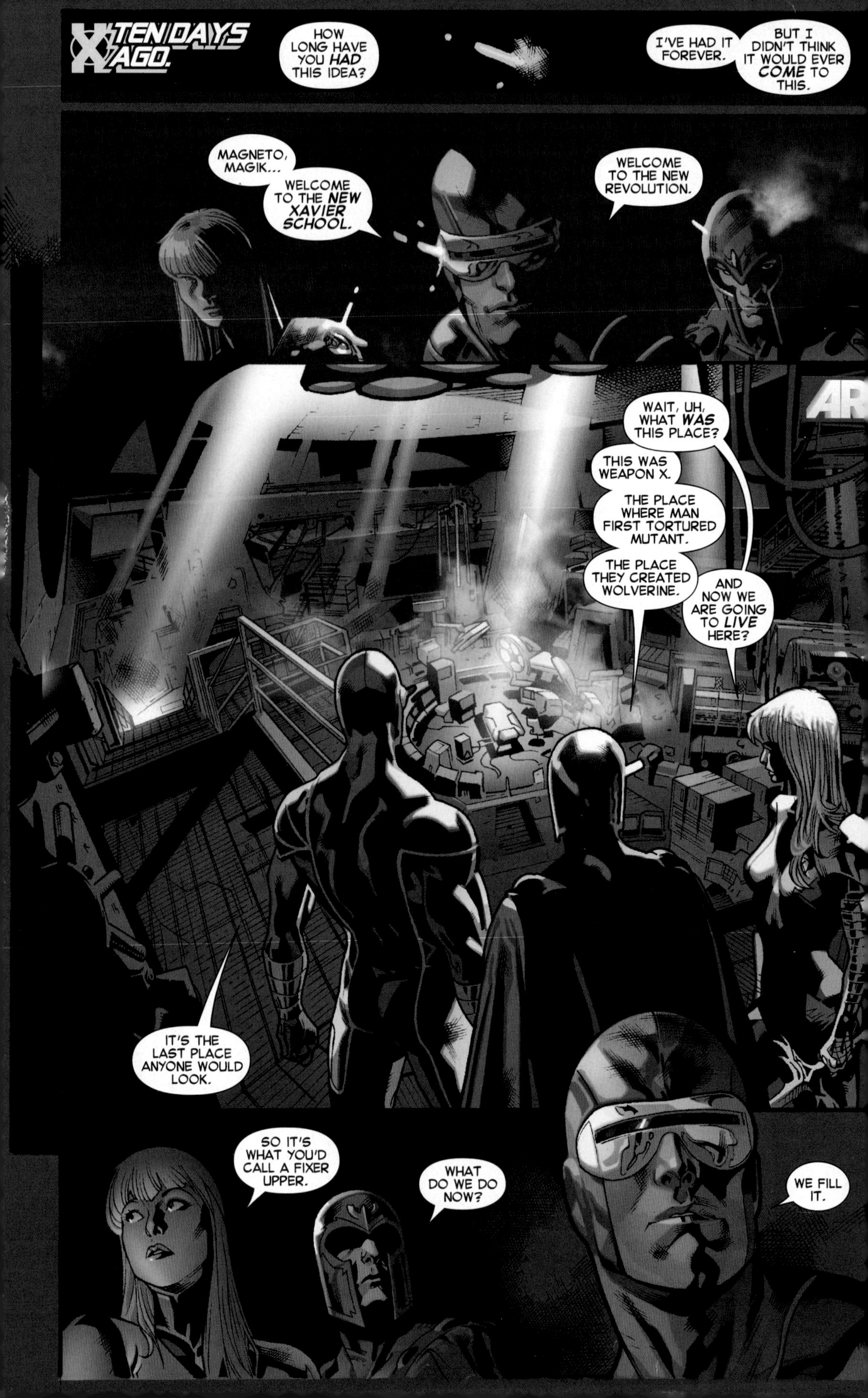

TEN DAYS AGO.
HOW LONG HAVE YOU HAD THIS IDEA?
I'VE HAD IT FOREVER.
BUT I DIDN'T THINK IT WOULD EVER COME TO THIS.
MAGNETO, MAGIK...
WELCOME TO THE NEW XAVIER SCHOOL.
WELCOME TO THE NEW REVOLUTION.
WAIT, UH, WHAT WAS THIS PLACE?
THIS WAS WEAPON X.
THE PLACE WHERE MAN FIRST TORTURED MUTANT.
THE PLACE THEY CREATED WOLVERINE.
AND NOW WE ARE GOING TO LIVE HERE?
IT'S THE LAST PLACE ANYONE WOULD LOOK.
SO IT'S WHAT YOU'D CALL A FIXER UPPER.
WHAT DO WE DO NOW?
WE FILL IT.

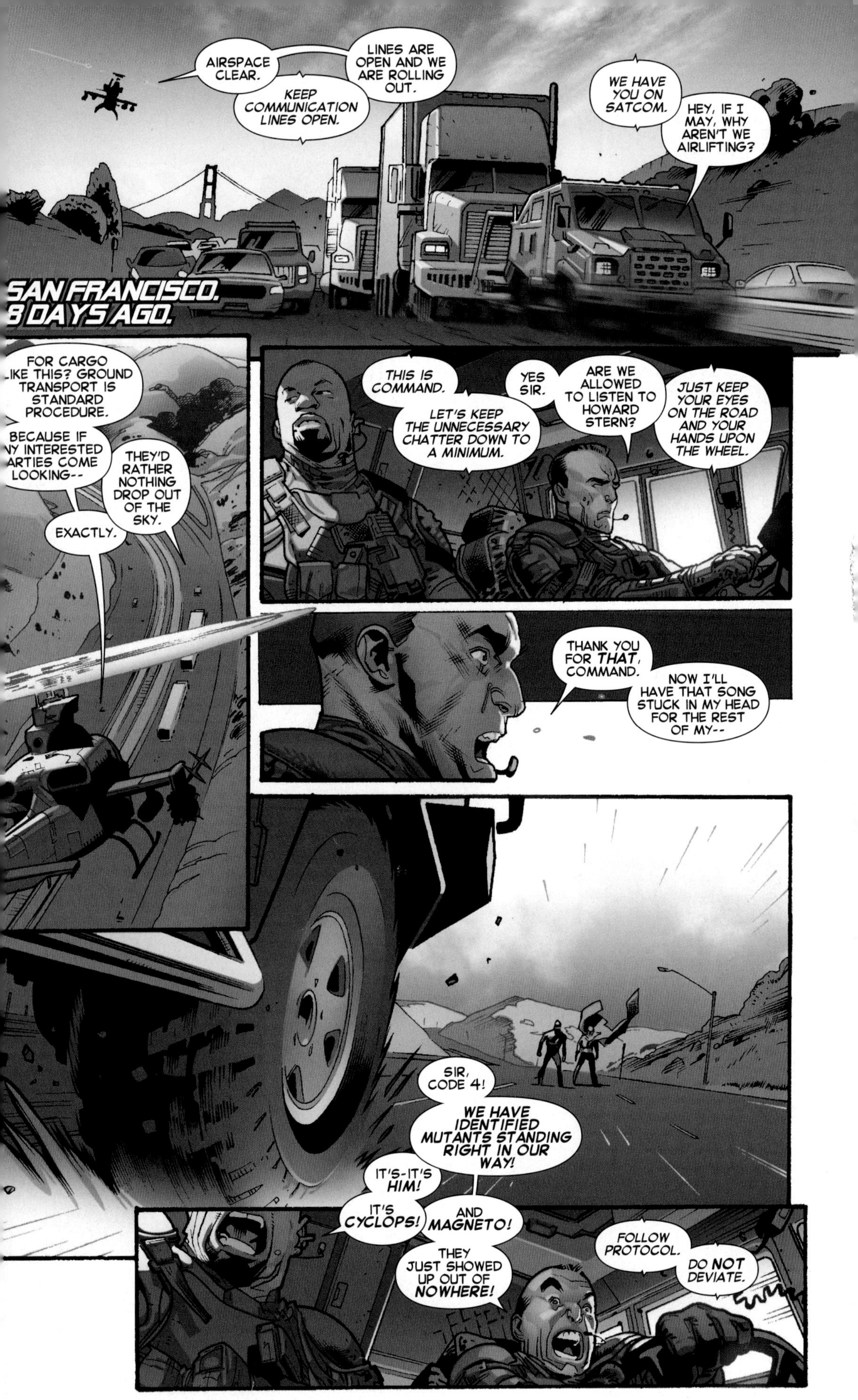
AIRSPACE CLEAR.
LINES ARE OPEN AND WE ARE ROLLING OUT.
KEEP COMMUNICATION LINES OPEN.
WE HAVE YOU ON SATCOM.
HEY, IF I MAY, WHY AREN'T WE AIRLIFTING?
SAN FRANCISCO. 8 DAYS AGO.
FOR CARGO LIKE THIS? GROUND TRANSPORT IS STANDARD PROCEDURE.
BECAUSE IF ANY INTERESTED PARTIES COME LOOKING--
THEY'D RATHER NOTHING DROP OUT OF THE SKY.
EXACTLY.
THIS IS COMMAND.
LET'S KEEP THE UNNECESSARY CHATTER DOWN TO A MINIMUM.
YES SIR.
ARE WE ALLOWED TO LISTEN TO HOWARD STERN?
JUST KEEP YOUR EYES ON THE ROAD AND YOUR HANDS UPON THE WHEEL.
THANK YOU FOR THAT, COMMAND.
NOW I'LL HAVE THAT SONG STUCK IN MY HEAD FOR THE REST OF MY--
SIR, CODE 4!
WE HAVE IDENTIFIED MUTANTS STANDING RIGHT IN OUR WAY!
IT'S-IT'S HIM!
IT'S CYCLOPS!
AND MAGNETO!
THEY JUST SHOWED UP OUT OF NOWHERE!
FOLLOW PROTOCOL.
DO NOT DEVIATE.

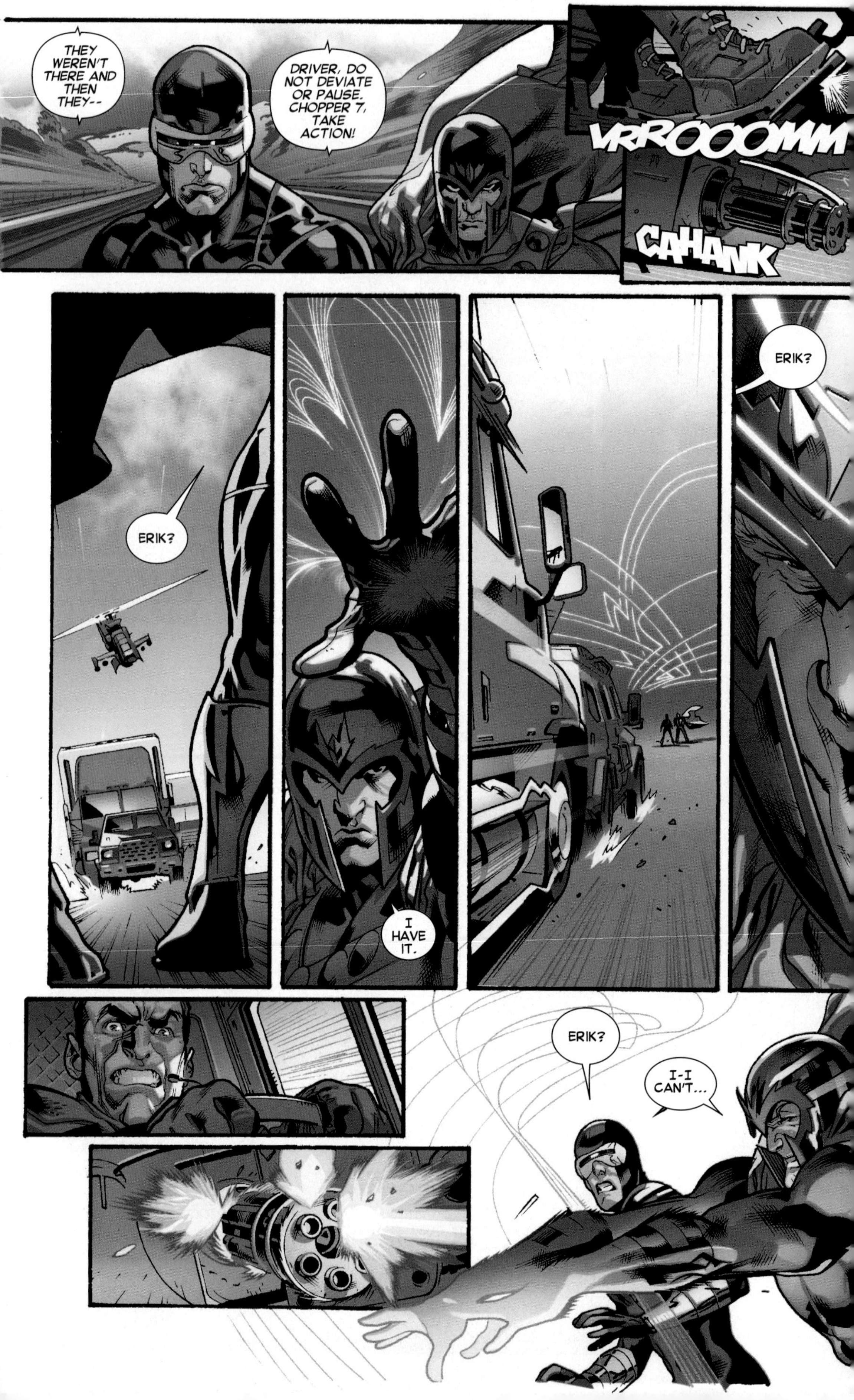
THEY WEREN'T THERE AND THEN THEY--
DRIVER, DO NOT DEVIATE OR PAUSE. CHOPPER 7, TAKE ACTION!
VRROOOMM
CAHANK
ERIK?
I HAVE IT.
ERIK?
ERIK?
I-I CAN'T...

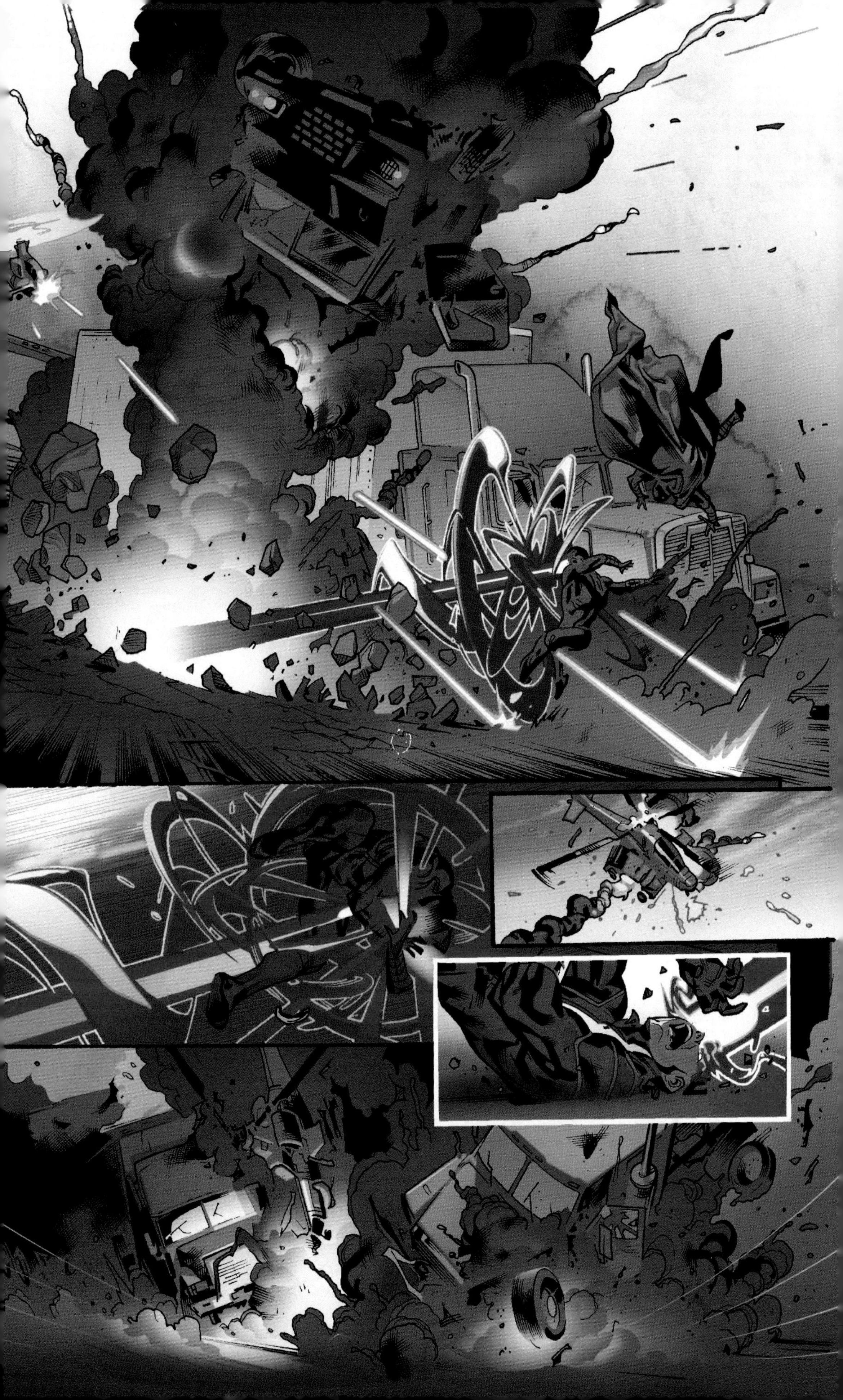

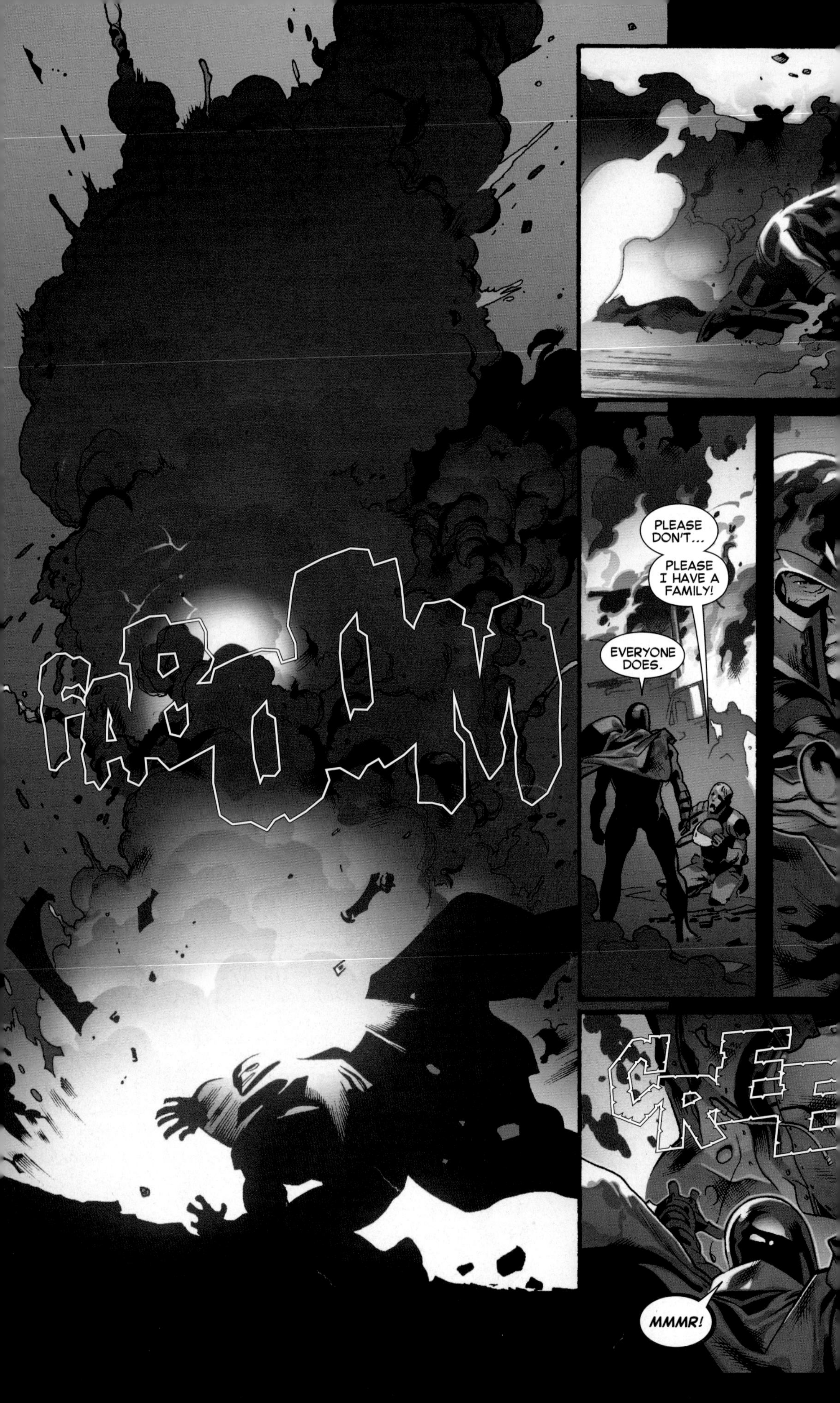
PLEASE DON'T...
PLEASE I HAVE A FAMILY!
EVERYONE DOES.
MMMR!

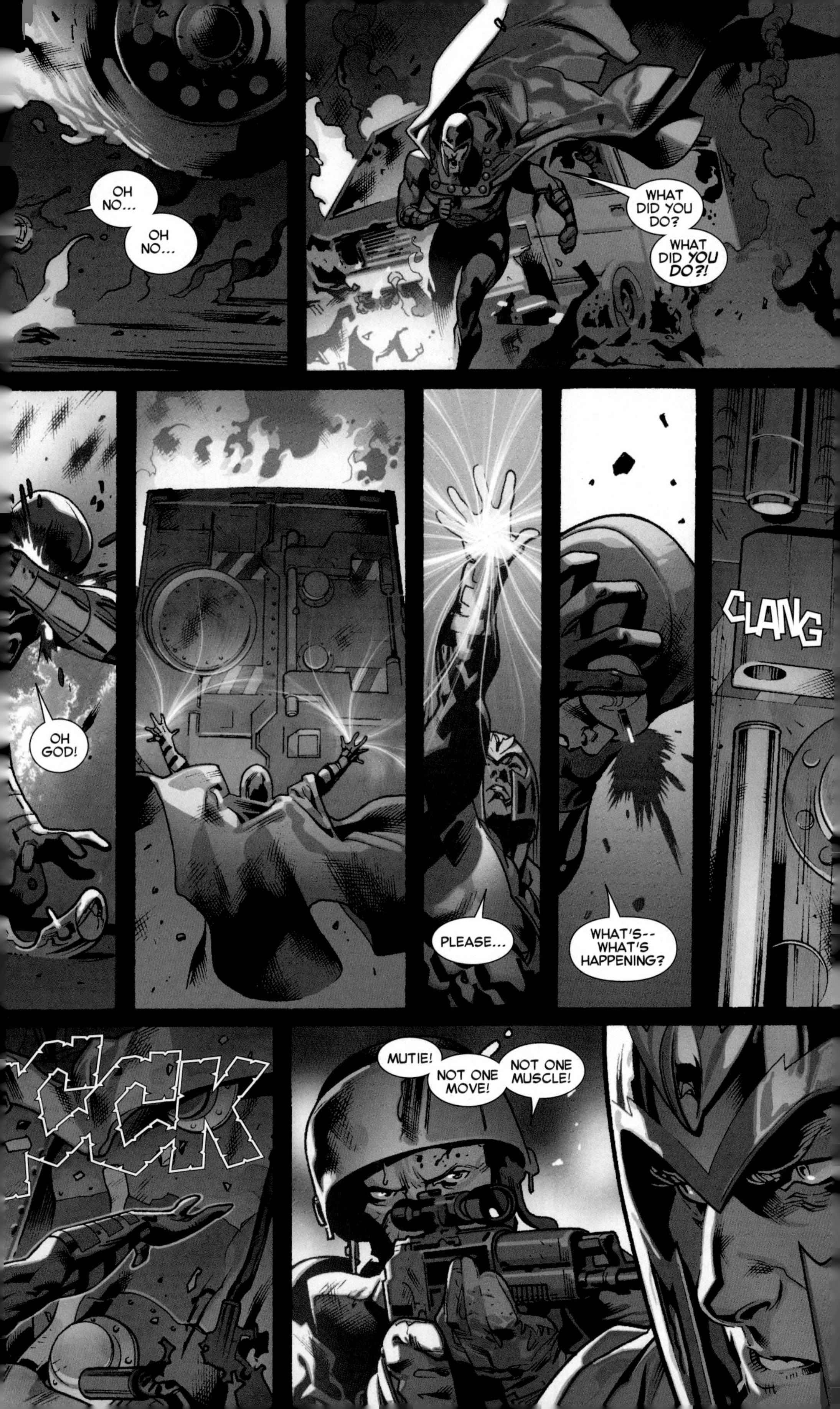
OH NO...
OH NO...
WHAT DID YOU DO?
WHAT DID YOU DO?!
OH GOD!
PLEASE...
WHAT'S-- WHAT'S HAPPENING?
CLANG
MUTIE!
NOT ONE MOVE!
NOT ONE MUSCLE!

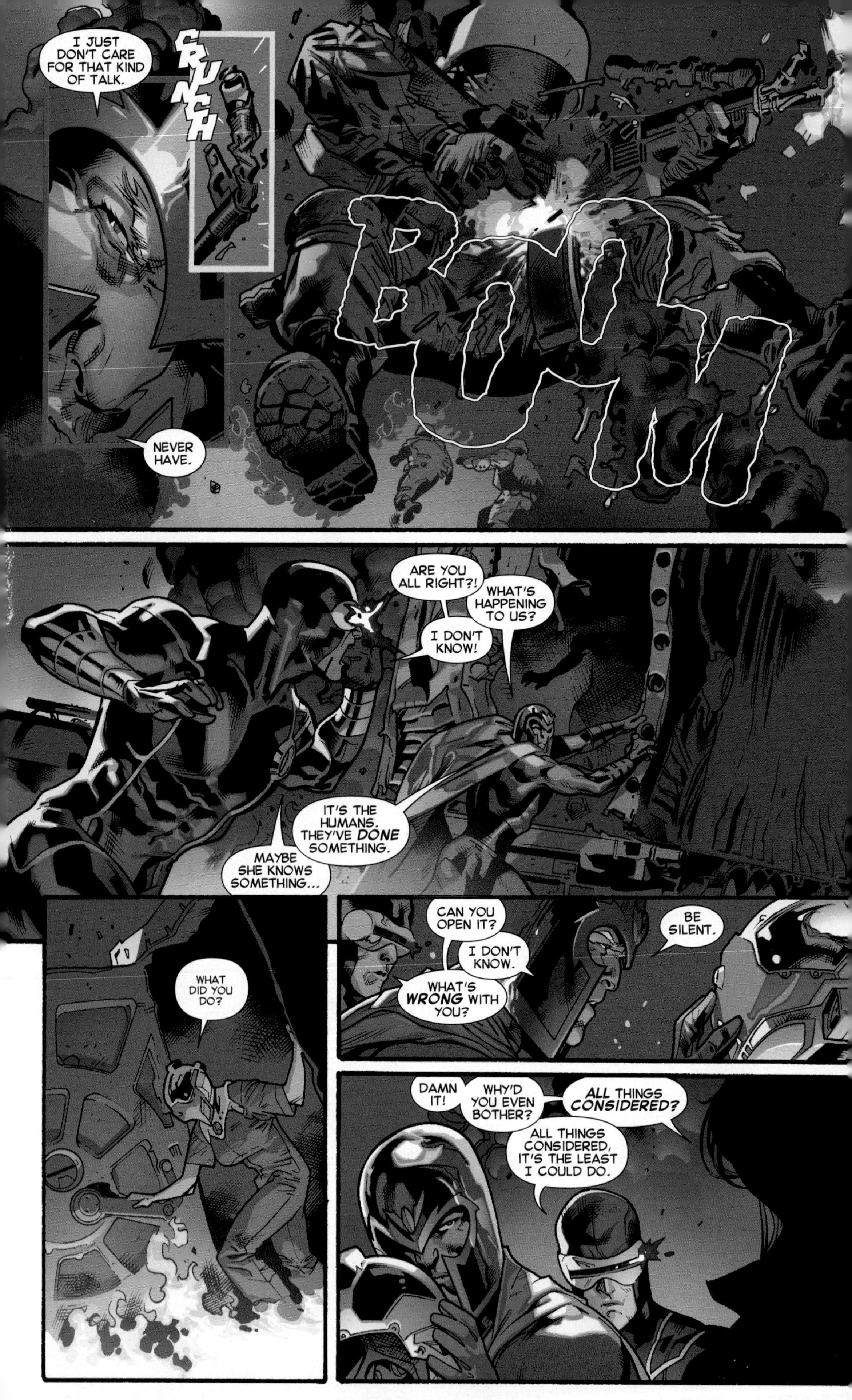
I JUST DON'T CARE FOR THAT KIND OF TALK.
CRUNCH
BOOM
NEVER HAVE.
ARE YOU ALL RIGHT?!
WHAT'S HAPPENING TO US?
I DON'T KNOW!
IT'S THE HUMANS. THEY'VE DONE SOMETHING.
MAYBE SHE KNOWS SOMETHING...
WHAT DID YOU DO?
CAN YOU OPEN IT?
I DON'T KNOW.
WHAT'S WRONG WITH YOU?
BE SILENT.
DAMN IT!
WHY'D YOU EVEN BOTHER?
ALL THINGS CONSIDERED?
ALL THINGS CONSIDERED, IT'S THE LEAST I COULD DO.

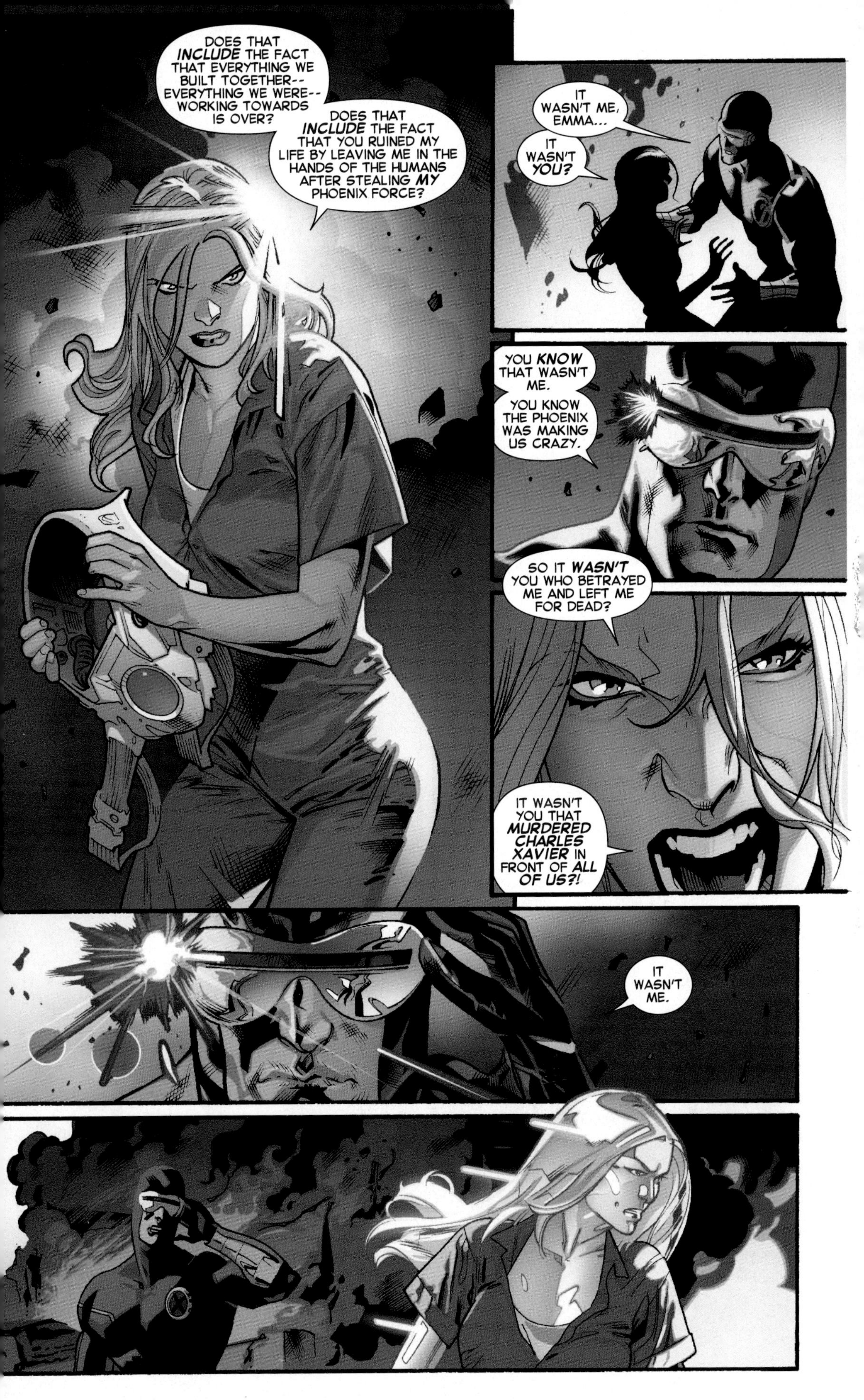
DOES THAT INCLUDE THE FACT THAT EVERYTHING WE BUILT TOGETHER-- EVERYTHING WE WERE-- WORKING TOWARDS IS OVER?
DOES THAT INCLUDE THE FACT THAT YOU RUINED MY LIFE BY LEAVING ME IN THE HANDS OF THE HUMANS AFTER STEALING MY PHOENIX FORCE?
IT WASN'T ME, EMMA...
IT WASN'T YOU?
YOU KNOW THAT WASN'T ME.
YOU KNOW THE PHOENIX WAS MAKING US CRAZY.
SO IT WASN'T YOU WHO BETRAYED ME AND LEFT ME FOR DEAD?
IT WASN'T YOU THAT MURDERED CHARLES XAVIER IN FRONT OF ALL OF US?!
IT WASN'T ME.

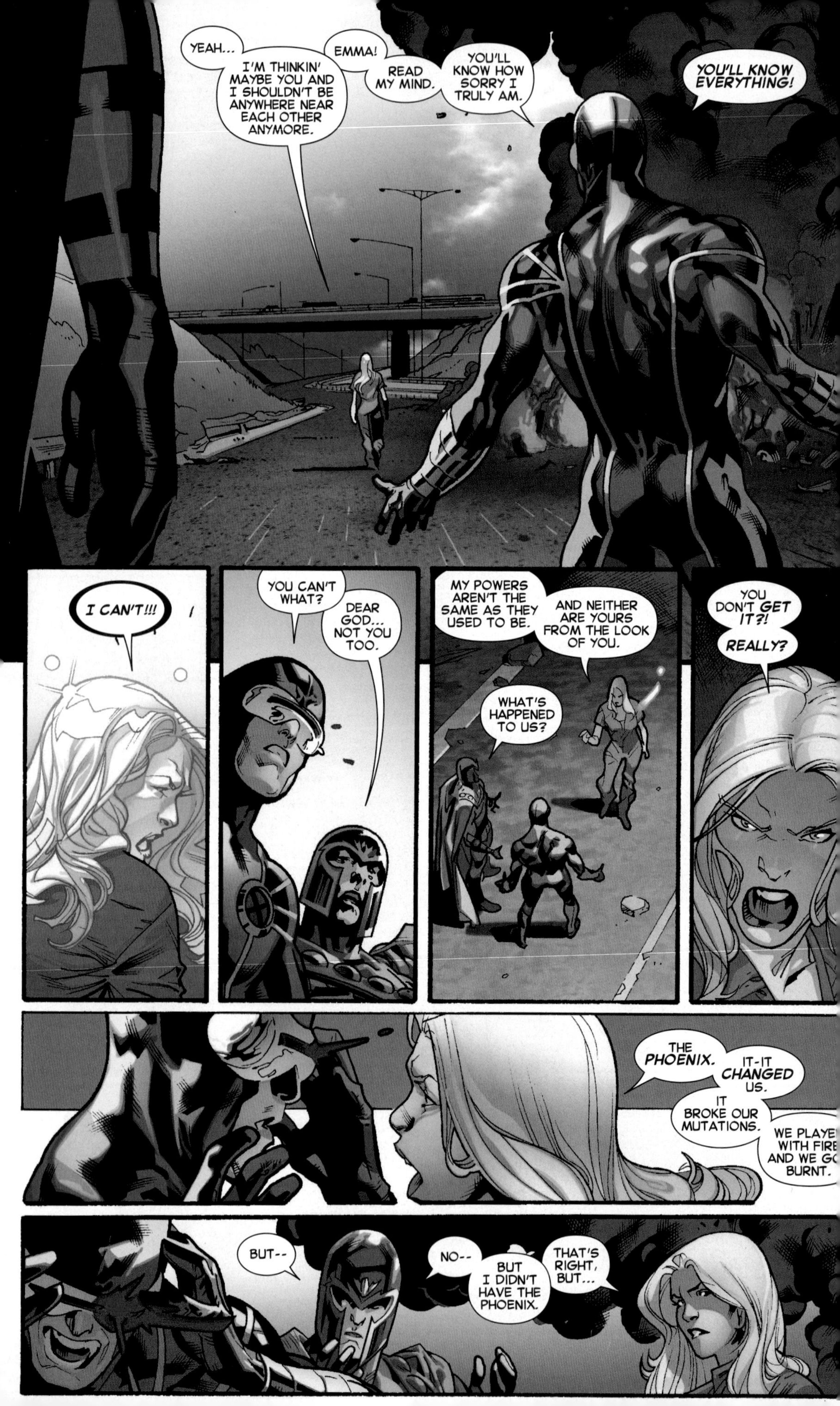
YEAH...
I'M THINKIN' MAYBE YOU AND I SHOULDN'T BE ANYWHERE NEAR EACH OTHER ANYMORE.
EMMA!
READ MY MIND.
YOU'LL KNOW HOW SORRY I TRULY AM.
YOU'LL KNOW EVERYTHING!
I CAN'T!!!
YOU CAN'T WHAT?
DEAR GOD... NOT YOU TOO.
MY POWERS AREN'T THE SAME AS THEY USED TO BE.
AND NEITHER ARE YOURS FROM THE LOOK OF YOU.
WHAT'S HAPPENED TO US?
YOU DON'T GET IT?!
REALLY?
THE PHOENIX.
IT-IT CHANGED US.
IT BROKE OUR MUTATIONS.
WE PLAYE WITH FIRE AND WE GO BURNT.
BUT--
NO--
BUT I DIDN'T HAVE THE PHOENIX.
THAT'S RIGHT, BUT...

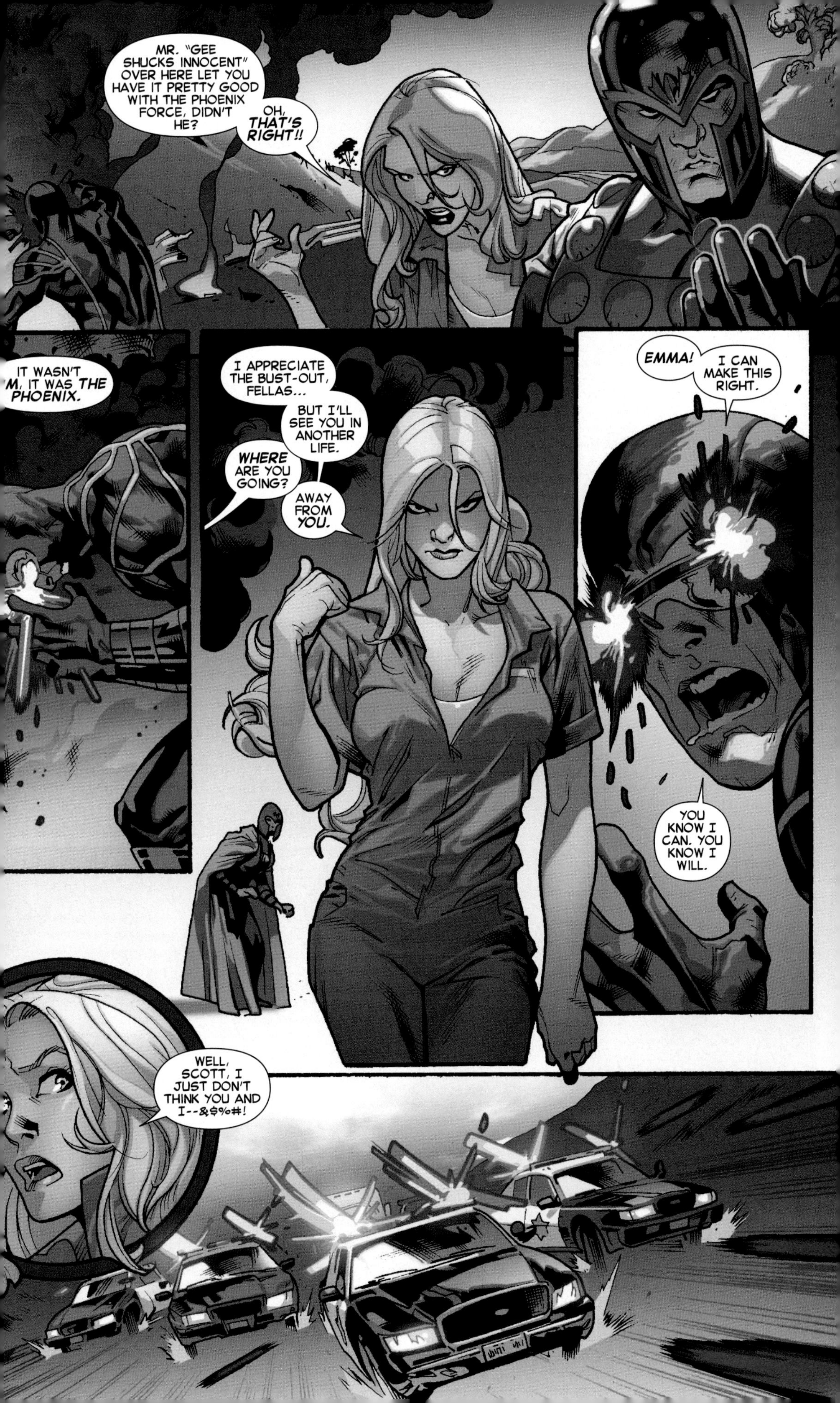
MR. "GEE SHUCKS INNOCENT" OVER HERE LET YOU HAVE IT PRETTY GOOD WITH THE PHOENIX FORCE, DIDN'T HE?
OH, THAT'S RIGHT!!
IT WASN'T M, IT WAS THE PHOENIX.
I APPRECIATE THE BUST-OUT, FELLAS...
BUT I'LL SEE YOU IN ANOTHER LIFE.
WHERE ARE YOU GOING?
AWAY FROM YOU.
EMMA!
I CAN MAKE THIS RIGHT.
YOU KNOW I CAN. YOU KNOW I WILL.
WELL, SCOTT, I JUST DON'T THINK YOU AND I--&$%#!

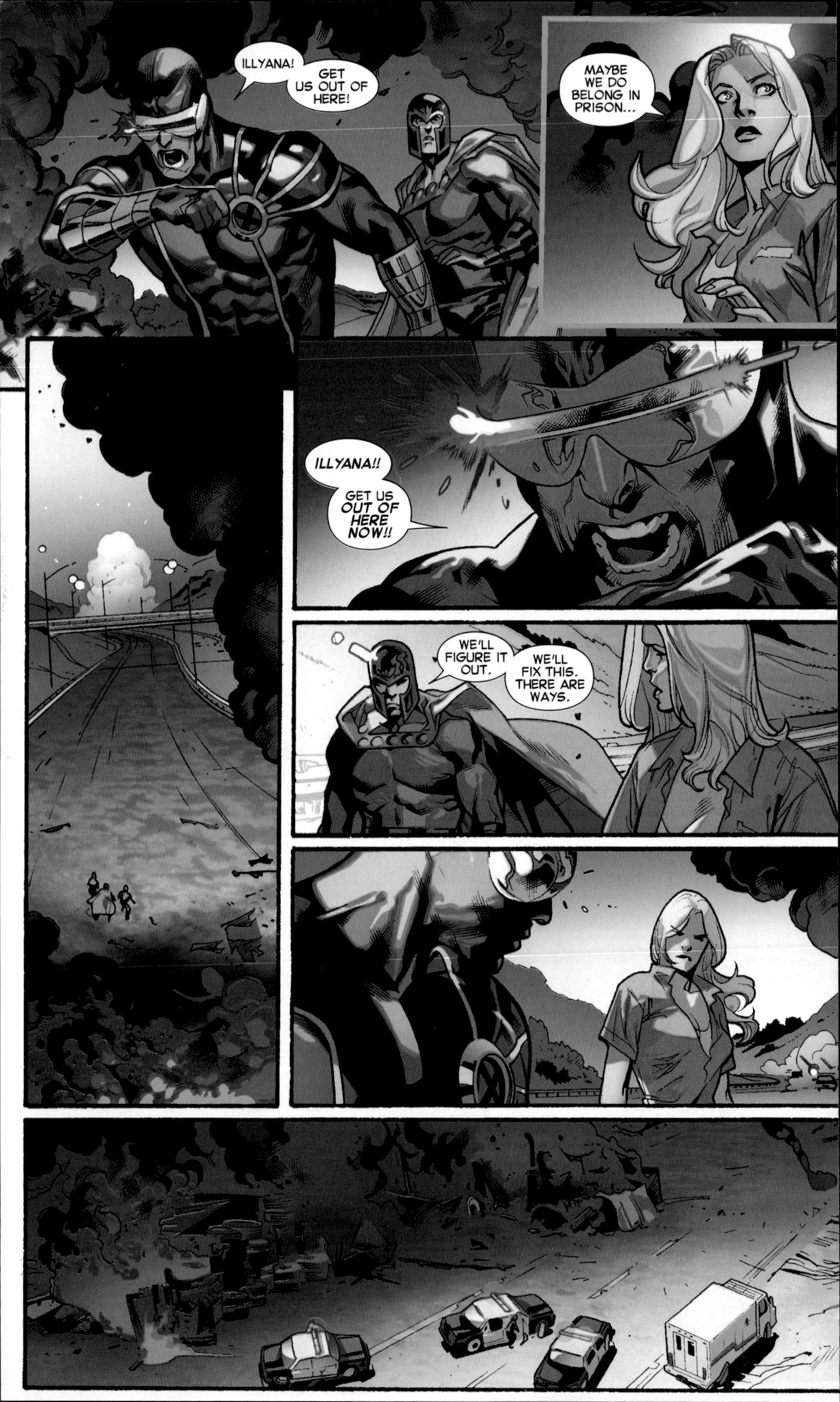
ILLYANA!
GET US OUT OF HERE!
MAYBE WE DO BELONG IN PRISON...
ILLYANA!!
GET US OUT OF HERE NOW!!
WE'LL FIGURE IT OUT.
WE'LL FIX THIS. THERE ARE WAYS.

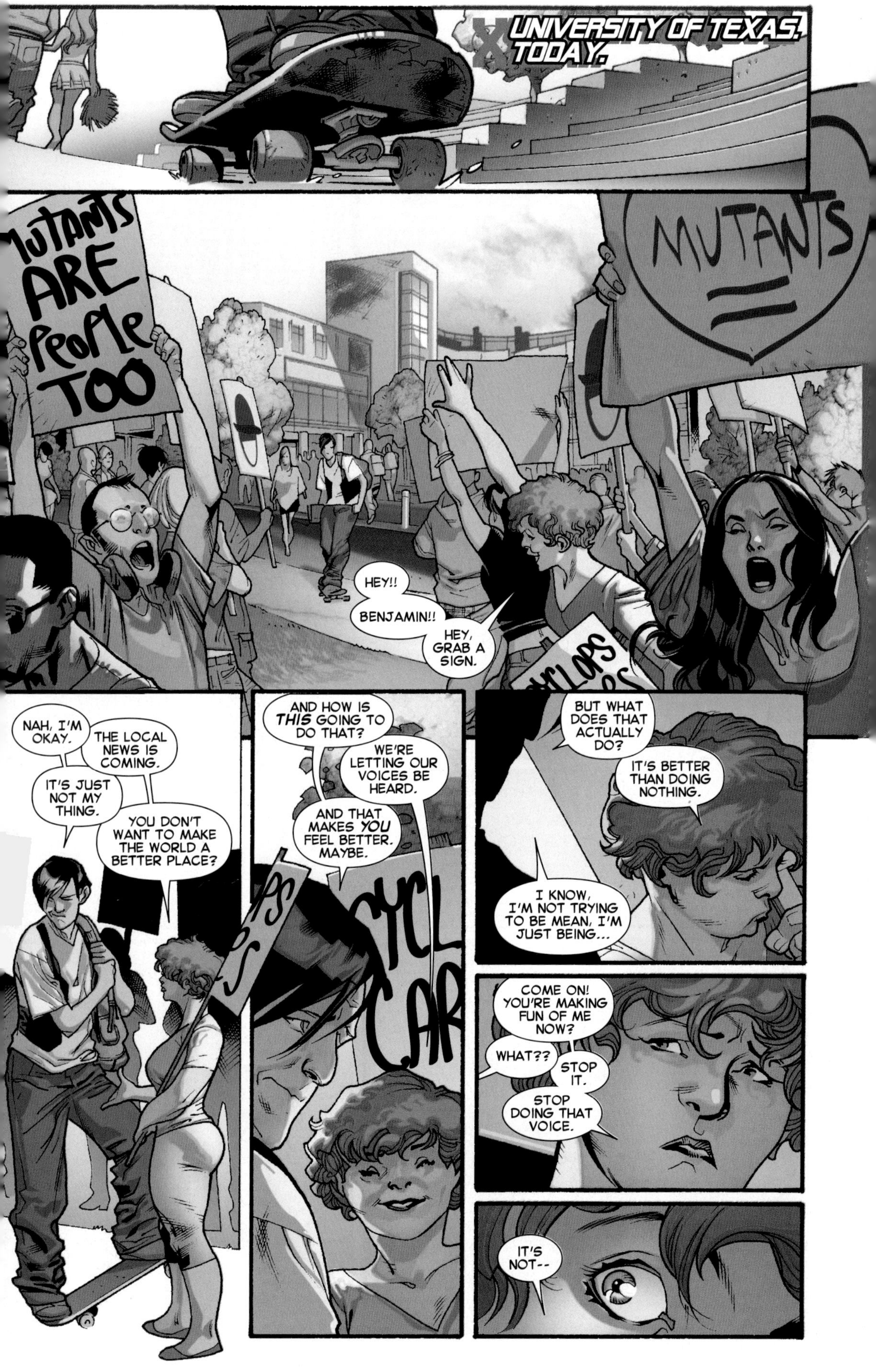
UNIVERSITY OF TEXAS. TODAY.
MUTANTS ARE PEOPLE TOO
MUTANTS =
HEY!!
BENJAMIN!!
HEY, GRAB A SIGN.
NAH, I'M OKAY.
THE LOCAL NEWS IS COMING.
IT'S JUST NOT MY THING.
YOU DON'T WANT TO MAKE THE WORLD A BETTER PLACE?
AND HOW IS THIS GOING TO DO THAT?
WE'RE LETTING OUR VOICES BE HEARD.
AND THAT MAKES YOU FEEL BETTER. MAYBE.
BUT WHAT DOES THAT ACTUALLY DO?
IT'S BETTER THAN DOING NOTHING.
I KNOW, I'M NOT TRYING TO BE MEAN, I'M JUST BEING...
COME ON! YOU'RE MAKING FUN OF ME NOW?
WHAT??
STOP IT.
STOP DOING THAT VOICE.
IT'S NOT--

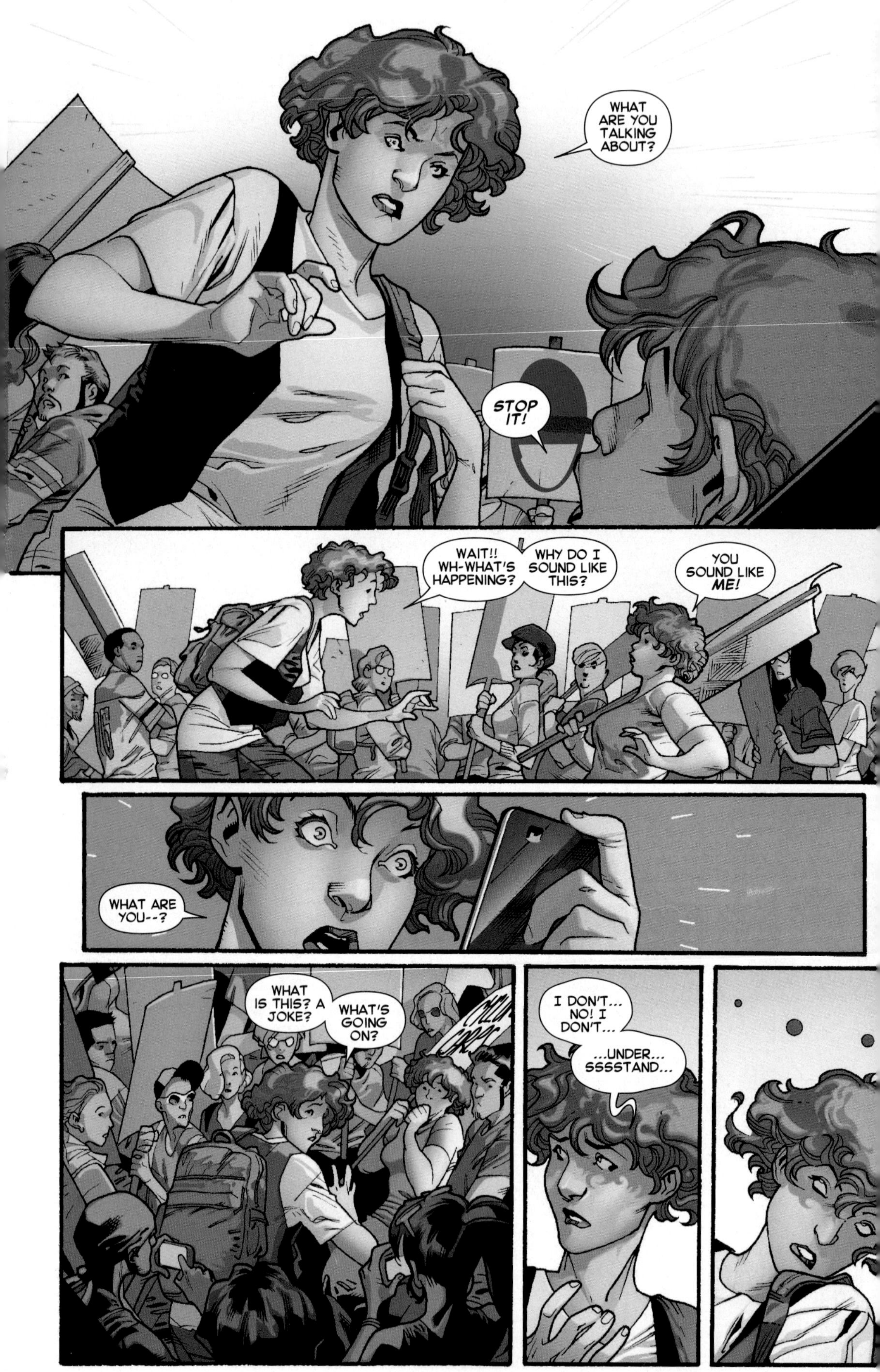
WHAT ARE YOU TALKING ABOUT?
STOP IT!
WAIT!! WH-WHAT'S HAPPENING?
WHY DO I SOUND LIKE THIS?
YOU SOUND LIKE *ME!*
WHAT ARE YOU--?
WHAT IS THIS? A JOKE?
WHAT'S GOING ON?
I DON'T... NO! I DON'T...
...UNDER... SSSSTAND...

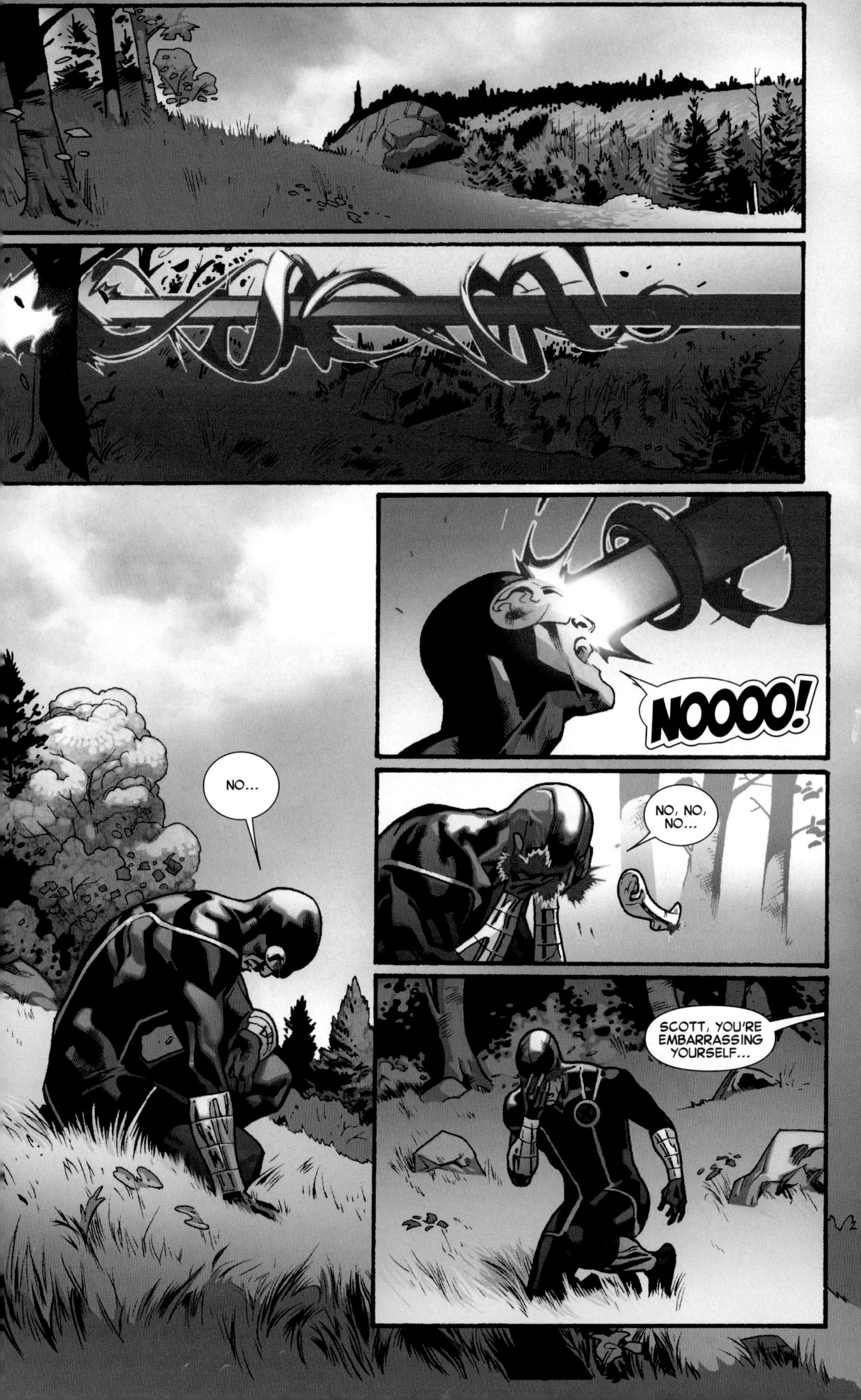
NOOOO!
NO...
NO, NO, NO...
SCOTT, YOU'RE EMBARRASSING YOURSELF...

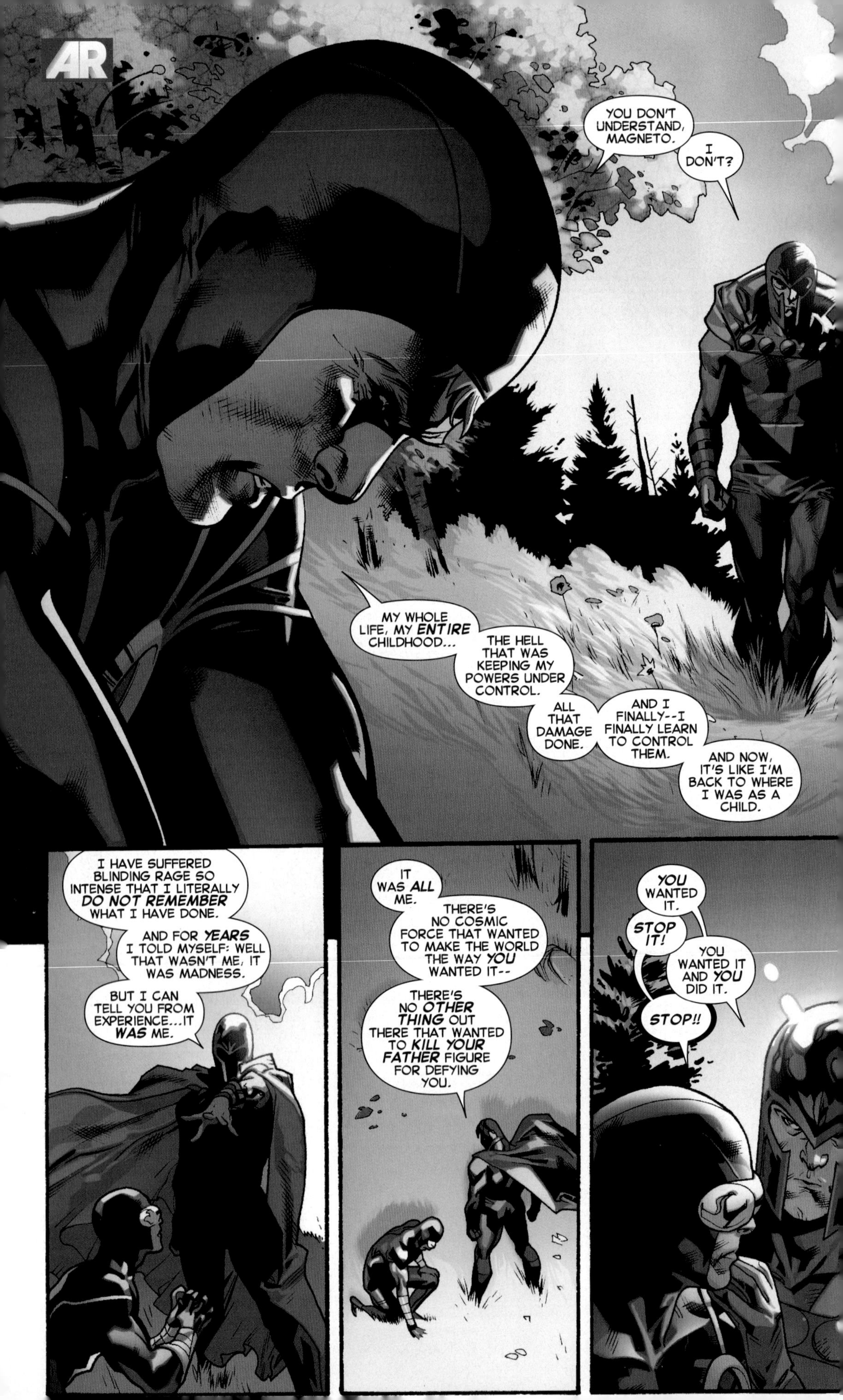
AR
YOU DON'T UNDERSTAND, MAGNETO.
I DON'T?
MY WHOLE LIFE, MY ENTIRE CHILDHOOD...
THE HELL THAT WAS KEEPING MY POWERS UNDER CONTROL.
ALL THAT DAMAGE DONE.
AND I FINALLY--I FINALLY LEARN TO CONTROL THEM.
AND NOW, IT'S LIKE I'M BACK TO WHERE I WAS AS A CHILD.
I HAVE SUFFERED BLINDING RAGE SO INTENSE THAT I LITERALLY DO NOT REMEMBER WHAT I HAVE DONE.
AND FOR YEARS I TOLD MYSELF: WELL THAT WASN'T ME, IT WAS MADNESS.
BUT I CAN TELL YOU FROM EXPERIENCE...IT WAS ME.
IT WAS ALL ME.
THERE'S NO COSMIC FORCE THAT WANTED TO MAKE THE WORLD THE WAY YOU WANTED IT--
THERE'S NO OTHER THING OUT THERE THAT WANTED TO KILL YOUR FATHER FIGURE FOR DEFYING YOU.
YOU WANTED IT.
STOP IT!
YOU WANTED IT AND YOU DID IT.
STOP!!

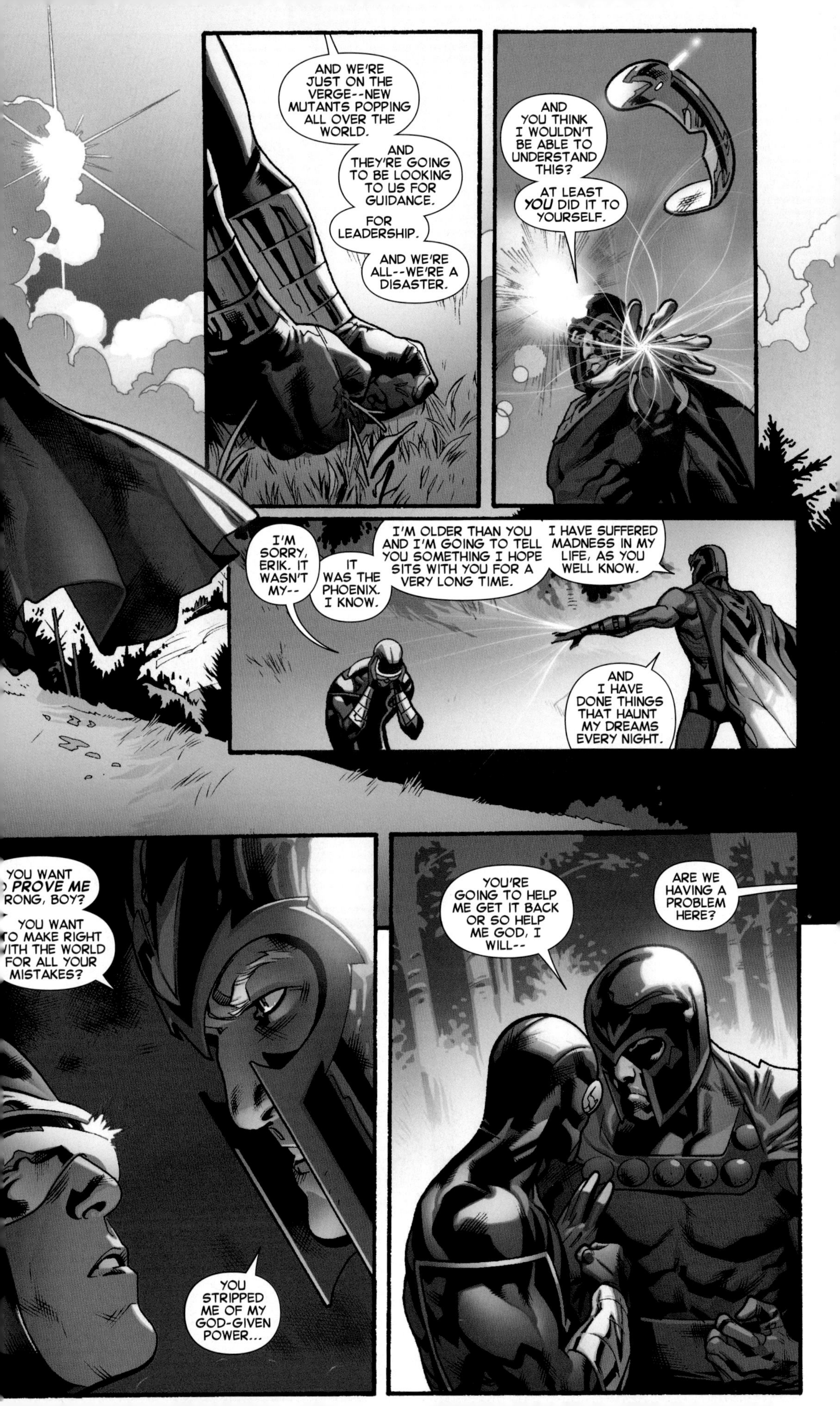

AND WE'RE JUST ON THE VERGE--NEW MUTANTS POPPING ALL OVER THE WORLD.
AND THEY'RE GOING TO BE LOOKING TO US FOR GUIDANCE.
FOR LEADERSHIP.
AND WE'RE ALL--WE'RE A DISASTER.
AND YOU THINK I WOULDN'T BE ABLE TO UNDERSTAND THIS?
AT LEAST *YOU* DID IT TO YOURSELF.
I'M SORRY, ERIK. IT WASN'T MY--
IT WAS THE PHOENIX. I KNOW.
I'M OLDER THAN YOU AND I'M GOING TO TELL YOU SOMETHING I HOPE SITS WITH YOU FOR A VERY LONG TIME.
I HAVE SUFFERED MADNESS IN MY LIFE, AS YOU WELL KNOW.
AND I HAVE DONE THINGS THAT HAUNT MY DREAMS EVERY NIGHT.
YOU WANT O ***PROVE ME*** RONG, BOY?
YOU WANT TO MAKE RIGHT WITH THE WORLD FOR ALL YOUR MISTAKES?
YOU STRIPPED ME OF MY GOD-GIVEN POWER...
YOU'RE GOING TO HELP ME GET IT BACK OR SO HELP ME GOD, I WILL--
ARE WE HAVING A PROBLEM HERE?

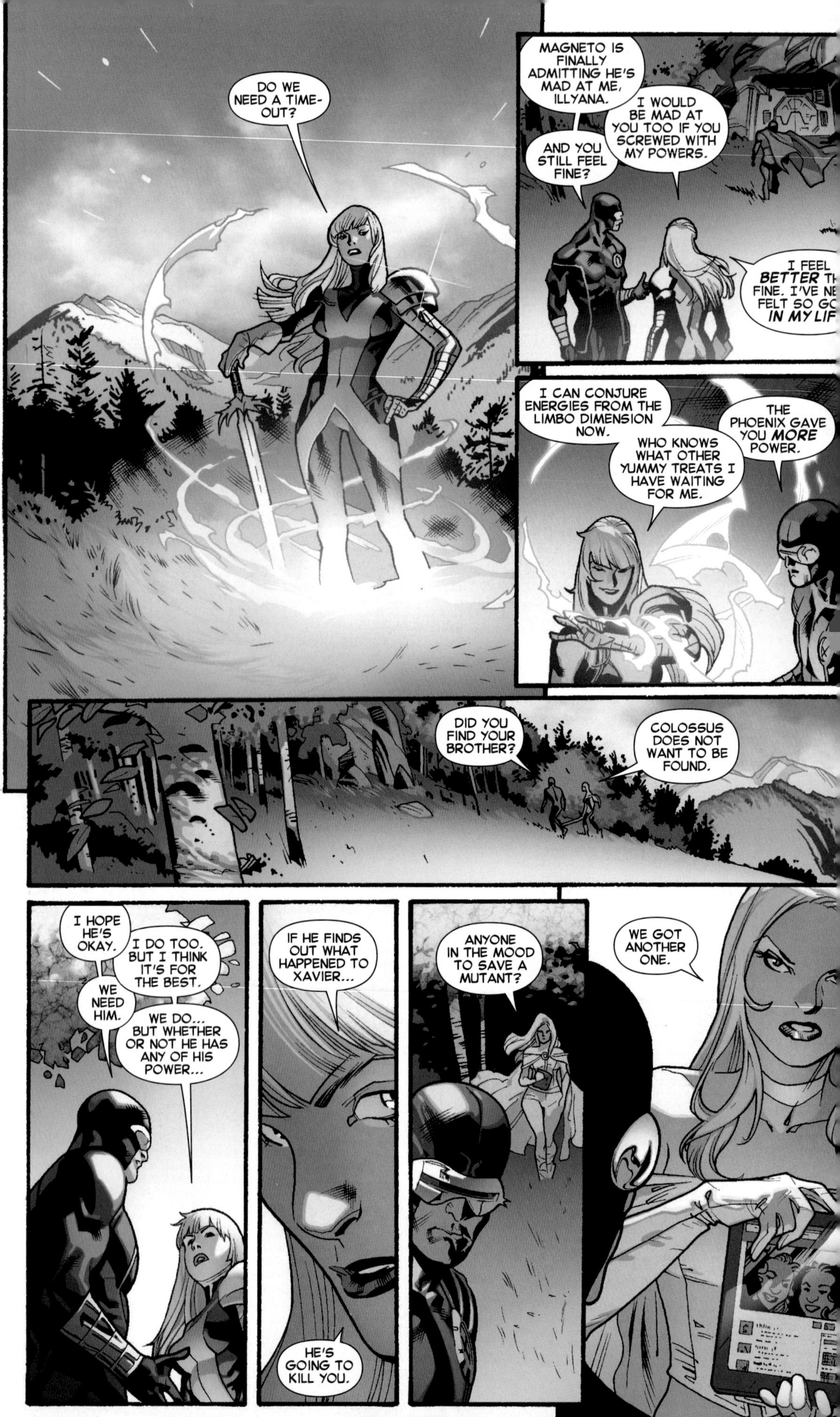

DO WE NEED A TIME-OUT?
MAGNETO IS FINALLY ADMITTING HE'S MAD AT ME, ILLYANA.
I WOULD BE MAD AT YOU TOO IF YOU SCREWED WITH MY POWERS.
AND YOU STILL FEEL FINE?
I CAN CONJURE ENERGIES FROM THE LIMBO DIMENSION NOW.
WHO KNOWS WHAT OTHER YUMMY TREATS I HAVE WAITING FOR ME.
THE PHOENIX GAVE YOU MORE POWER.
DID YOU FIND YOUR BROTHER?
COLOSSUS DOES NOT WANT TO BE FOUND.
I HOPE HE'S OKAY.
I DO TOO. BUT I THINK IT'S FOR THE BEST.
WE NEED HIM.
WE DO... BUT WHETHER OR NOT HE HAS ANY OF HIS POWER...
IF HE FINDS OUT WHAT HAPPENED TO XAVIER...
HE'S GOING TO KILL YOU.
ANYONE IN THE MOOD TO SAVE A MUTANT?
WE GOT ANOTHER ONE.

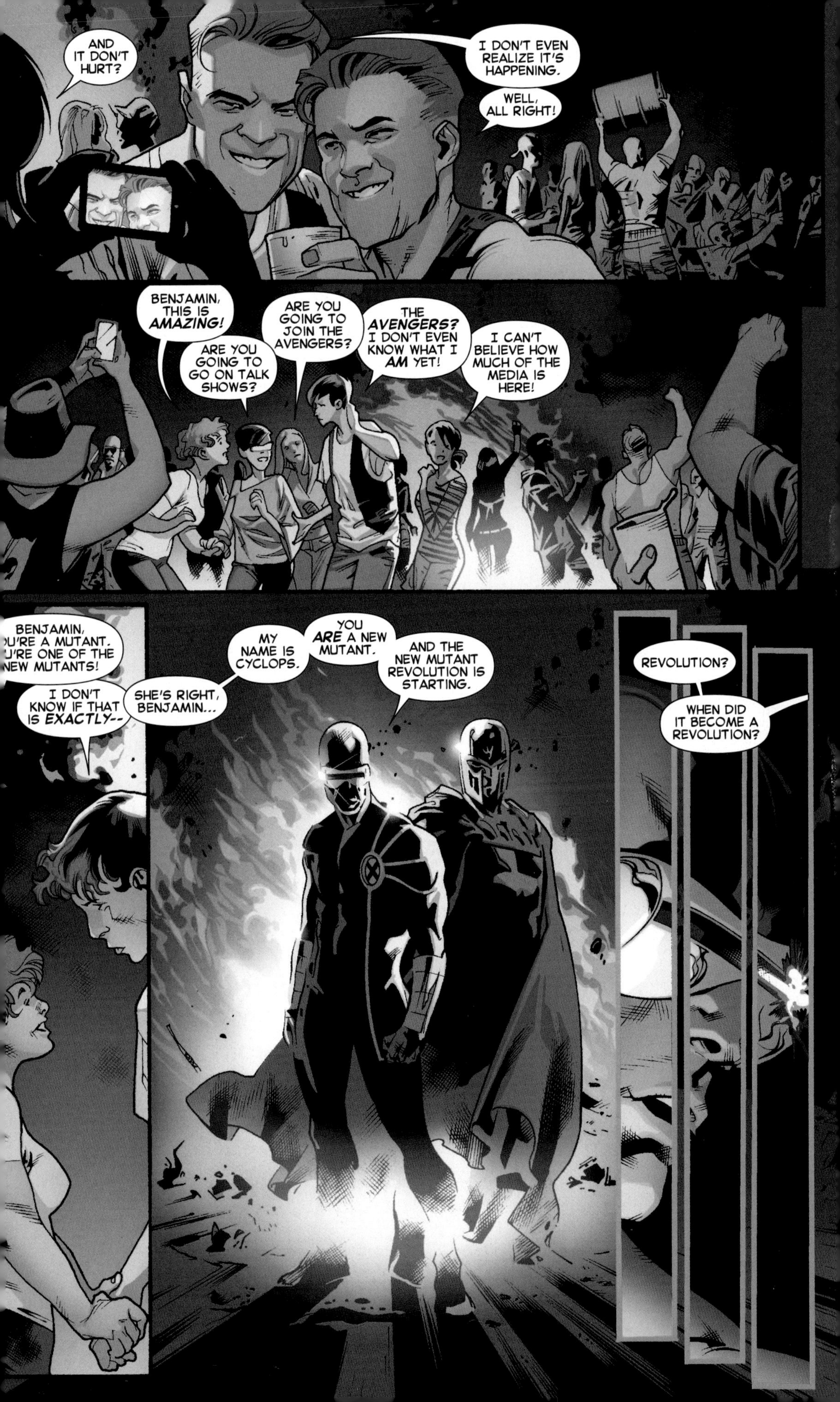
AND IT DON'T HURT?
I DON'T EVEN REALIZE IT'S HAPPENING.
WELL, ALL RIGHT!
BENJAMIN, THIS IS AMAZING!
ARE YOU GOING TO GO ON TALK SHOWS?
ARE YOU GOING TO JOIN THE AVENGERS?
THE AVENGERS? I DON'T EVEN KNOW WHAT I AM YET!
I CAN'T BELIEVE HOW MUCH OF THE MEDIA IS HERE!
BENJAMIN, YOU'RE A MUTANT. YOU'RE ONE OF THE NEW MUTANTS!
I DON'T KNOW IF THAT IS EXACTLY--
SHE'S RIGHT, BENJAMIN...
MY NAME IS CYCLOPS.
YOU ARE A NEW MUTANT.
AND THE NEW MUTANT REVOLUTION IS STARTING.
REVOLUTION?
WHEN DID IT BECOME A REVOLUTION?

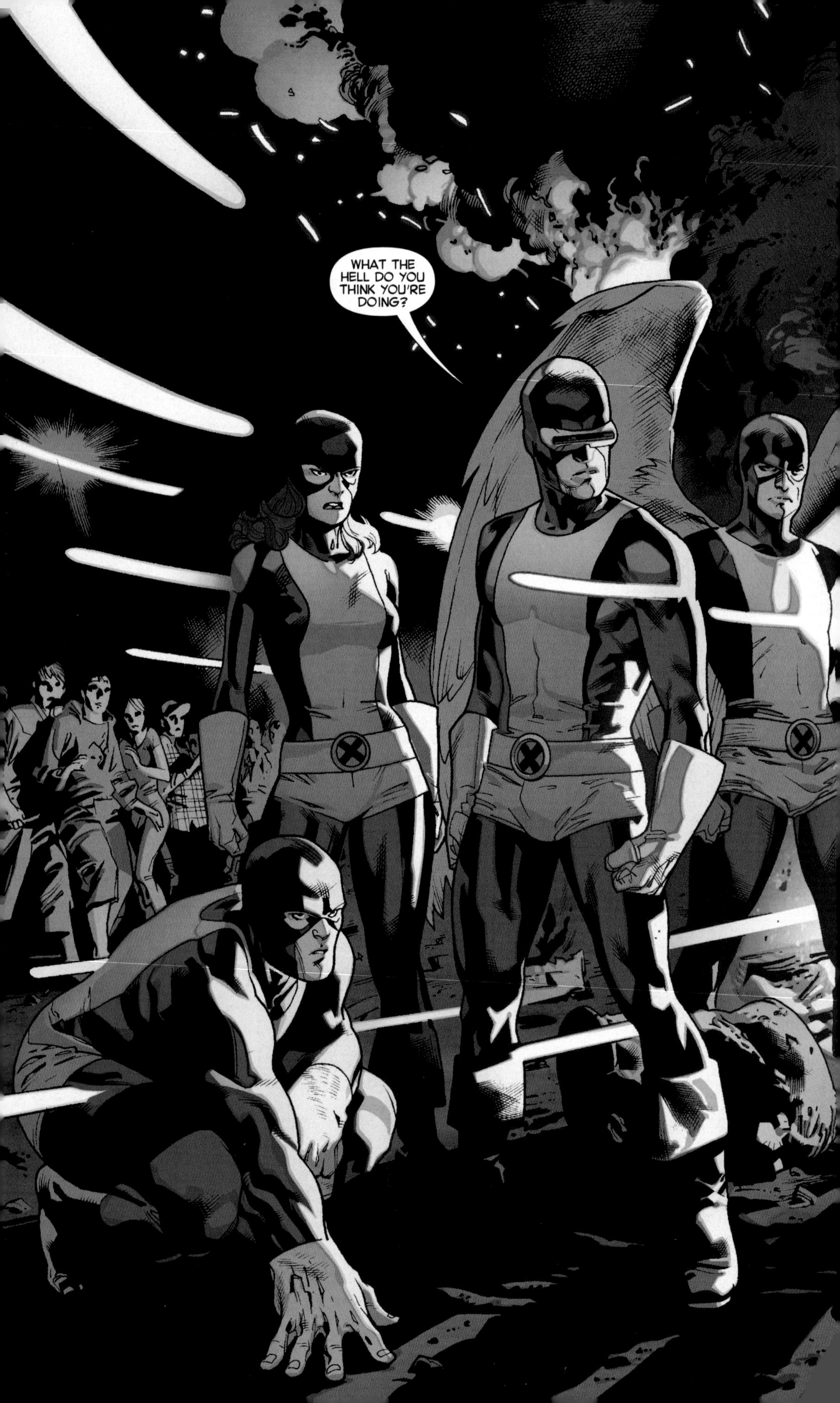
WHAT THE HELL DO YOU THINK YOU'RE DOING?

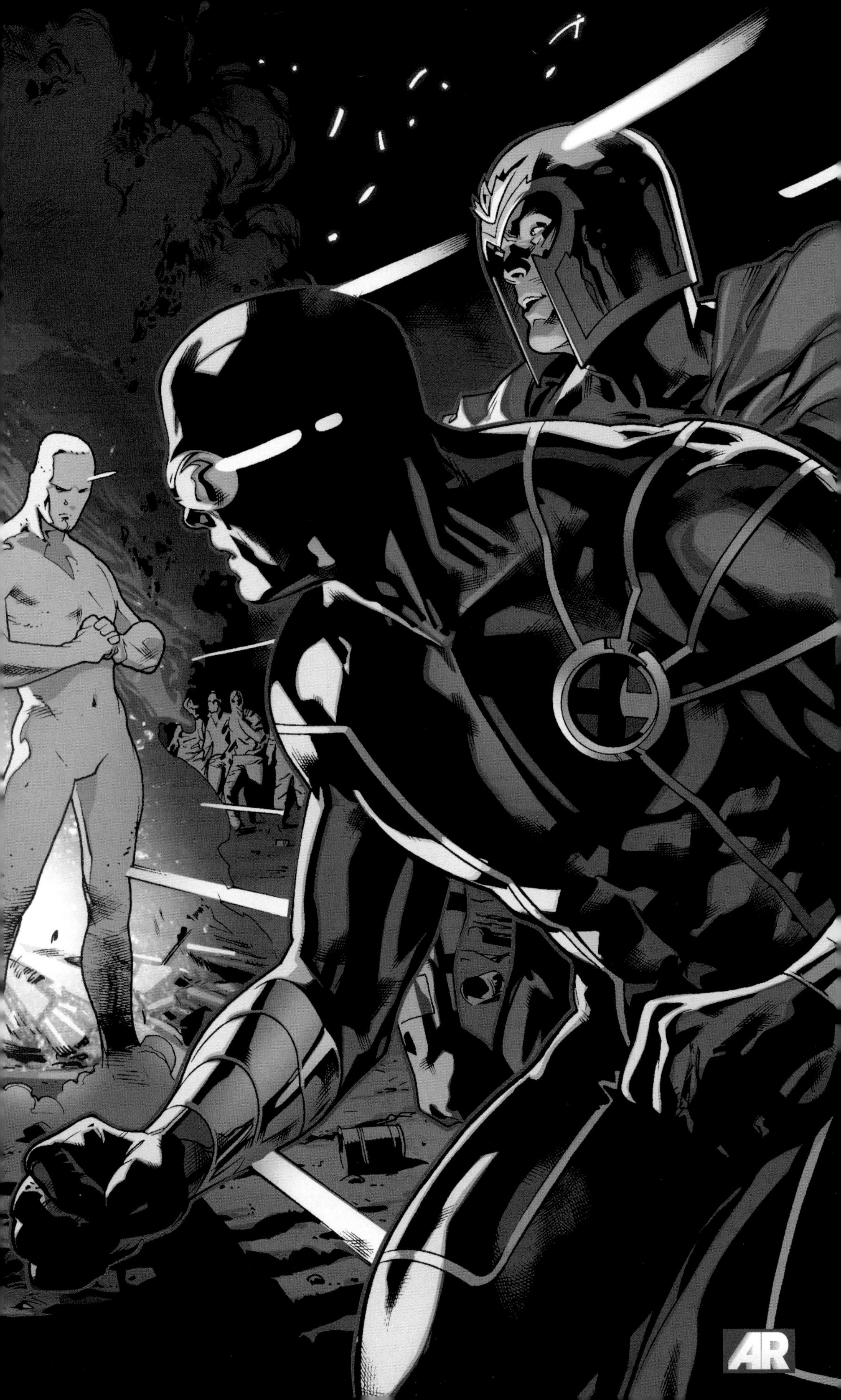

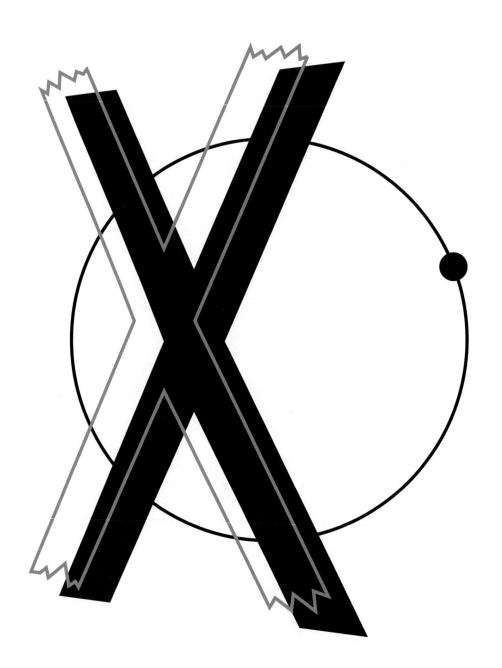

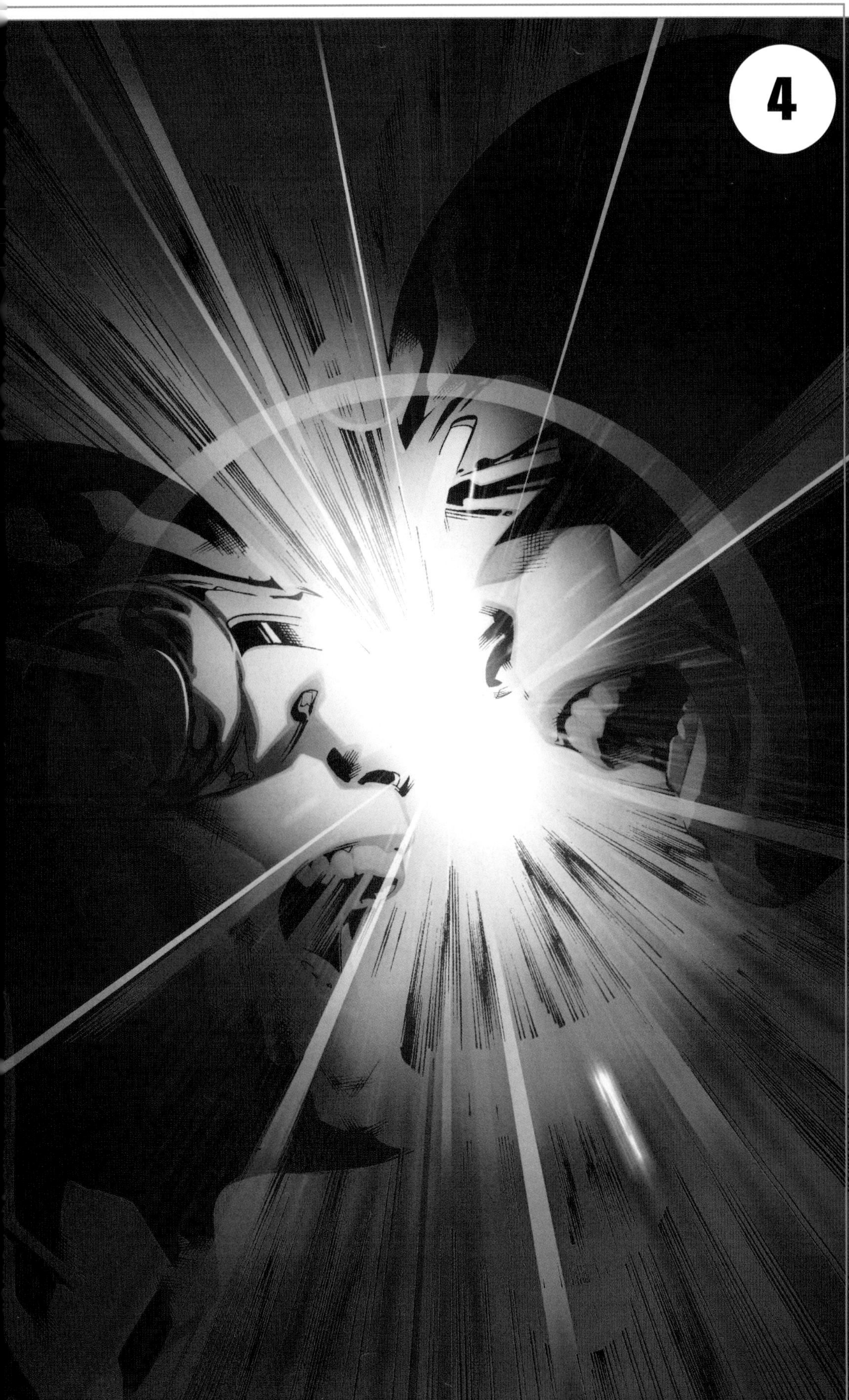
4

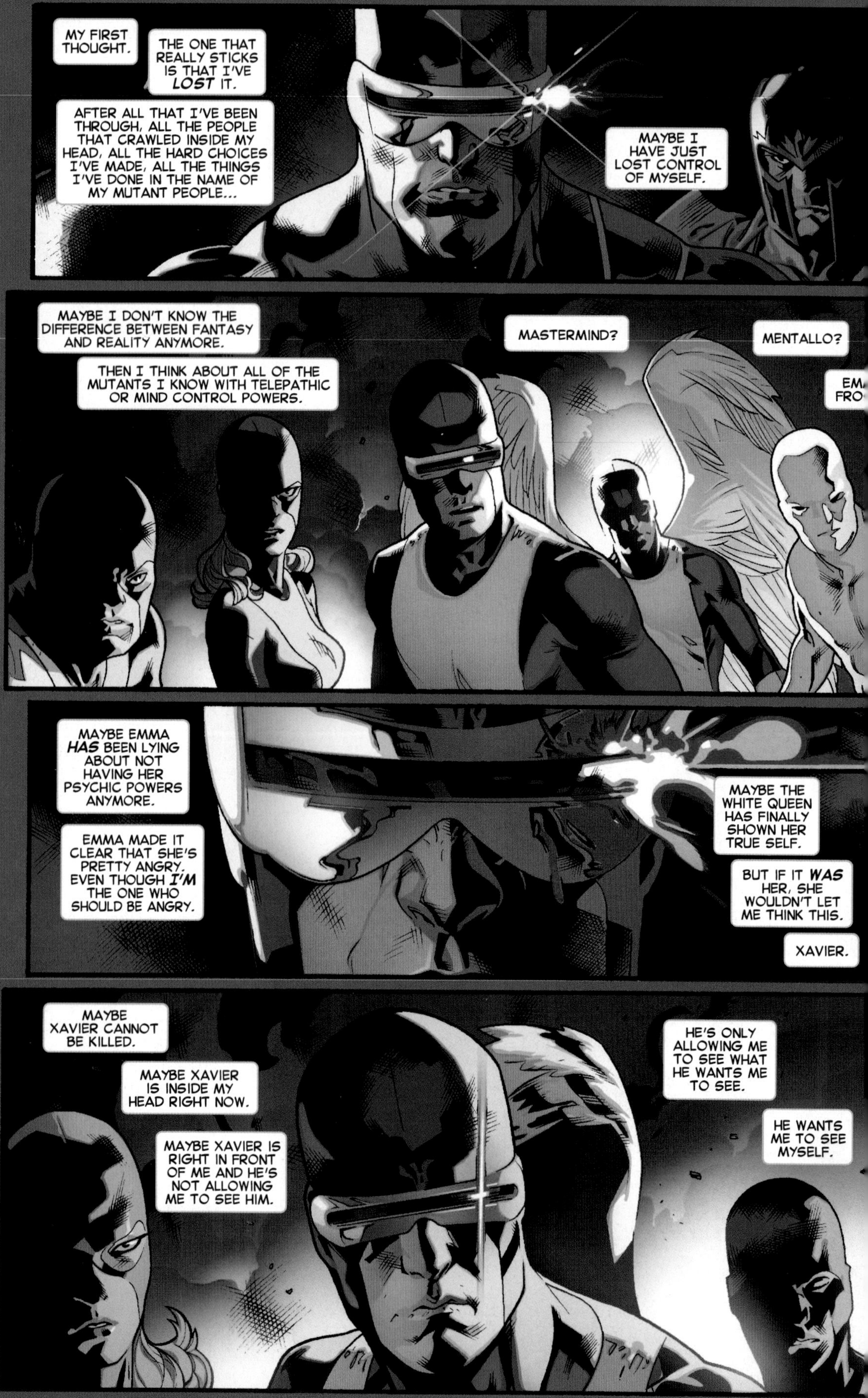
MY FIRST THOUGHT.
THE ONE THAT REALLY STICKS IS THAT I'VE *LOST* IT.
AFTER ALL THAT I'VE BEEN THROUGH, ALL THE PEOPLE THAT CRAWLED INSIDE MY HEAD, ALL THE HARD CHOICES I'VE MADE, ALL THE THINGS I'VE DONE IN THE NAME OF MY MUTANT PEOPLE...
MAYBE I HAVE JUST LOST CONTROL OF MYSELF.
MAYBE I DON'T KNOW THE DIFFERENCE BETWEEN FANTASY AND REALITY ANYMORE.
THEN I THINK ABOUT ALL OF THE MUTANTS I KNOW WITH TELEPATHIC OR MIND CONTROL POWERS.
MASTERMIND?
MENTALLO?
MAYBE EMMA *HAS* BEEN LYING ABOUT NOT HAVING HER PSYCHIC POWERS ANYMORE.
EMMA MADE IT CLEAR THAT SHE'S PRETTY ANGRY. EVEN THOUGH *I'M* THE ONE WHO SHOULD BE ANGRY.
MAYBE THE WHITE QUEEN HAS FINALLY SHOWN HER TRUE SELF.
BUT IF IT *WAS* HER, SHE WOULDN'T LET ME THINK THIS.
XAVIER.
MAYBE XAVIER CANNOT BE KILLED.
MAYBE XAVIER IS INSIDE MY HEAD RIGHT NOW.
MAYBE XAVIER IS RIGHT IN FRONT OF ME AND HE'S NOT ALLOWING ME TO SEE HIM.
HE'S ONLY ALLOWING ME TO SEE WHAT HE WANTS ME TO SEE.
HE WANTS ME TO SEE MYSELF.

WANTS ME SEE WHO I S WHEN HE OVED ME.
WHEN I WAS EVERYTHING THAT HE WANTED ME TO BE.
HE WANTS ME TO SEE THE ORIGINAL X-MEN.
HE WANTS ME TO SEE US WHEN WE WERE PURE.
WHEN WE DIDN'T KNOW ANY BETTER.
WHEN WE DIDN'T KNOW WHAT THE WORLD WAS REALLY LIKE.
BUT I KNOW IN MY HEART THAT XAVIER'S DEAD.
AND I KNOW, IF I REALLY THINK ABOUT IT, I KNOW THAT NO MATTER HOW ANGRY EMMA IS--SHE WOULD NEVER DO THIS.
O I HAVE TO REALLY THINK ABOUT WHO OULD DO THIS.
WHO WOULD PUNISH ME THIS VICIOUSLY.
THEN I THINK ABOUT SHAPE-SHIFTERS.
I THINK ABOUT MYSTIQUE.
BUT THERE WOULD HAVE TO BE FIVE SHAPE-SHIFTERS, WOULDN'T THERE?
AND THEY WOULD HAVE TO BE FANTASTIC.
NO.
SOMEHOW THIS IS REAL.
I AM LOOKING RIGHT AT MYSELF.

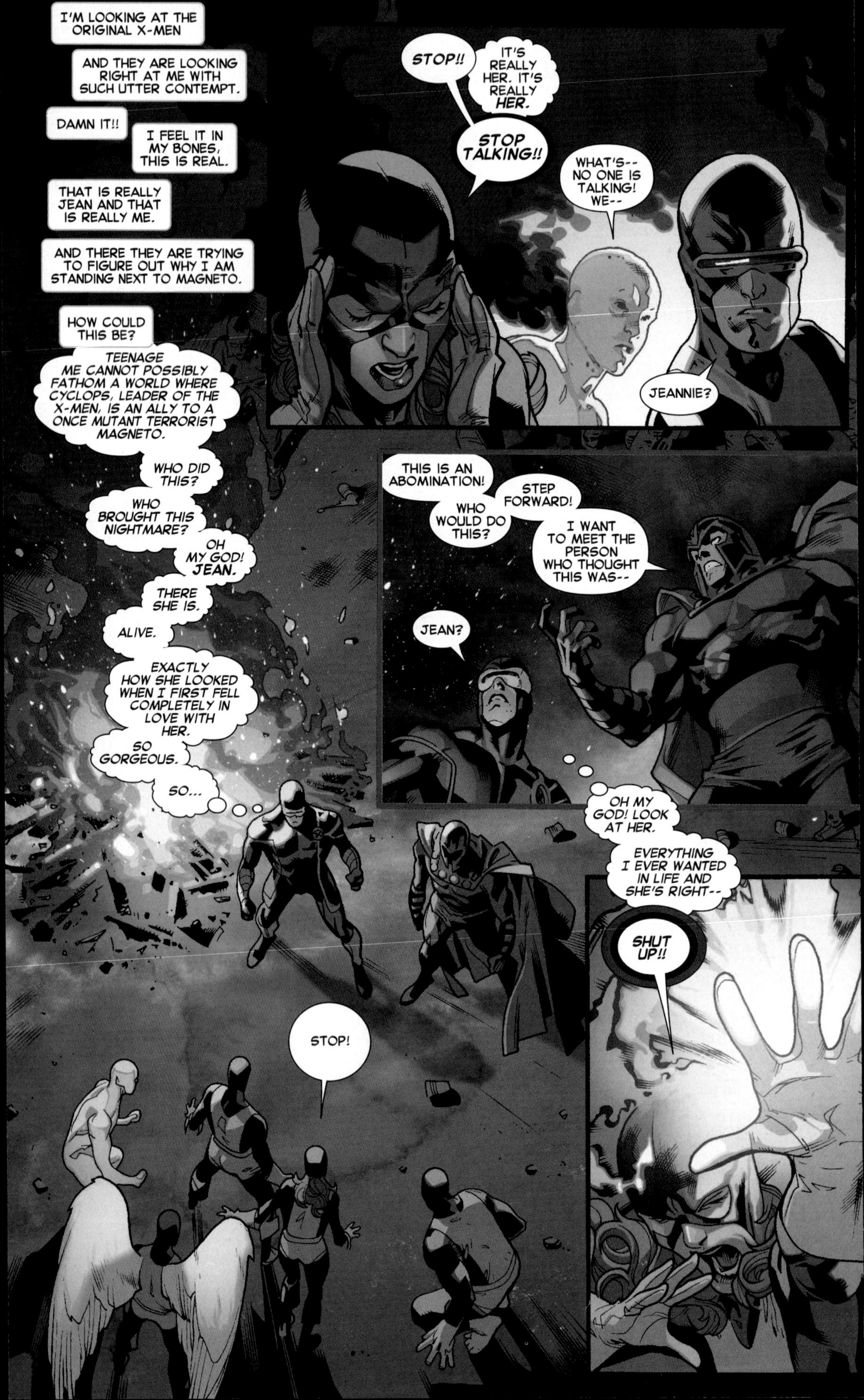
I'M LOOKING AT THE ORIGINAL X-MEN
AND THEY ARE LOOKING RIGHT AT ME WITH SUCH UTTER CONTEMPT.
DAMN IT!!
I FEEL IT IN MY BONES, THIS IS REAL.
THAT IS REALLY JEAN AND THAT IS REALLY ME.
AND THERE THEY ARE TRYING TO FIGURE OUT WHY I AM STANDING NEXT TO MAGNETO.
HOW COULD THIS BE?
TEENAGE ME CANNOT POSSIBLY FATHOM A WORLD WHERE CYCLOPS, LEADER OF THE X-MEN, IS AN ALLY TO A ONCE MUTANT TERRORIST MAGNETO.
STOP!!
IT'S REALLY HER. IT'S REALLY HER.
STOP TALKING!!
WHAT'S-- NO ONE IS TALKING! WE--
JEANNIE?
WHO DID THIS?
WHO BROUGHT THIS NIGHTMARE?
OH MY GOD! JEAN.
THERE SHE IS.
ALIVE.
EXACTLY HOW SHE LOOKED WHEN I FIRST FELL COMPLETELY IN LOVE WITH HER.
SO GORGEOUS.
SO...
THIS IS AN ABOMINATION!
WHO WOULD DO THIS?
STEP FORWARD!
I WANT TO MEET THE PERSON WHO THOUGHT THIS WAS--
JEAN?
OH MY GOD! LOOK AT HER.
EVERYTHING I EVER WANTED IN LIFE AND SHE'S RIGHT--
STOP!
SHUT UP!!

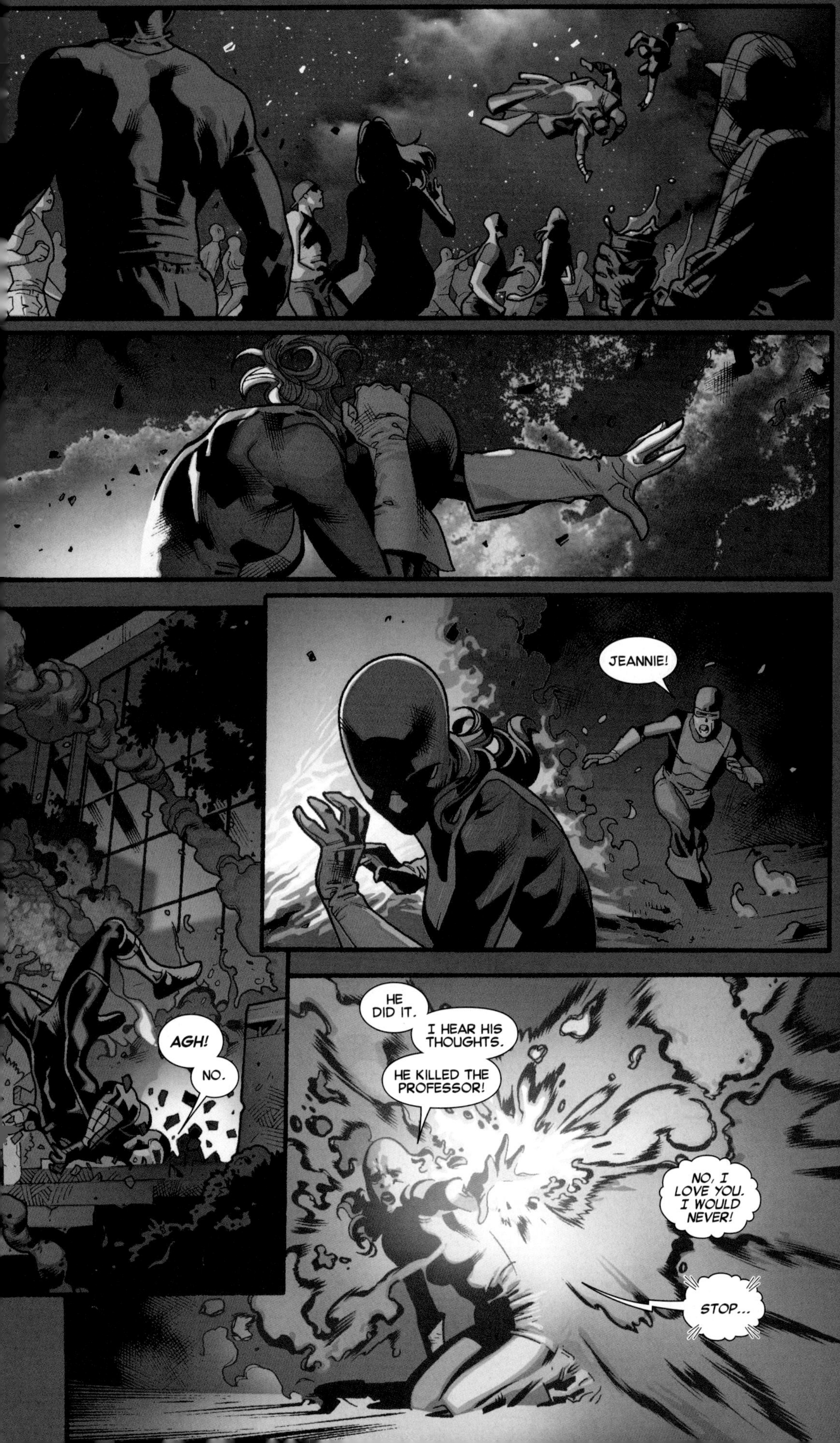
JEANNIE!
AGH!
NO.
HE DID IT.
I HEAR HIS THOUGHTS.
HE KILLED THE PROFESSOR!
NO, I LOVE YOU. I WOULD NEVER!
STOP...

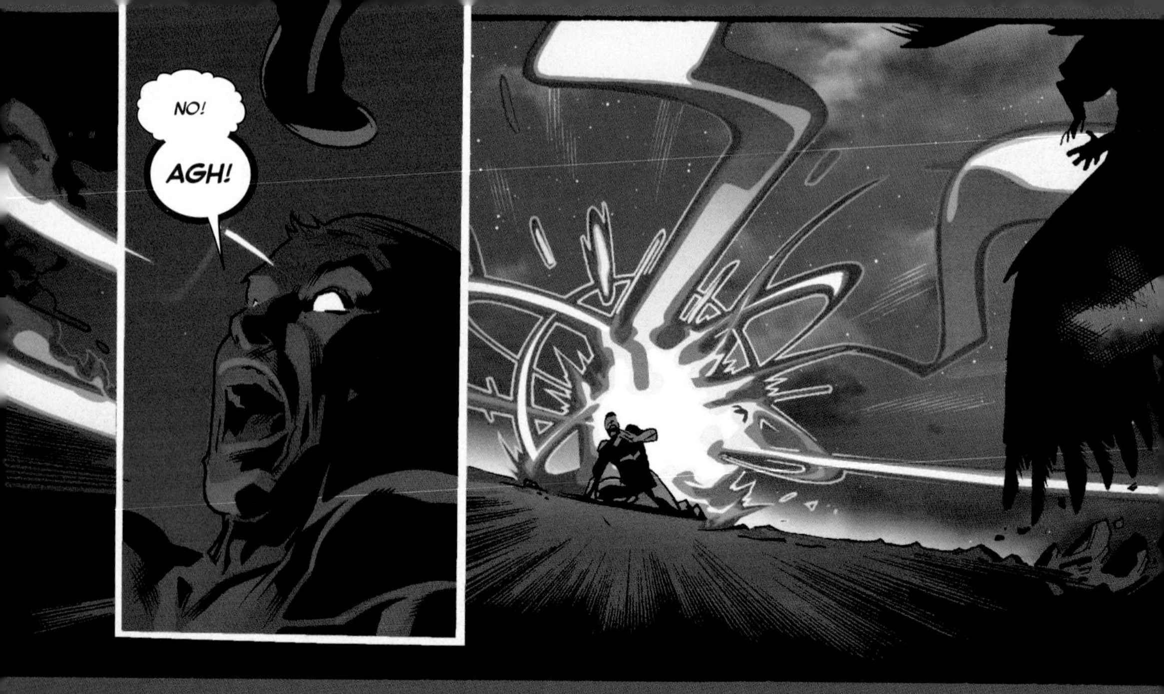
NO!
AGH!

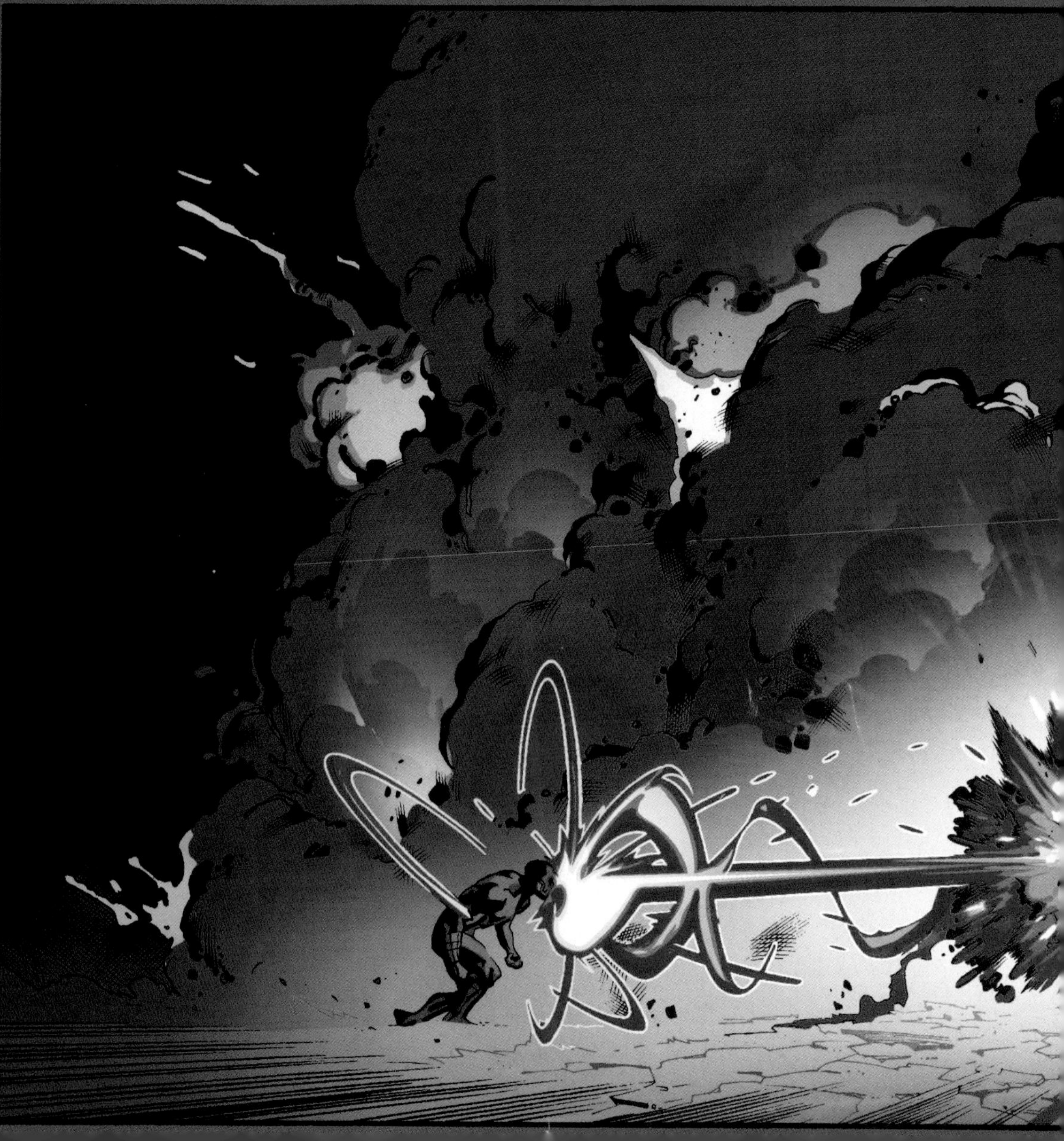

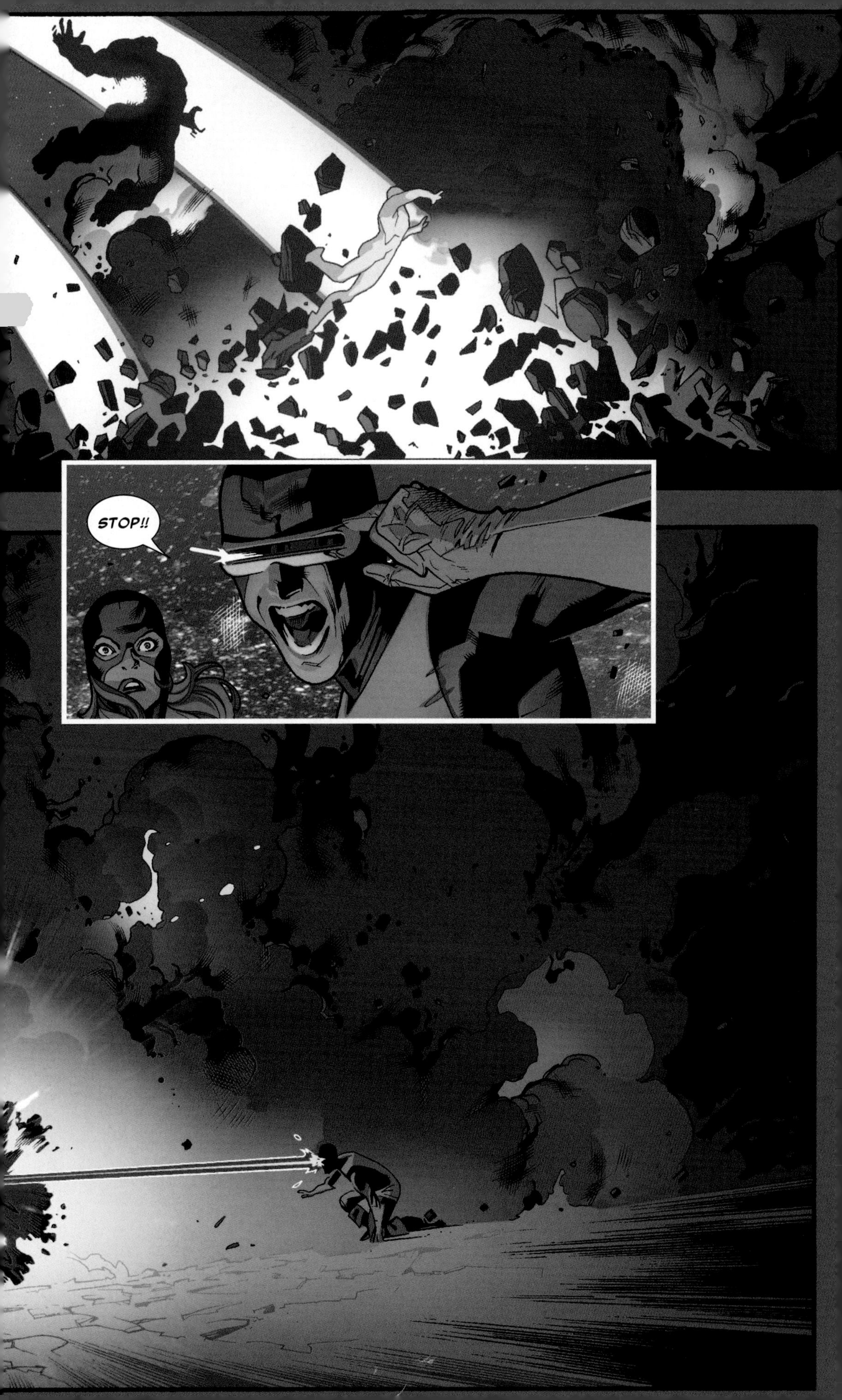
STOP!!

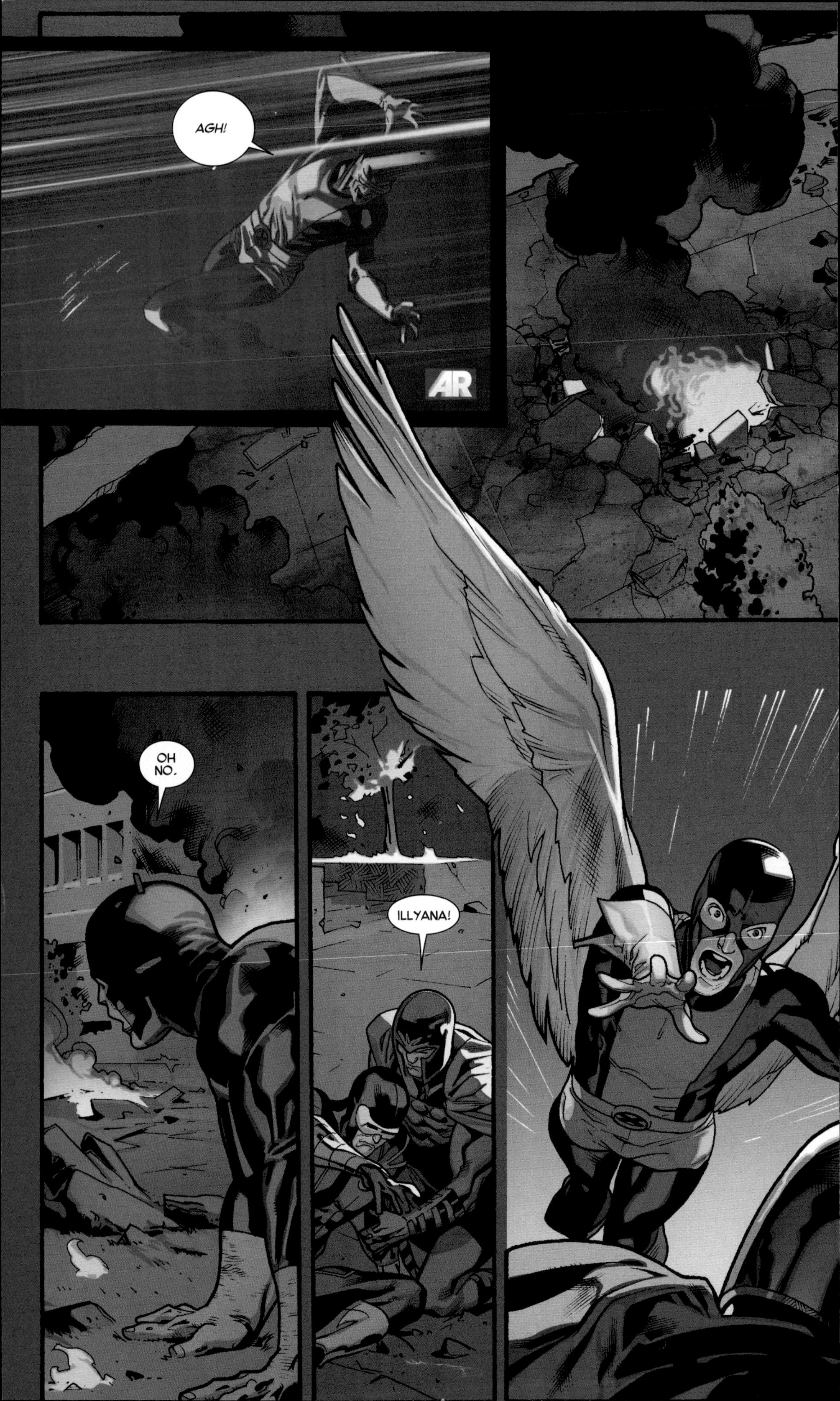

AGH!
AR
OH NO.
ILLYANA!

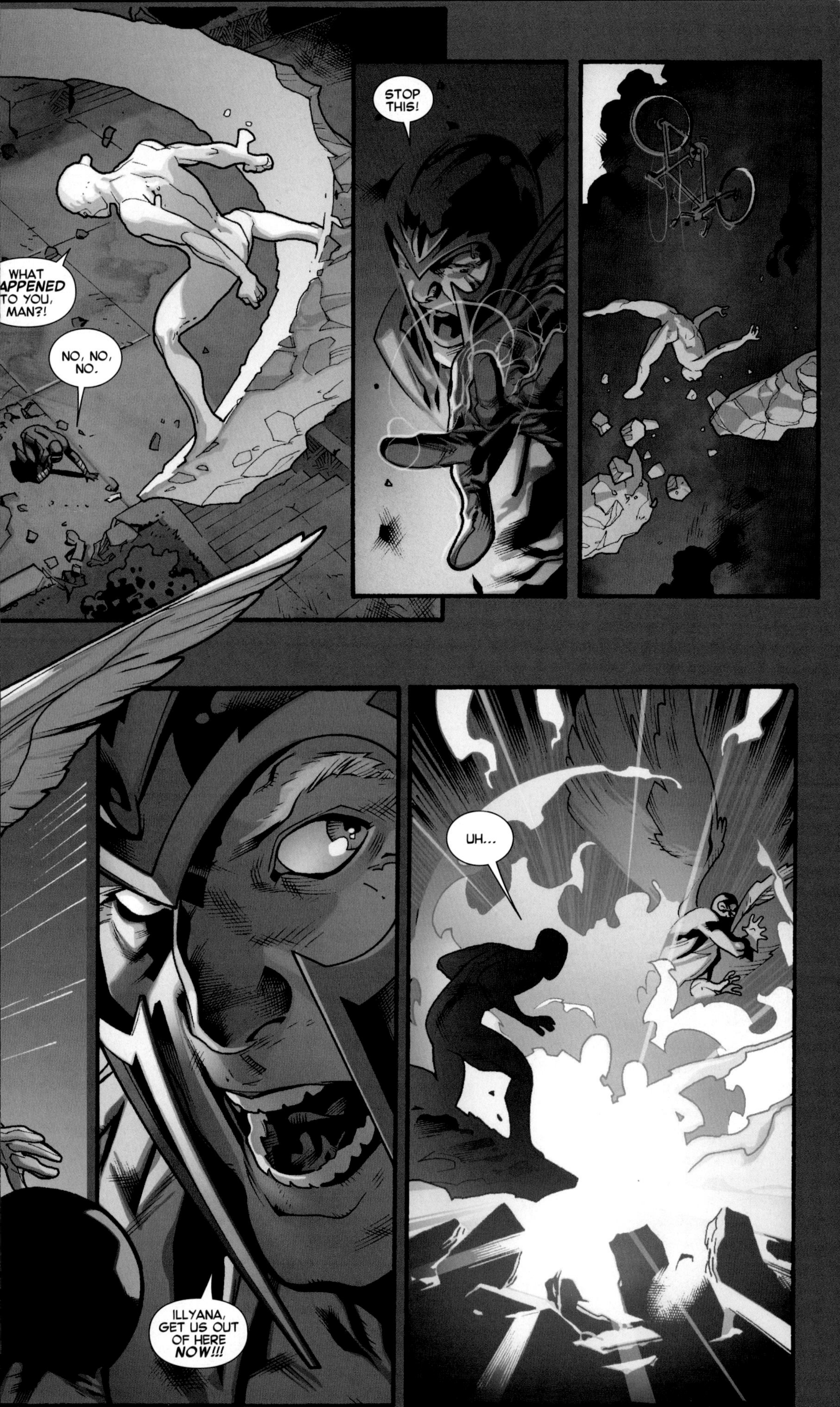
WHAT HAPPENED TO YOU, MAN?!
NO, NO, NO.
STOP THIS!
UH...
ILLYANA, GET US OUT OF HERE NOW!!!

HE RAN AWAY? MAGNETO RAN AWAY?!

SINCE WHEN DOES HE DO THAT?

THIS ISN'T THE FUTURE! THIS IS PLANET BACKWARDS!

I CAN'T BELIEVE SCOTT JUST ATTACKED US LIKE THAT.

BENJAMIN?

OH MY GOD, BENJAMIN!! ARE YOU OKAY?

I--

WHAT IS GOING ON?

I HAVE NO IDEA.

YOU TURN INTO A MUTANT AND THE FRICKIN' X-MEN SHOW UP AND START BEATING THE HELL OUT OF EACH OTHER?

AND THEN THEY JUST LEAVE?

THIS IS CRAZY.

WERE THEY HERE FOR ME?

IT LOOKED LIKE IT, RIGHT?

UH, YEAH.

I TH THIS M YOU ACTUA MUTA

I MEA THAT V CYCLO

TWO CYCLOPS.

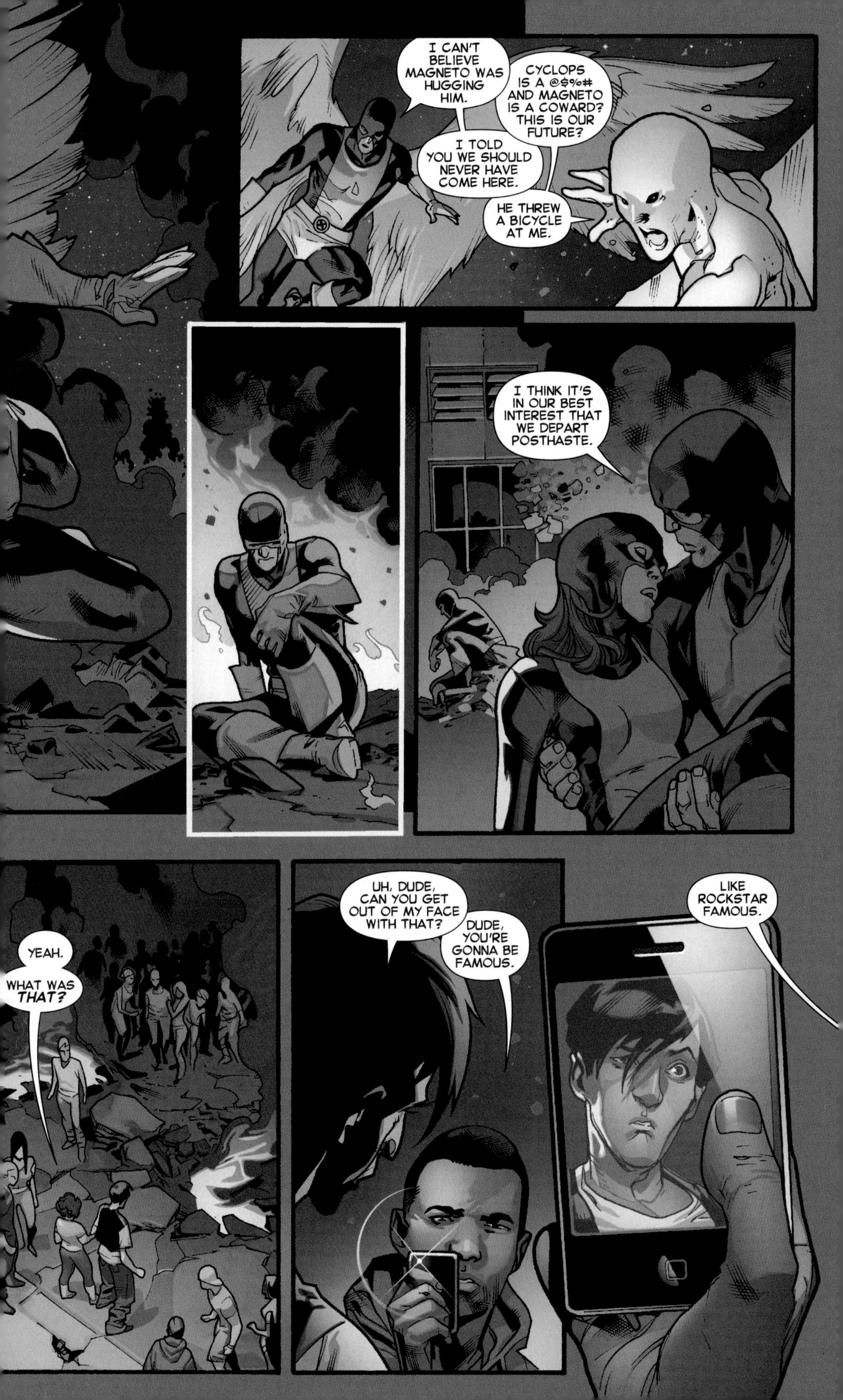
I CAN'T BELIEVE MAGNETO WAS HUGGING HIM.
CYCLOPS IS A @$%# AND MAGNETO IS A COWARD? THIS IS OUR FUTURE?
I TOLD YOU WE SHOULD NEVER HAVE COME HERE.
HE THREW A BICYCLE AT ME.
I THINK IT'S IN OUR BEST INTEREST THAT WE DEPART POSTHASTE.
YEAH.
WHAT WAS *THAT?*
UH, DUDE, CAN YOU GET OUT OF MY FACE WITH THAT?
DUDE, YOU'RE GONNA BE FAMOUS.
LIKE ROCKSTAR FAMOUS.

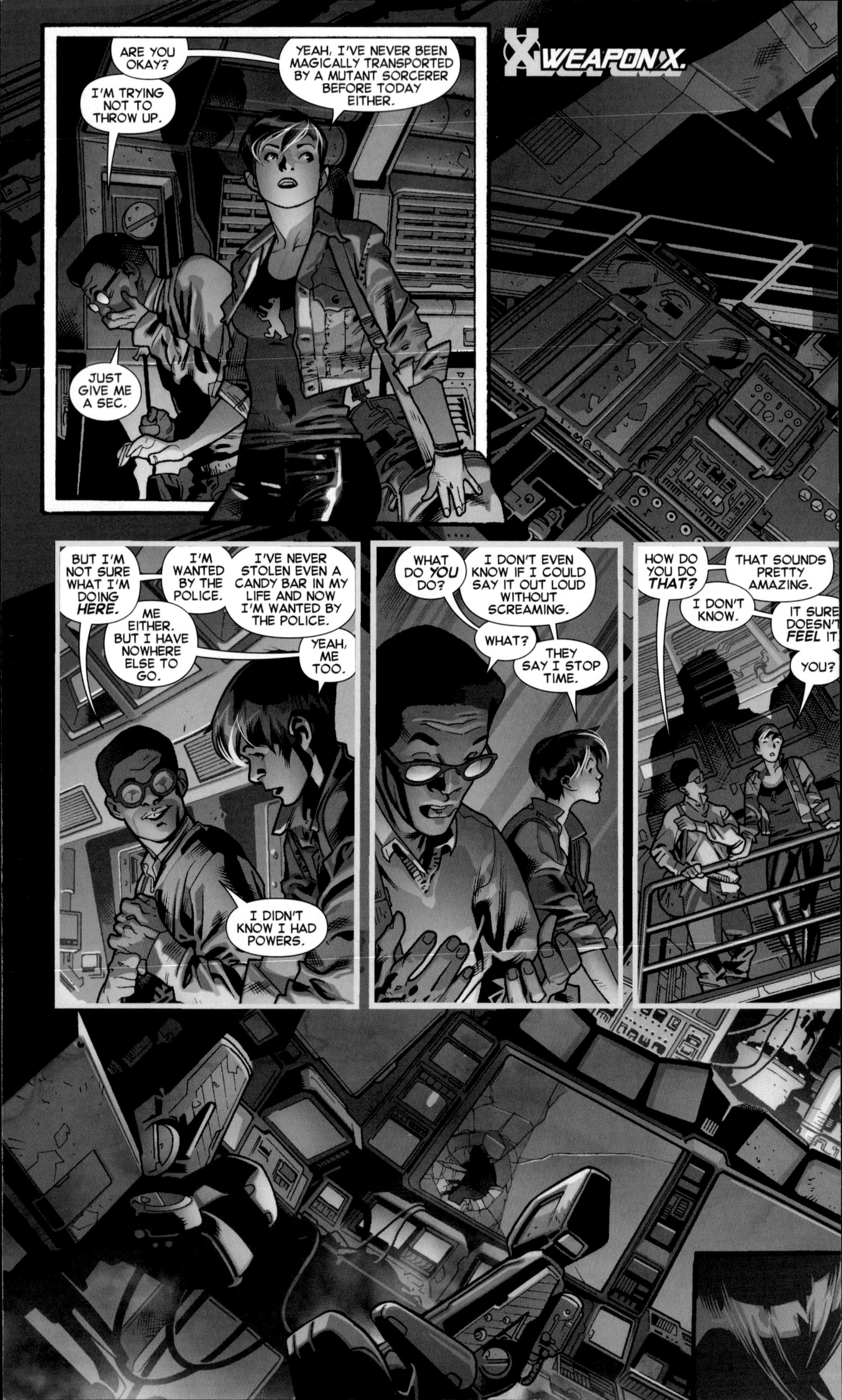
WEAPON X.
ARE YOU OKAY?
YEAH, I'VE NEVER BEEN MAGICALLY TRANSPORTED BY A MUTANT SORCERER BEFORE TODAY EITHER.
I'M TRYING NOT TO THROW UP.
JUST GIVE ME A SEC.
BUT I'M NOT SURE WHAT I'M DOING HERE.
I'M WANTED BY THE POLICE.
I'VE NEVER STOLEN EVEN A CANDY BAR IN MY LIFE AND NOW I'M WANTED BY THE POLICE.
ME EITHER. BUT I HAVE NOWHERE ELSE TO GO.
YEAH, ME TOO.
I DIDN'T KNOW I HAD POWERS.
WHAT DO YOU DO?
I DON'T EVEN KNOW IF I COULD SAY IT OUT LOUD WITHOUT SCREAMING.
WHAT?
THEY SAY I STOP TIME.
HOW DO YOU DO THAT?
THAT SOUNDS PRETTY AMAZING.
I DON'T KNOW.
IT SURE DOESN'T FEEL IT.
YOU?

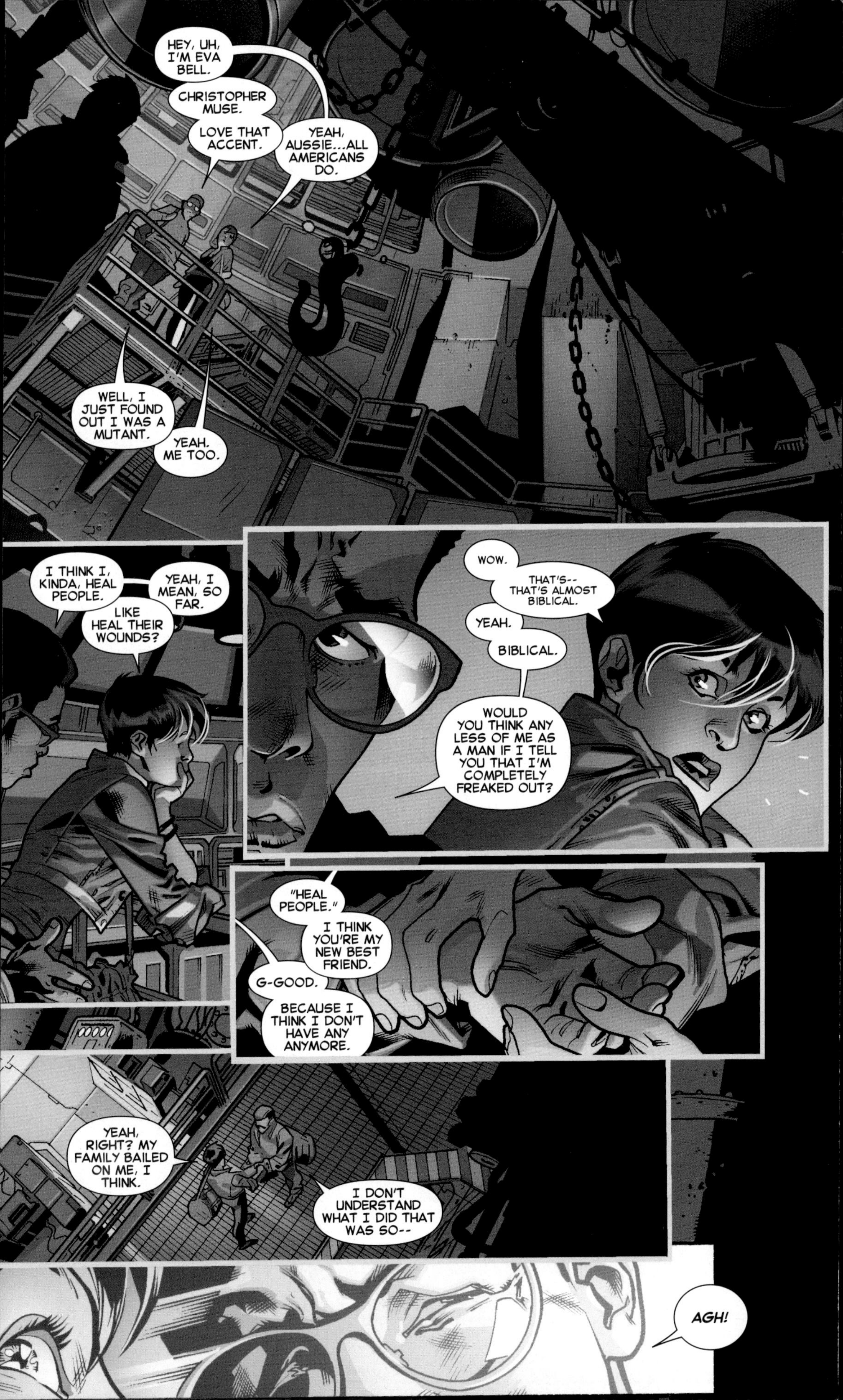

HEY, UH, I'M EVA BELL.
CHRISTOPHER MUSE.
LOVE THAT ACCENT.
YEAH, AUSSIE...ALL AMERICANS DO.
WELL, I JUST FOUND OUT I WAS A MUTANT.
YEAH. ME TOO.
I THINK I, KINDA, HEAL PEOPLE.
YEAH, I MEAN, SO FAR.
LIKE HEAL THEIR WOUNDS?
WOW.
THAT'S-- THAT'S ALMOST BIBLICAL.
YEAH.
BIBLICAL.
WOULD YOU THINK ANY LESS OF ME AS A MAN IF I TELL YOU THAT I'M COMPLETELY FREAKED OUT?
"HEAL PEOPLE."
I THINK YOU'RE MY NEW BEST FRIEND.
G-GOOD.
BECAUSE I THINK I DON'T HAVE ANY ANYMORE.
YEAH, RIGHT? MY FAMILY BAILED ON ME, I THINK.
I DON'T UNDERSTAND WHAT I DID THAT WAS SO--
AGH!

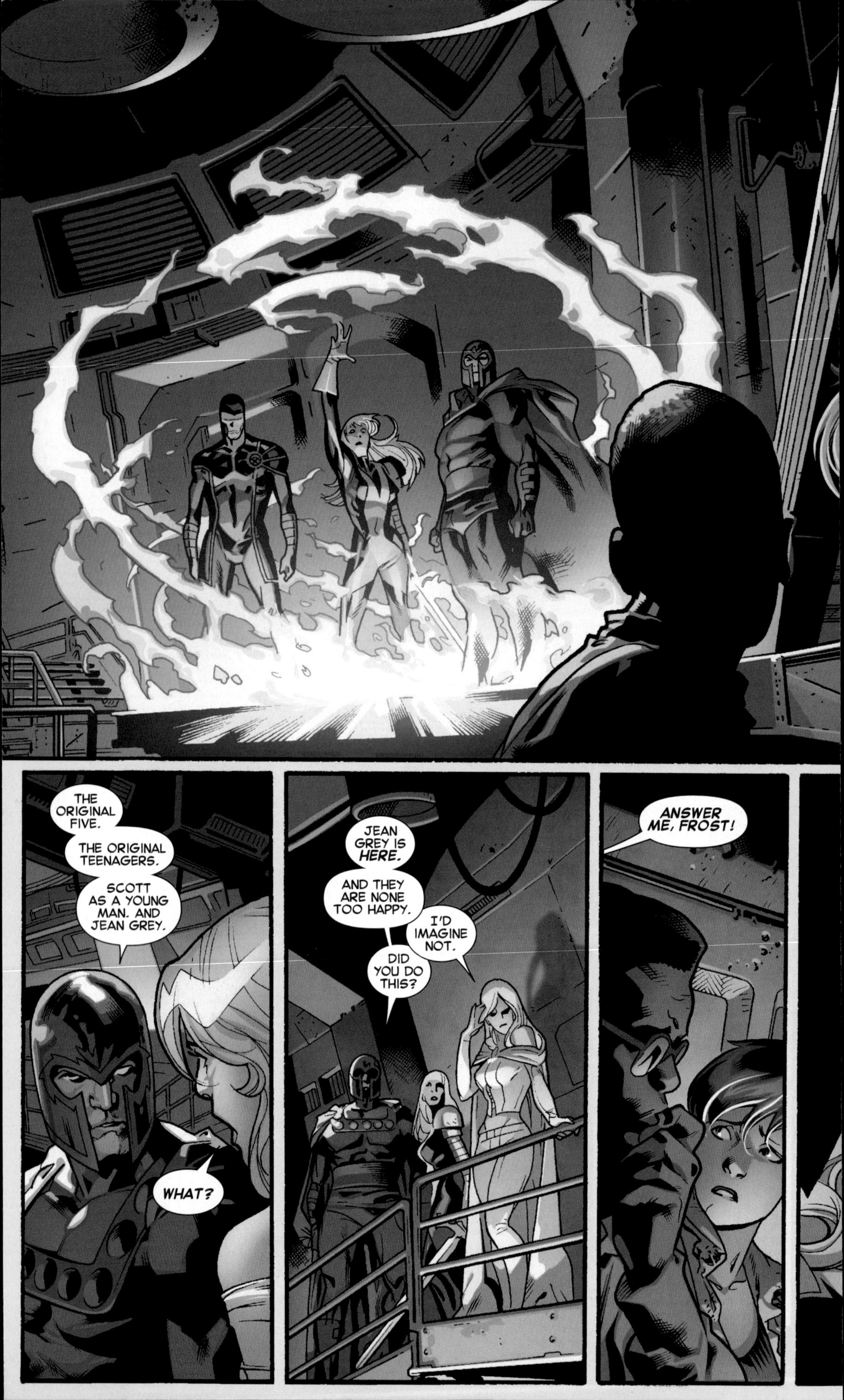
THE ORIGINAL FIVE.
THE ORIGINAL TEENAGERS.
SCOTT AS A YOUNG MAN. AND JEAN GREY.
WHAT?
JEAN GREY IS HERE.
AND THEY ARE NONE TOO HAPPY.
I'D IMAGINE NOT.
DID YOU DO THIS?
ANSWER ME, FROST!

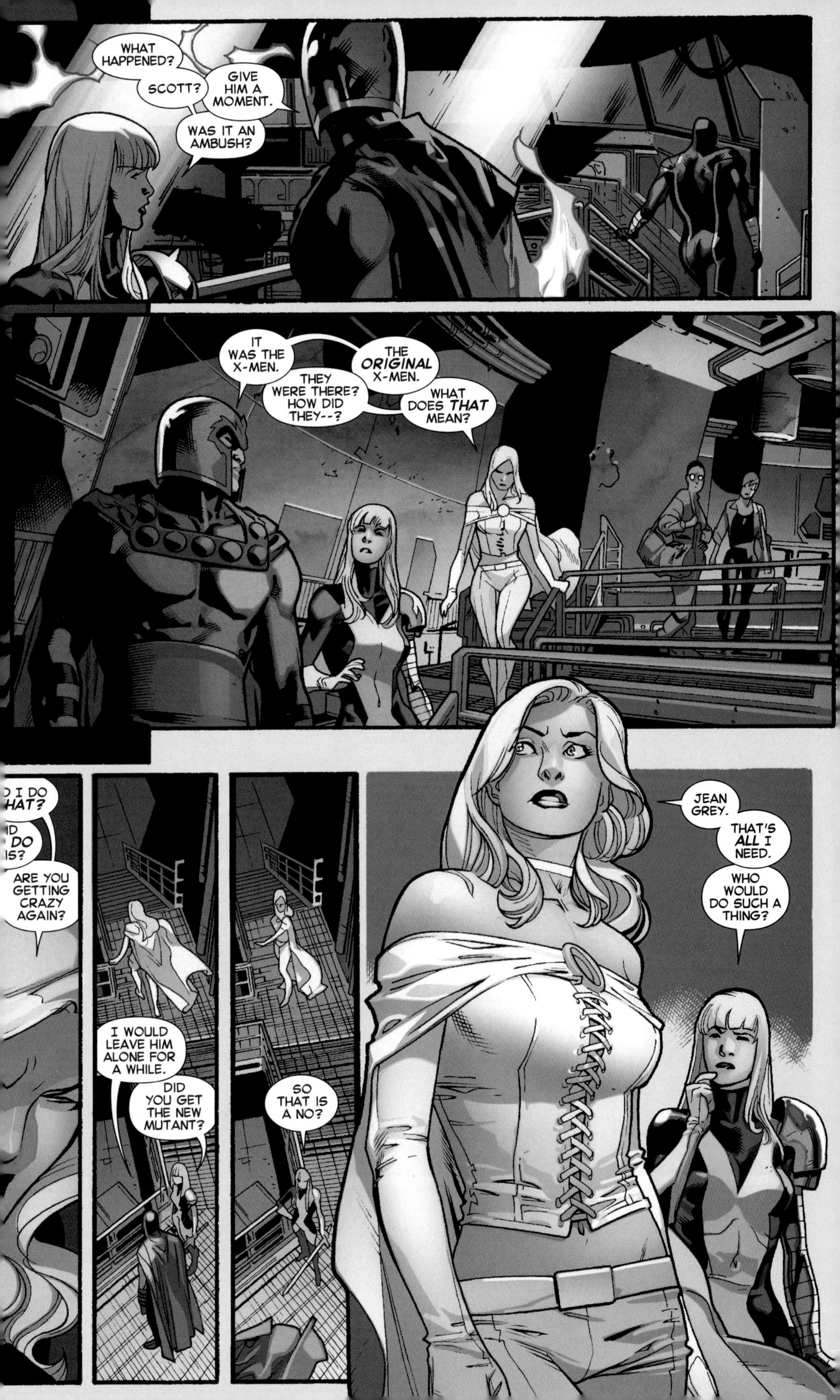
WHAT HAPPENED?
SCOTT?
GIVE HIM A MOMENT.
WAS IT AN AMBUSH?
IT WAS THE X-MEN.
THE ORIGINAL X-MEN.
THEY WERE THERE? HOW DID THEY--?
WHAT DOES THAT MEAN?
ARE YOU GETTING CRAZY AGAIN?
I WOULD LEAVE HIM ALONE FOR A WHILE.
DID YOU GET THE NEW MUTANT?
SO THAT IS A NO?
JEAN GREY.
THAT'S ALL I NEED.
WHO WOULD DO SUCH A THING?

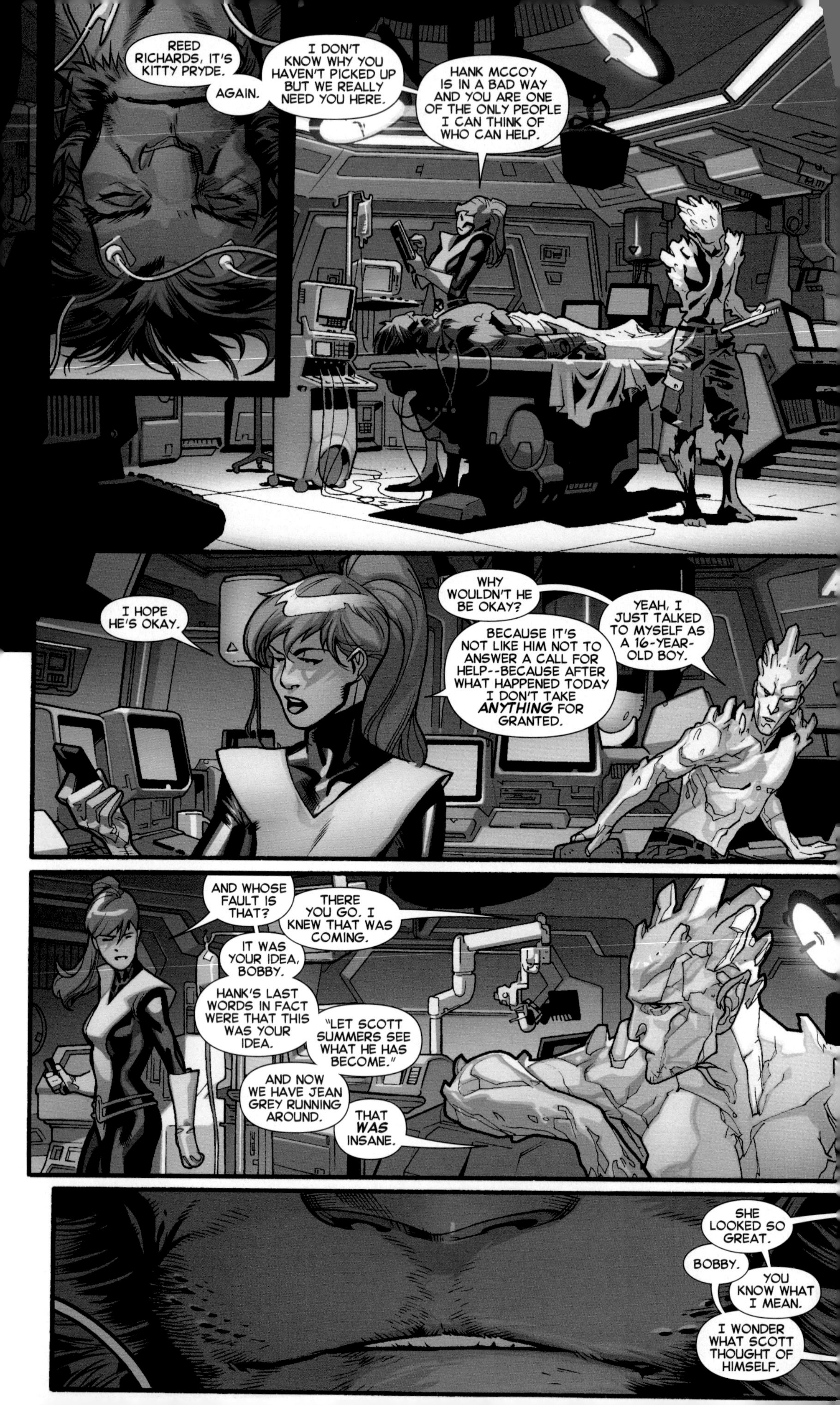

REED RICHARDS, IT'S KITTY PRYDE.
AGAIN.
I DON'T KNOW WHY YOU HAVEN'T PICKED UP BUT WE REALLY NEED YOU HERE.
HANK McCOY IS IN A BAD WAY AND YOU ARE ONE OF THE ONLY PEOPLE I CAN THINK OF WHO CAN HELP.
I HOPE HE'S OKAY.
WHY WOULDN'T HE BE OKAY?
BECAUSE IT'S NOT LIKE HIM NOT TO ANSWER A CALL FOR HELP--BECAUSE AFTER WHAT HAPPENED TODAY I DON'T TAKE ANYTHING FOR GRANTED.
YEAH, I JUST TALKED TO MYSELF AS A 16-YEAR-OLD BOY.
AND WHOSE FAULT IS THAT?
THERE YOU GO. I KNEW THAT WAS COMING.
IT WAS YOUR IDEA, BOBBY.
HANK'S LAST WORDS IN FACT WERE THAT THIS WAS YOUR IDEA.
"LET SCOTT SUMMERS SEE WHAT HE HAS BECOME."
AND NOW WE HAVE JEAN GREY RUNNING AROUND.
THAT WAS INSANE.
SHE LOOKED SO GREAT.
BOBBY.
YOU KNOW WHAT I MEAN.
I WONDER WHAT SCOTT THOUGHT OF HIMSELF.

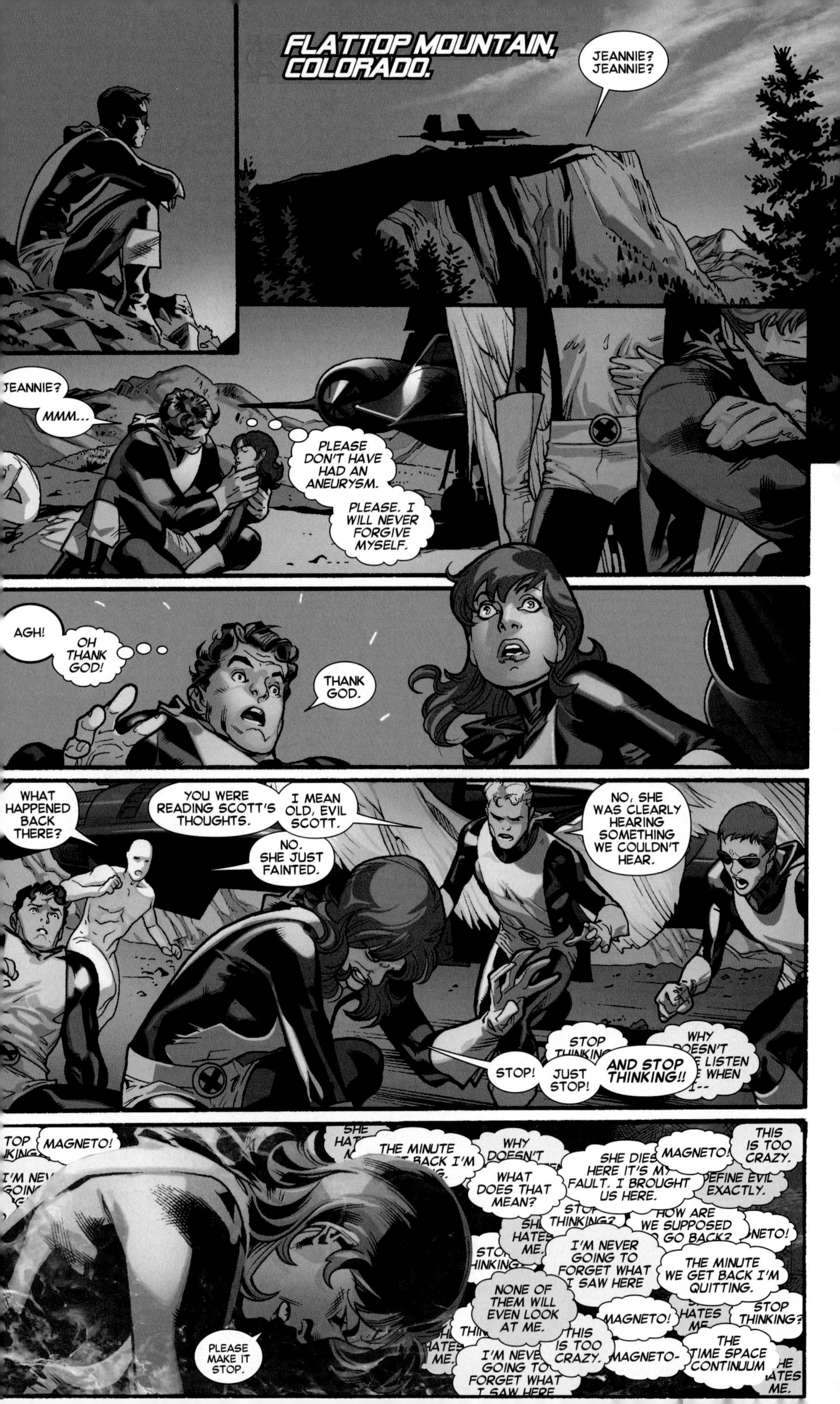

FLATTOP MOUNTAIN, COLORADO.
JEANNIE? JEANNIE?
JEANNIE?
MMM...
PLEASE DON'T HAVE HAD AN ANEURYSM.
PLEASE. I WILL NEVER FORGIVE MYSELF.
AGH!
OH THANK GOD!
THANK GOD.
WHAT HAPPENED BACK THERE?
YOU WERE READING SCOTT'S THOUGHTS.
I MEAN OLD, EVIL SCOTT.
NO. SHE JUST FAINTED.
NO, SHE WAS CLEARLY HEARING SOMETHING WE COULDN'T HEAR.
STOP!
JUST STOP!
AND STOP THINKING!!
MAGNETO!
WHAT DOES THAT MEAN?
SHE DIES HERE IT'S MY FAULT. I BROUGHT US HERE.
MAGNETO!
THIS IS TOO CRAZY.
EXACTLY.
I'M NEVER GOING TO FORGET WHAT I SAW HERE
THE MINUTE WE GET BACK I'M QUITTING.
NONE OF THEM WILL EVEN LOOK AT ME.
MAGNETO!
STOP THINKING?
THIS IS TOO CRAZY.
MAGNETO-
THE TIME SPACE CONTINUUM
PLEASE MAKE IT STOP.

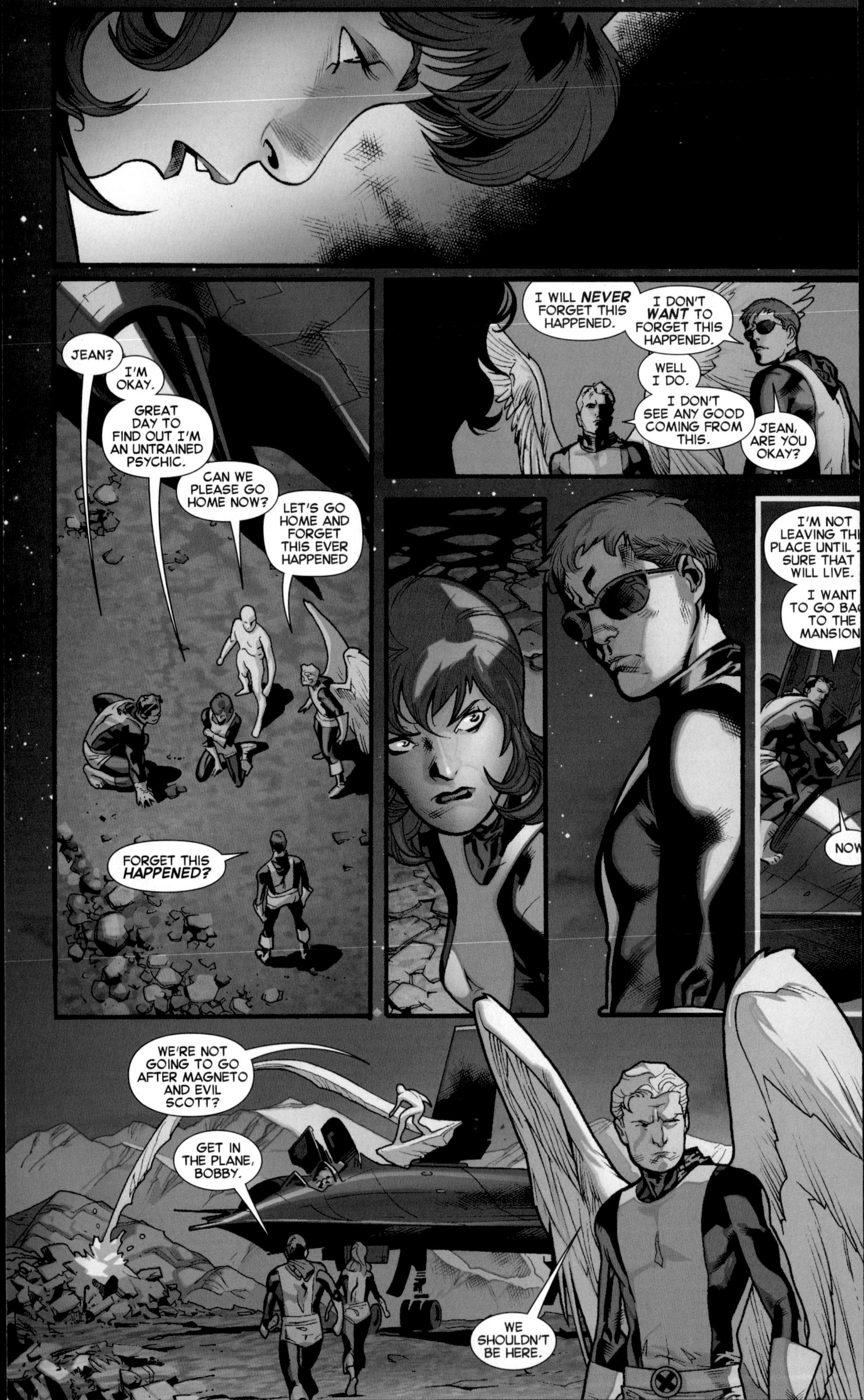
JEAN?
I'M OKAY.
GREAT DAY TO FIND OUT I'M AN UNTRAINED PSYCHIC.
CAN WE PLEASE GO HOME NOW?
LET'S GO HOME AND FORGET THIS EVER HAPPENED
FORGET THIS *HAPPENED?*
I WILL *NEVER* FORGET THIS HAPPENED.
I DON'T *WANT* TO FORGET THIS HAPPENED.
WELL I DO.
I DON'T SEE ANY GOOD COMING FROM THIS.
JEAN, ARE YOU OKAY?
WE'RE NOT GOING TO GO AFTER MAGNETO AND EVIL SCOTT?
GET IN THE PLANE, BOBBY.
WE SHOULDN'T BE HERE.

NOT NOW, EMMA.

I KNOW.

I JUST WANT YOU TO KNOW I DIDN'T DO THIS.

DO YOU KNOW WHO DID?

NO.

YOU KNOW THE DIFFERENCE BETWEEN REAL AND NOT REAL.

WAS IT REAL?

YES.

SHE WAS JUST STANDING *RIGHT THERE*.

YES.

HER AND THE YOUNG YOU.

YES.

WHAT DID THEY WANT?

EMMA, GO AWAY.

I'M SERIOUS.

IF WE KNOW WHAT THEY WANT THEN WE KNOW WHO DID THIS.

THEY WANTED TO SEE FOR THEMSELVES WHAT I HAVE BECOME.

SO.

IF THAT'S THE MOTIVE N ALL WE HAVE ASK IS WHO-- HO HAS THE REWITHAL AND ECHNOLOGY?

HANK MCCOY.

HAT'S HAT I UGHT TOO.

WHY?

BECAUSE YOU KILLED CHARLES XAVIER.

AND HE CAN'T KILL YOU BACK SO HE'S GOING TO PUNISH YOU.

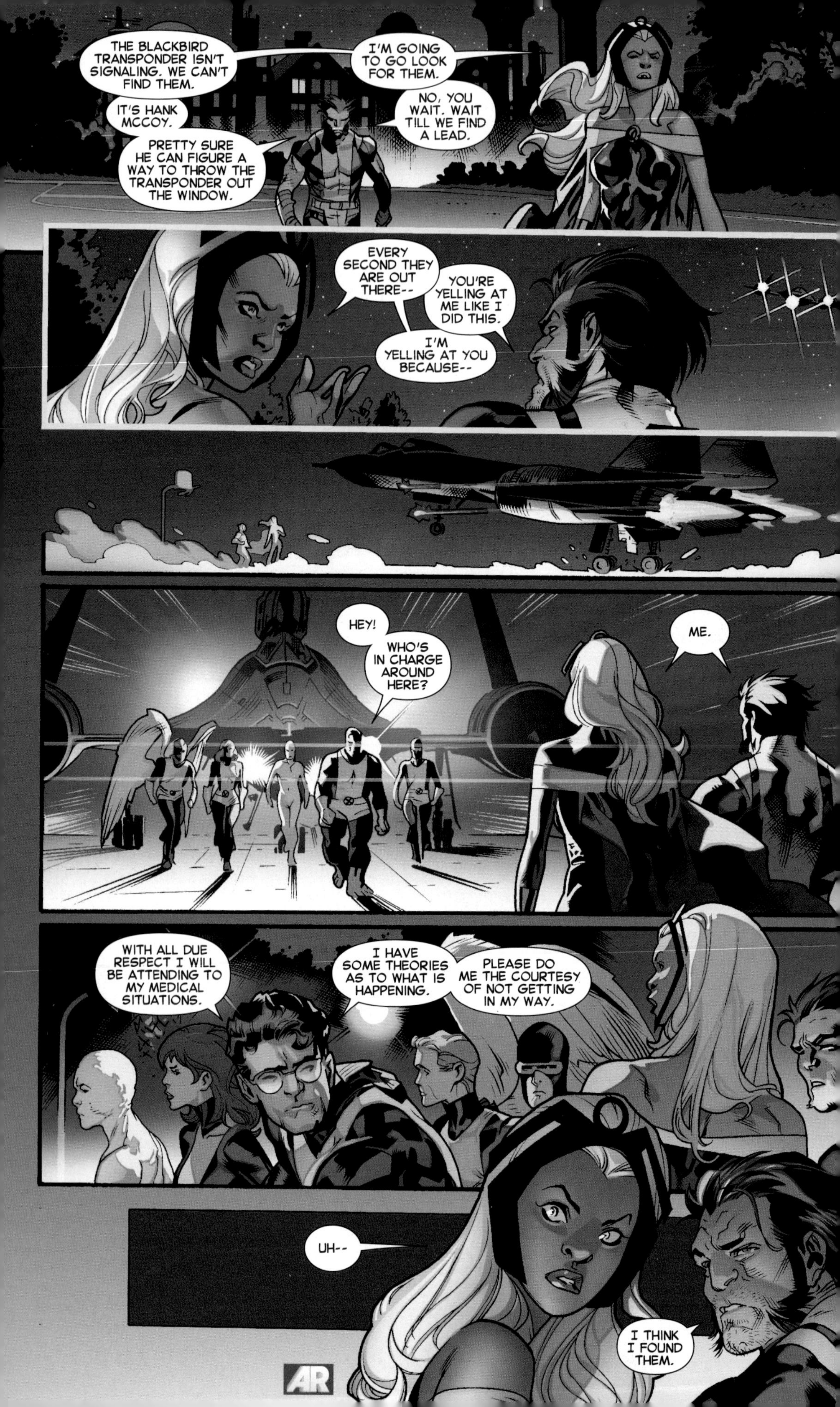
THE BLACKBIRD TRANSPONDER ISN'T SIGNALING. WE CAN'T FIND THEM.
I'M GOING TO GO LOOK FOR THEM.
IT'S HANK McCOY.
NO, YOU WAIT. WAIT TILL WE FIND A LEAD.
PRETTY SURE HE CAN FIGURE A WAY TO THROW THE TRANSPONDER OUT THE WINDOW.
EVERY SECOND THEY ARE OUT THERE--
YOU'RE YELLING AT ME LIKE I DID THIS.
I'M YELLING AT YOU BECAUSE--
HEY!
WHO'S IN CHARGE AROUND HERE?
ME.
WITH ALL DUE RESPECT I WILL BE ATTENDING TO MY MEDICAL SITUATIONS.
I HAVE SOME THEORIES AS TO WHAT IS HAPPENING.
PLEASE DO ME THE COURTESY OF NOT GETTING IN MY WAY.
UH--
I THINK I FOUND THEM.

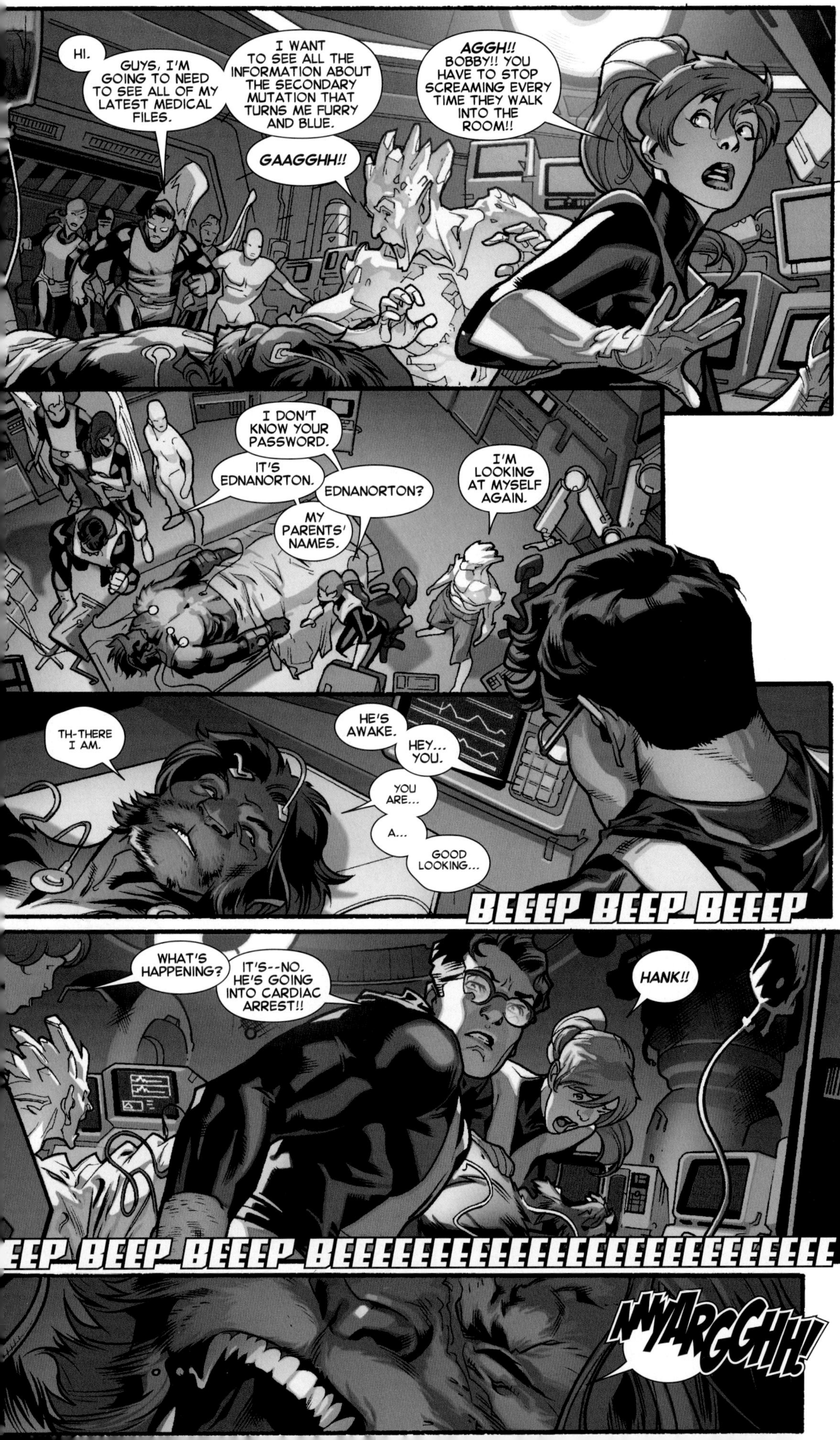

HI.
GUYS, I'M GOING TO NEED TO SEE ALL OF MY LATEST MEDICAL FILES.
I WANT TO SEE ALL THE INFORMATION ABOUT THE SECONDARY MUTATION THAT TURNS ME FURRY AND BLUE.
GAAGGHH!!
AGGH!! BOBBY!! YOU HAVE TO STOP SCREAMING EVERY TIME THEY WALK INTO THE ROOM!!
I DON'T KNOW YOUR PASSWORD.
IT'S EDNANORTON.
EDNANORTON?
MY PARENTS' NAMES.
I'M LOOKING AT MYSELF AGAIN.
TH-THERE I AM.
HE'S AWAKE.
HEY... YOU.
YOU ARE...
A...
GOOD LOOKING...
BEEEP BEEP BEEEP
WHAT'S HAPPENING?
IT'S--NO. HE'S GOING INTO CARDIAC ARREST!!
HANK!!
EEP BEEP BEEEP BEEEEEEEEEEEEEEEEEEEEEEEEEEE
NNYARGGHH!

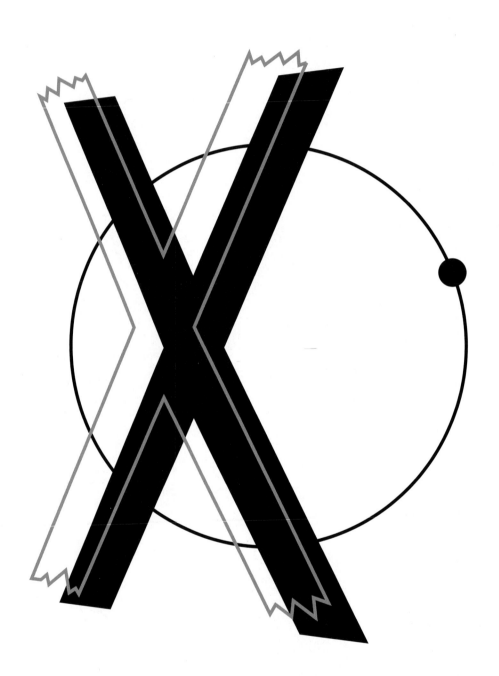

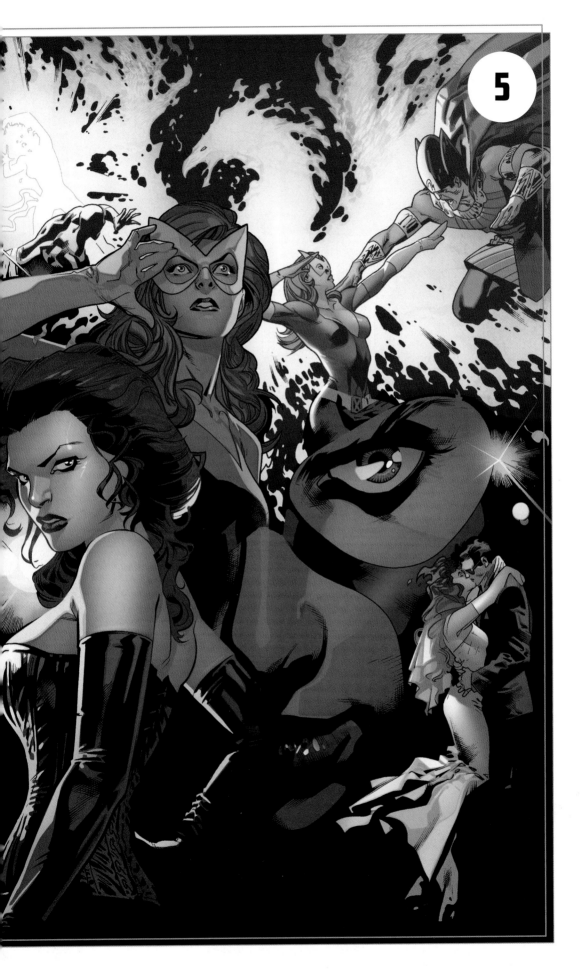

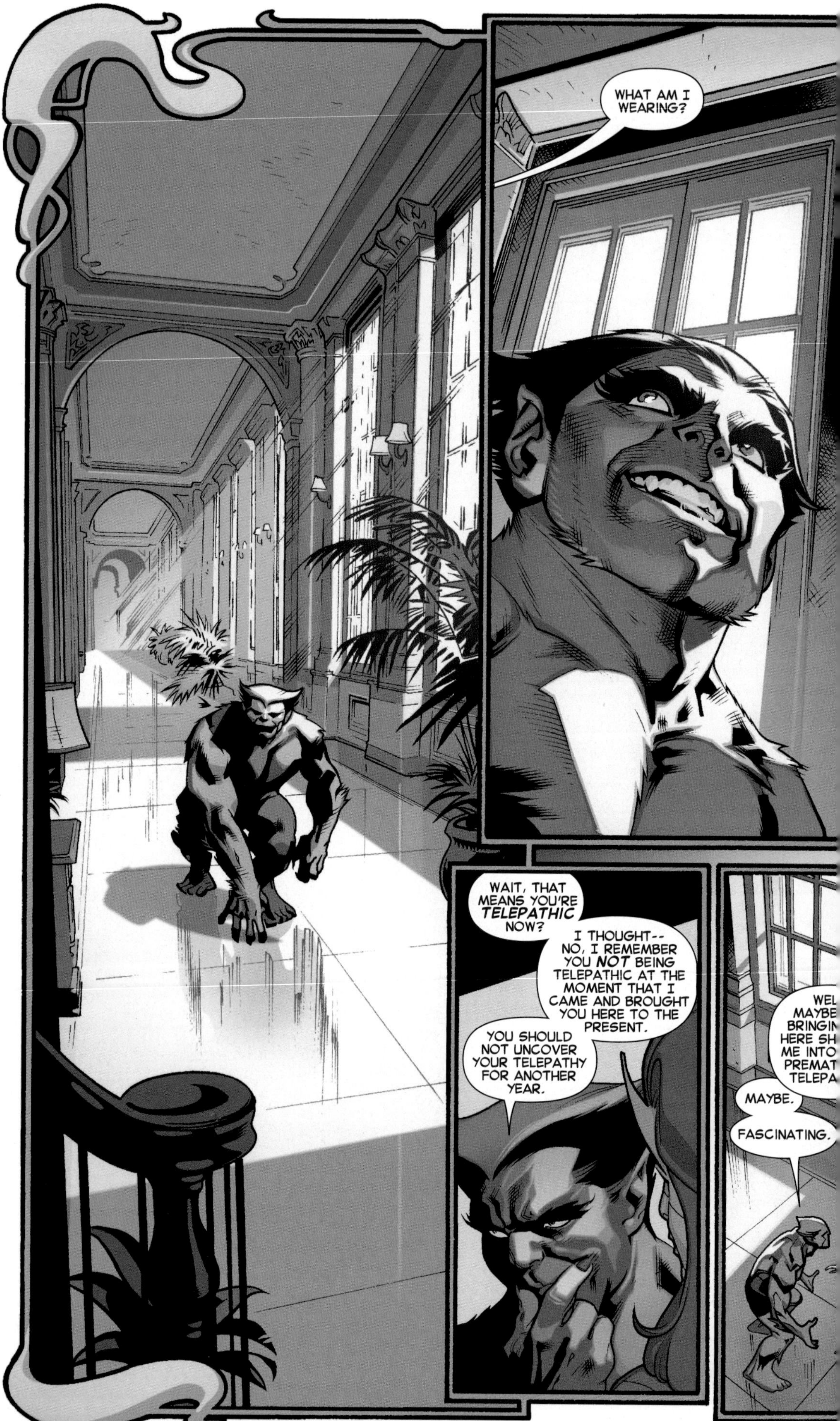

WHAT AM I WEARING?
WAIT, THAT MEANS YOU'RE *TELEPATHIC* NOW?
I THOUGHT-- NO, I REMEMBER YOU *NOT* BEING TELEPATHIC AT THE MOMENT THAT I CAME AND BROUGHT YOU HERE TO THE PRESENT.
YOU SHOULD NOT UNCOVER YOUR TELEPATHY FOR ANOTHER YEAR.
MAYBE.
FASCINATING.

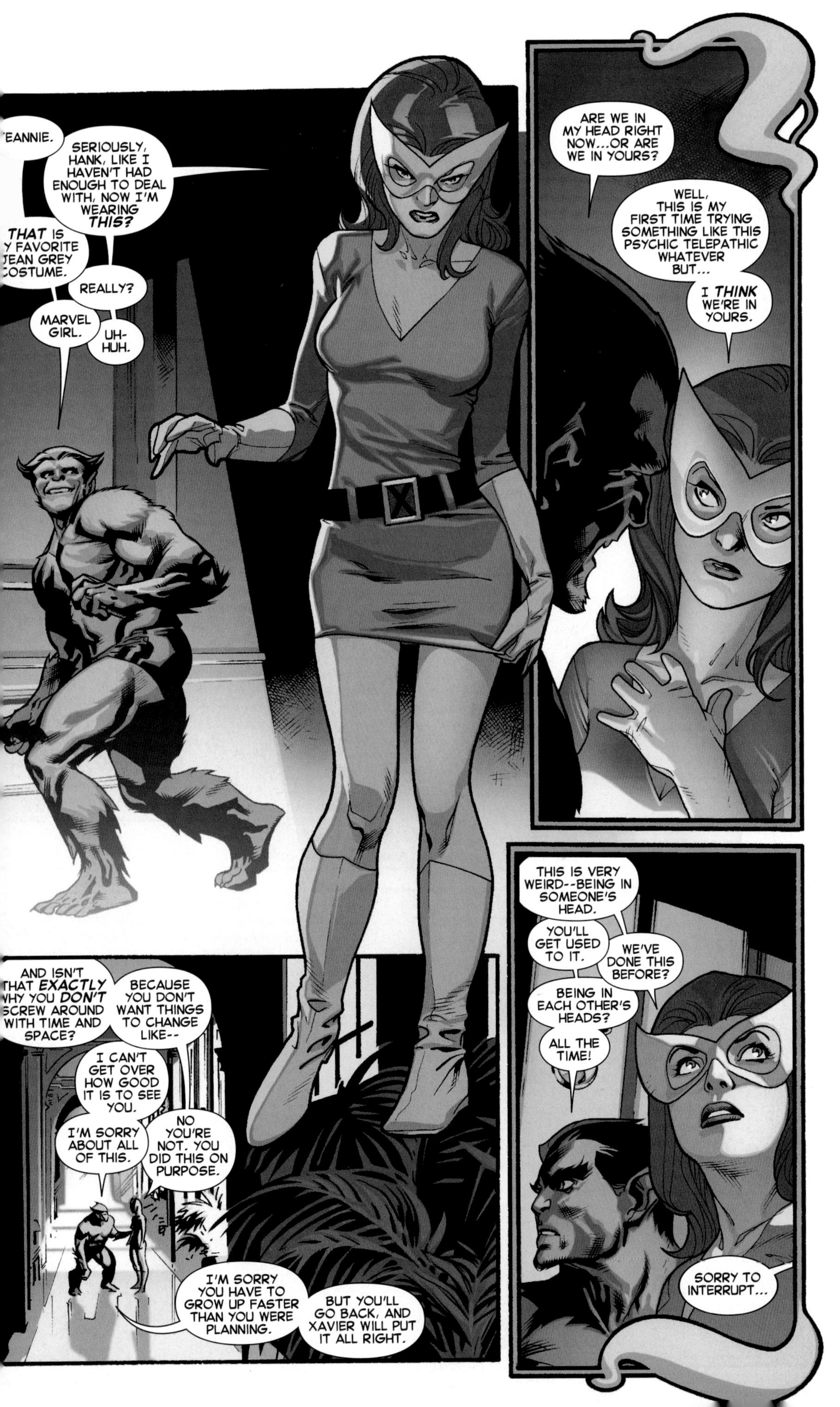

JEANNIE.
SERIOUSLY, HANK, LIKE I HAVEN'T HAD ENOUGH TO DEAL WITH, NOW I'M WEARING THIS?
THAT IS MY FAVORITE JEAN GREY COSTUME.
REALLY?
MARVEL GIRL.
UH-HUH.
ARE WE IN MY HEAD RIGHT NOW...OR ARE WE IN YOURS?
WELL, THIS IS MY FIRST TIME TRYING SOMETHING LIKE THIS PSYCHIC TELEPATHIC WHATEVER BUT...
I THINK WE'RE IN YOURS.
AND ISN'T THAT EXACTLY WHY YOU DON'T SCREW AROUND WITH TIME AND SPACE?
BECAUSE YOU DON'T WANT THINGS TO CHANGE LIKE--
I CAN'T GET OVER HOW GOOD IT IS TO SEE YOU.
I'M SORRY ABOUT ALL OF THIS.
NO YOU'RE NOT. YOU DID THIS ON PURPOSE.
I'M SORRY YOU HAVE TO GROW UP FASTER THAN YOU WERE PLANNING.
BUT YOU'LL GO BACK, AND XAVIER WILL PUT IT ALL RIGHT.
THIS IS VERY WEIRD--BEING IN SOMEONE'S HEAD.
YOU'LL GET USED TO IT.
WE'VE DONE THIS BEFORE?
BEING IN EACH OTHER'S HEADS?
ALL THE TIME!
SORRY TO INTERRUPT...

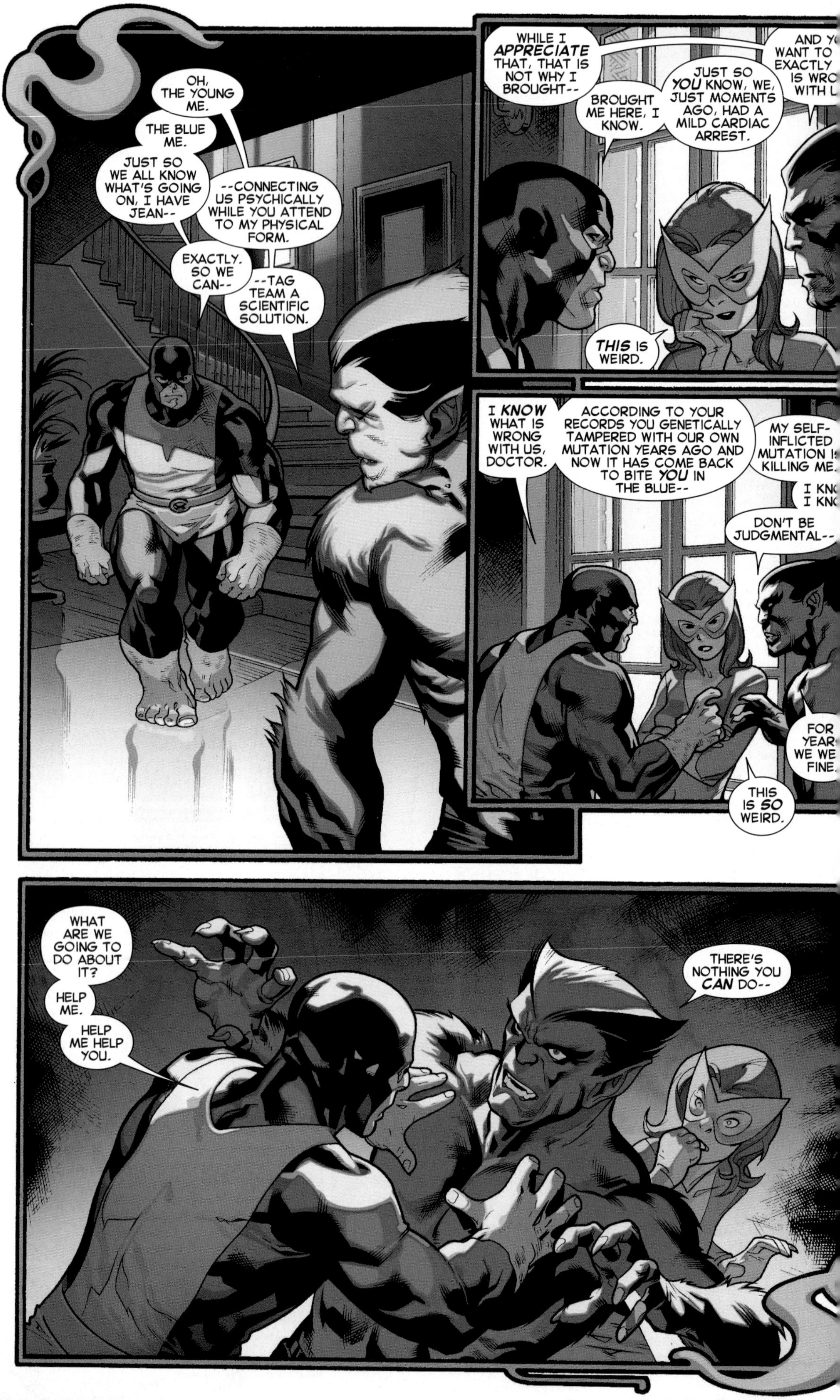

OH, THE YOUNG ME.
THE BLUE ME.
JUST SO WE ALL KNOW WHAT'S GOING ON, I HAVE JEAN--
--CONNECTING US PSYCHICALLY WHILE YOU ATTEND TO MY PHYSICAL FORM.
EXACTLY. SO WE CAN--
--TAG TEAM A SCIENTIFIC SOLUTION.
WHILE I *APPRECIATE* THAT, THAT IS NOT WHY I BROUGHT--
BROUGHT ME HERE, I KNOW.
JUST SO *YOU* KNOW, WE, JUST MOMENTS AGO, HAD A MILD CARDIAC ARREST.
AND YO WANT TO EXACTLY IS WRO WITH U
THIS IS WEIRD.
I *KNOW* WHAT IS WRONG WITH US, DOCTOR.
ACCORDING TO YOUR RECORDS YOU GENETICALLY TAMPERED WITH OUR OWN MUTATION YEARS AGO AND NOW IT HAS COME BACK TO BITE *YOU* IN THE BLUE--
MY SELF-INFLICTED MUTATION I KILLING ME.
I KNO I KNO
DON'T BE JUDGMENTAL--
FOR YEAR WE WE FINE.
THIS IS *SO* WEIRD.
WHAT ARE WE GOING TO DO ABOUT IT?
HELP ME.
HELP ME HELP YOU.
THERE'S NOTHING YOU *CAN* DO--

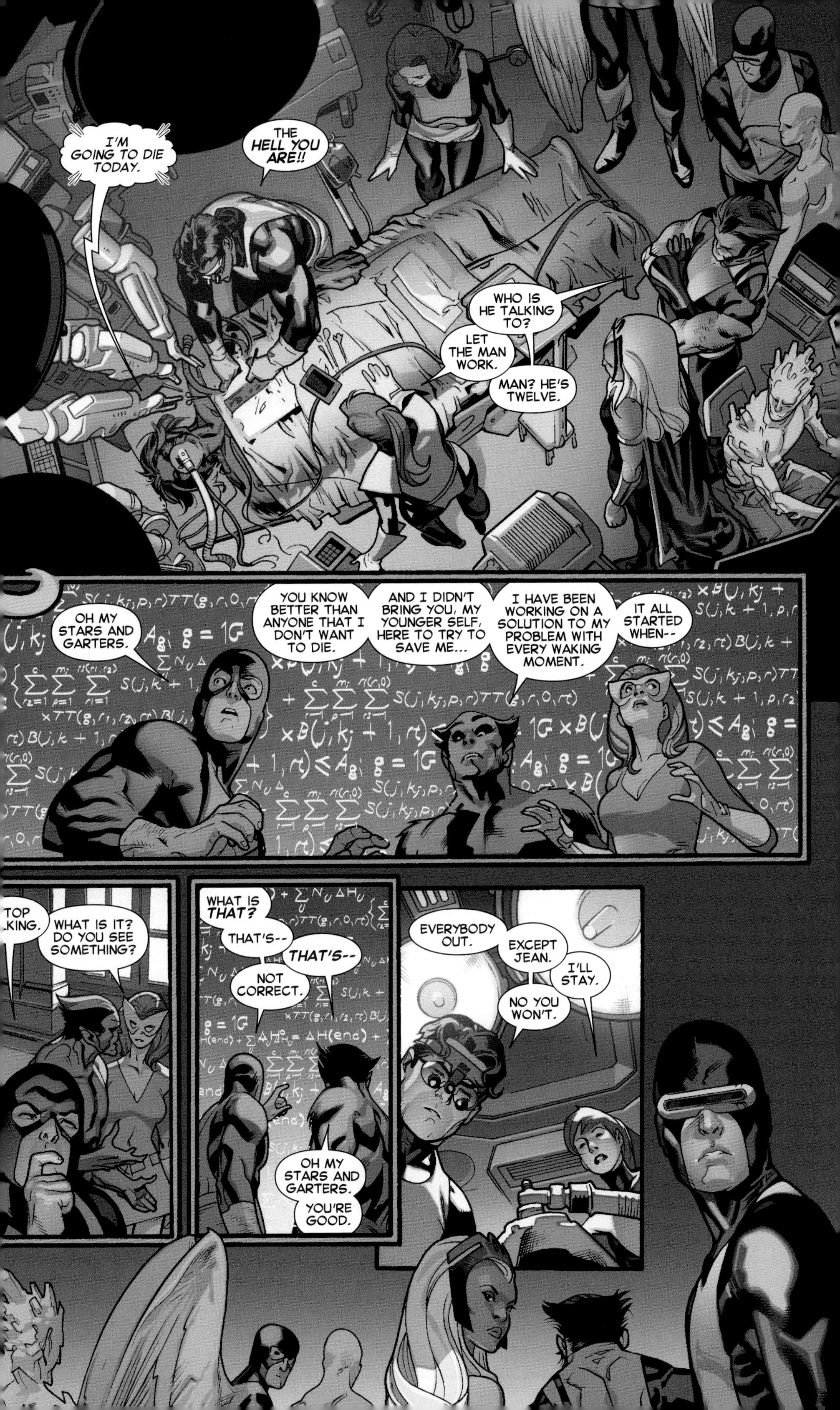

I'M GOING TO DIE TODAY.
THE HELL YOU ARE!!
WHO IS HE TALKING TO?
LET THE MAN WORK.
MAN? HE'S TWELVE.
OH MY STARS AND GARTERS.
YOU KNOW BETTER THAN ANYONE THAT I DON'T WANT TO DIE.
AND I DIDN'T BRING YOU, MY YOUNGER SELF, HERE TO TRY TO SAVE ME...
I HAVE BEEN WORKING ON A SOLUTION TO MY PROBLEM WITH EVERY WAKING MOMENT.
IT ALL STARTED WHEN--
TOP
KING.
WHAT IS IT? DO YOU SEE SOMETHING?
WHAT IS THAT?
THAT'S--
THAT'S--
NOT CORRECT.
OH MY STARS AND GARTERS.
YOU'RE GOOD.
EVERYBODY OUT.
EXCEPT JEAN.
I'LL STAY.
NO YOU WON'T.

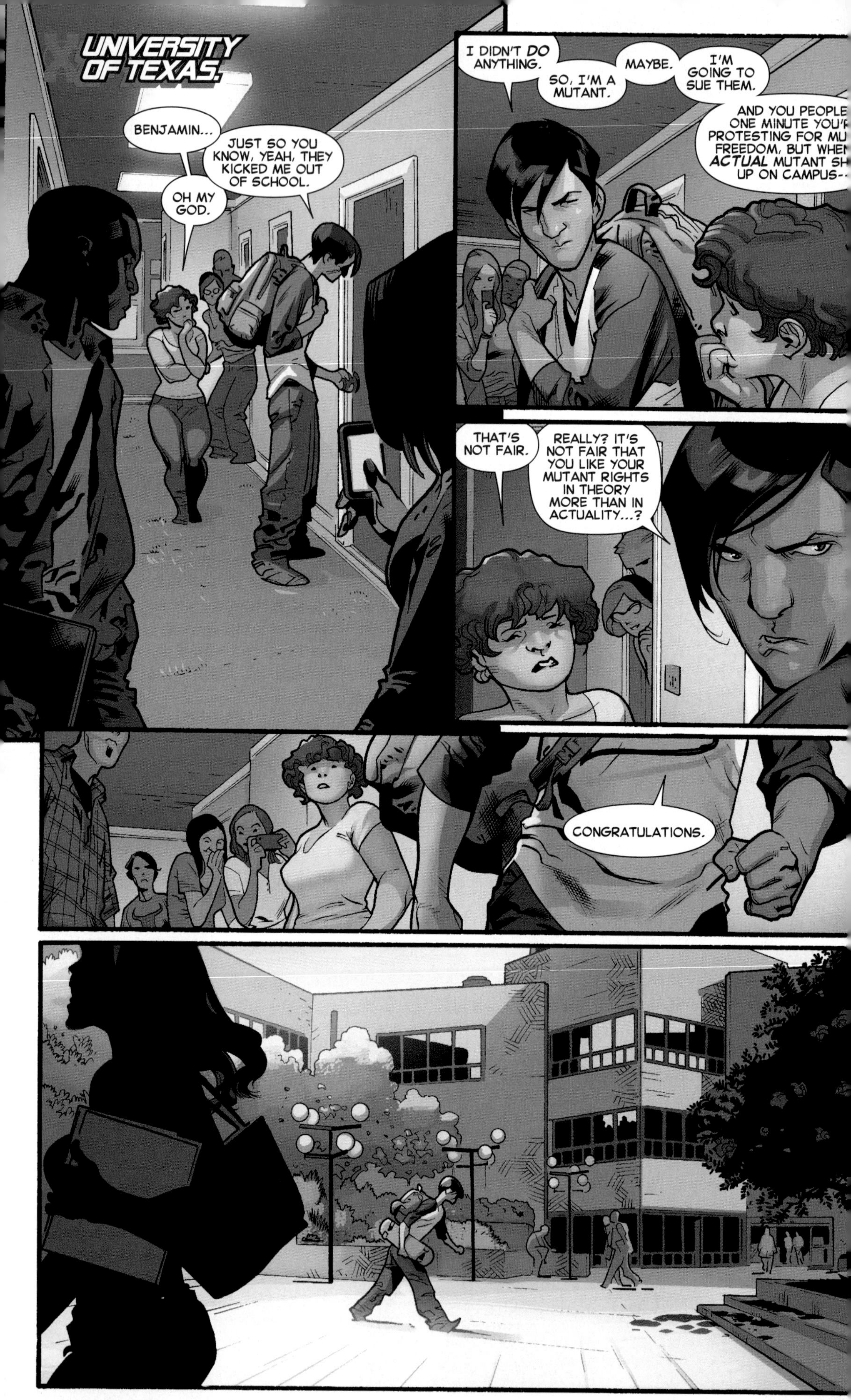
UNIVERSITY OF TEXAS.
BENJAMIN...
JUST SO YOU KNOW, YEAH, THEY KICKED ME OUT OF SCHOOL.
OH MY GOD.
I DIDN'T DO ANYTHING.
SO, I'M A MUTANT.
MAYBE.
I'M GOING TO SUE THEM.
THAT'S NOT FAIR.
REALLY? IT'S NOT FAIR THAT YOU LIKE YOUR MUTANT RIGHTS IN THEORY MORE THAN IN ACTUALITY...?
CONGRATULATIONS.

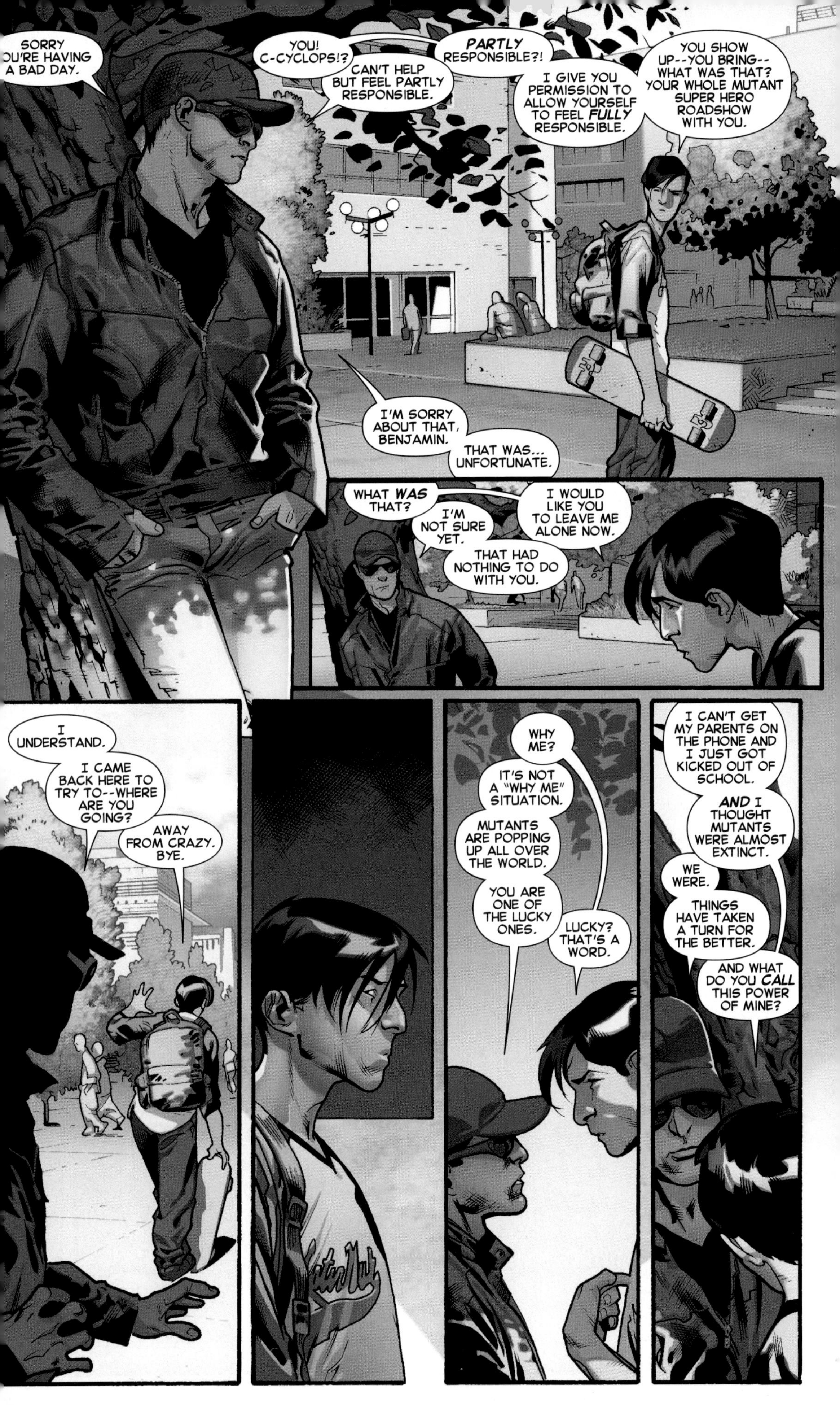

SORRY YOU'RE HAVING A BAD DAY.
YOU! C-CYCLOPS!?
CAN'T HELP BUT FEEL PARTLY RESPONSIBLE.
PARTLY RESPONSIBLE?!
I GIVE YOU PERMISSION TO ALLOW YOURSELF TO FEEL FULLY RESPONSIBLE.
YOU SHOW UP--YOU BRING--WHAT WAS THAT? YOUR WHOLE MUTANT SUPER HERO ROADSHOW WITH YOU.
I'M SORRY ABOUT THAT, BENJAMIN.
THAT WAS... UNFORTUNATE.
WHAT WAS THAT?
I'M NOT SURE YET.
I WOULD LIKE YOU TO LEAVE ME ALONE NOW.
THAT HAD NOTHING TO DO WITH YOU.
I UNDERSTAND.
I CAME BACK HERE TO TRY TO--WHERE ARE YOU GOING?
AWAY FROM CRAZY. BYE.
WHY ME?
IT'S NOT A "WHY ME" SITUATION.
MUTANTS ARE POPPING UP ALL OVER THE WORLD.
YOU ARE ONE OF THE LUCKY ONES.
LUCKY? THAT'S A WORD.
I CAN'T GET MY PARENTS ON THE PHONE AND I JUST GOT KICKED OUT OF SCHOOL.
AND I THOUGHT MUTANTS WERE ALMOST EXTINCT.
WE WERE.
THINGS HAVE TAKEN A TURN FOR THE BETTER.
AND WHAT DO YOU CALL THIS POWER OF MINE?

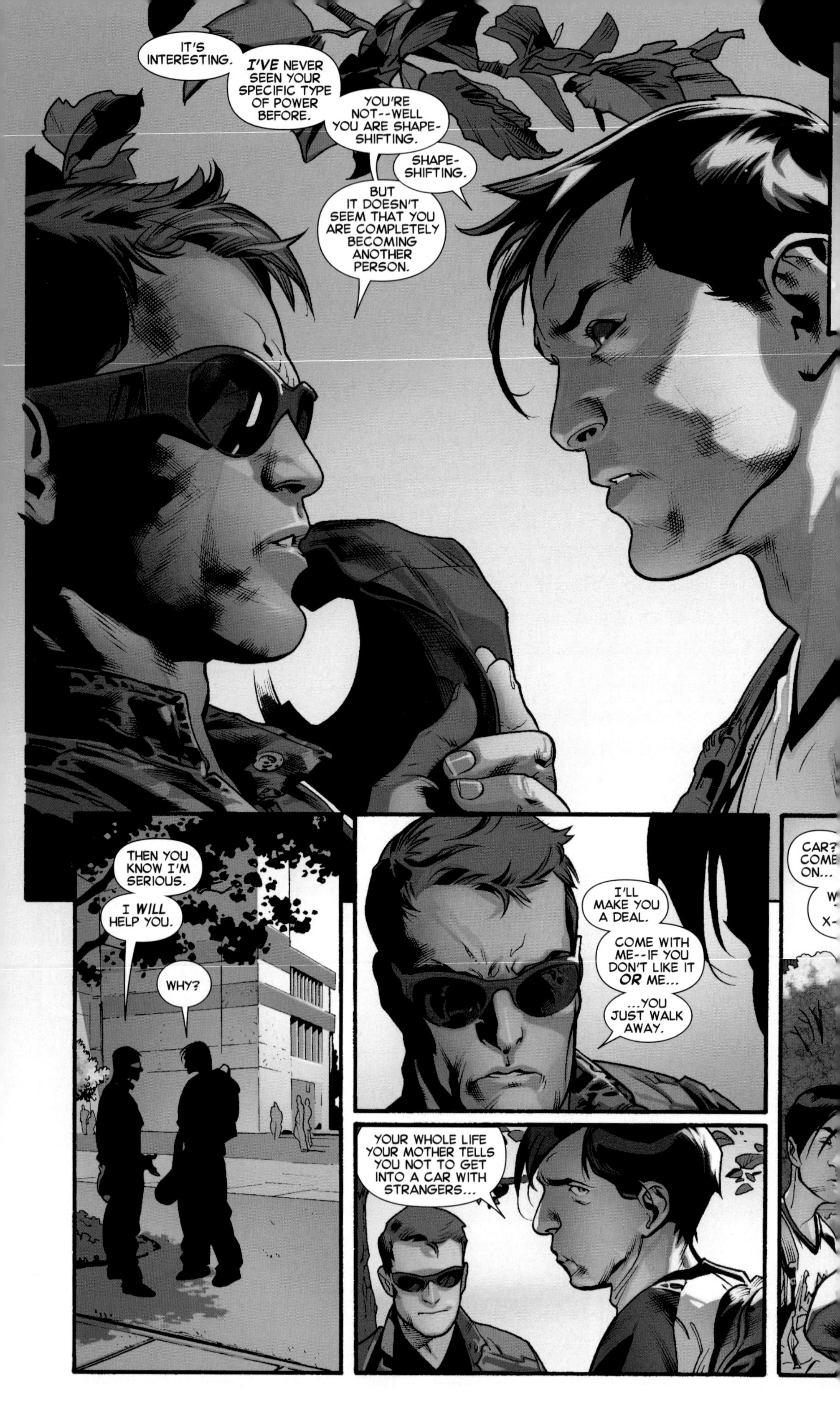
IT'S INTERESTING.
I'VE NEVER SEEN YOUR SPECIFIC TYPE OF POWER BEFORE.
YOU'RE NOT--WELL YOU ARE SHAPE-SHIFTING.
SHAPE-SHIFTING.
BUT IT DOESN'T SEEM THAT YOU ARE COMPLETELY BECOMING ANOTHER PERSON.
THEN YOU KNOW I'M SERIOUS.
I WILL HELP YOU.
WHY?
I'LL MAKE YOU A DEAL.
COME WITH ME--IF YOU DON'T LIKE IT OR ME...
...YOU JUST WALK AWAY.
YOUR WHOLE LIFE YOUR MOTHER TELLS YOU NOT TO GET INTO A CAR WITH STRANGERS...
CAR? COME ON...

5

IT'S MORE LIKE YOU ARE BECOMING SOMETHING...IT'S LIKE YOU'RE BECOMING ONE WITH YOUR ENVIRONMENT.

YOU'RE ADAPTING PHYSICALLY TO YOUR SURROUNDINGS.

AND I AM SCARED OUT OF MY MIND.

I GET THAT, BENJAMIN.

I'VE BEEN WHERE YOU ARE.

IN A WAY I'M THERE RIGHT NOW.

WE DON'T KNOW THE FULL EXTENT OF YOUR POWER OR WHAT ELSE YOU ARE CAPABLE OF.

BUT YOU NEED GUIDANCE AND TRAINING.

I'M OFFERING IT TO YOU.

I HAVE THE INTERNET.

I KNOW WHO YOU ARE, SCOTT SUMMERS.

I KNOW WHAT YOU'VE DONE.

LYANA, O FOR KUP AND IVERY.

WHAT ARE WE-- WHOA.

JUST BREATHE.

THIS FEELS A LITTLE ODD.

BUT IT'S OVER LIKE THAT.

WELCOME, BENJAMIN DEEDS...

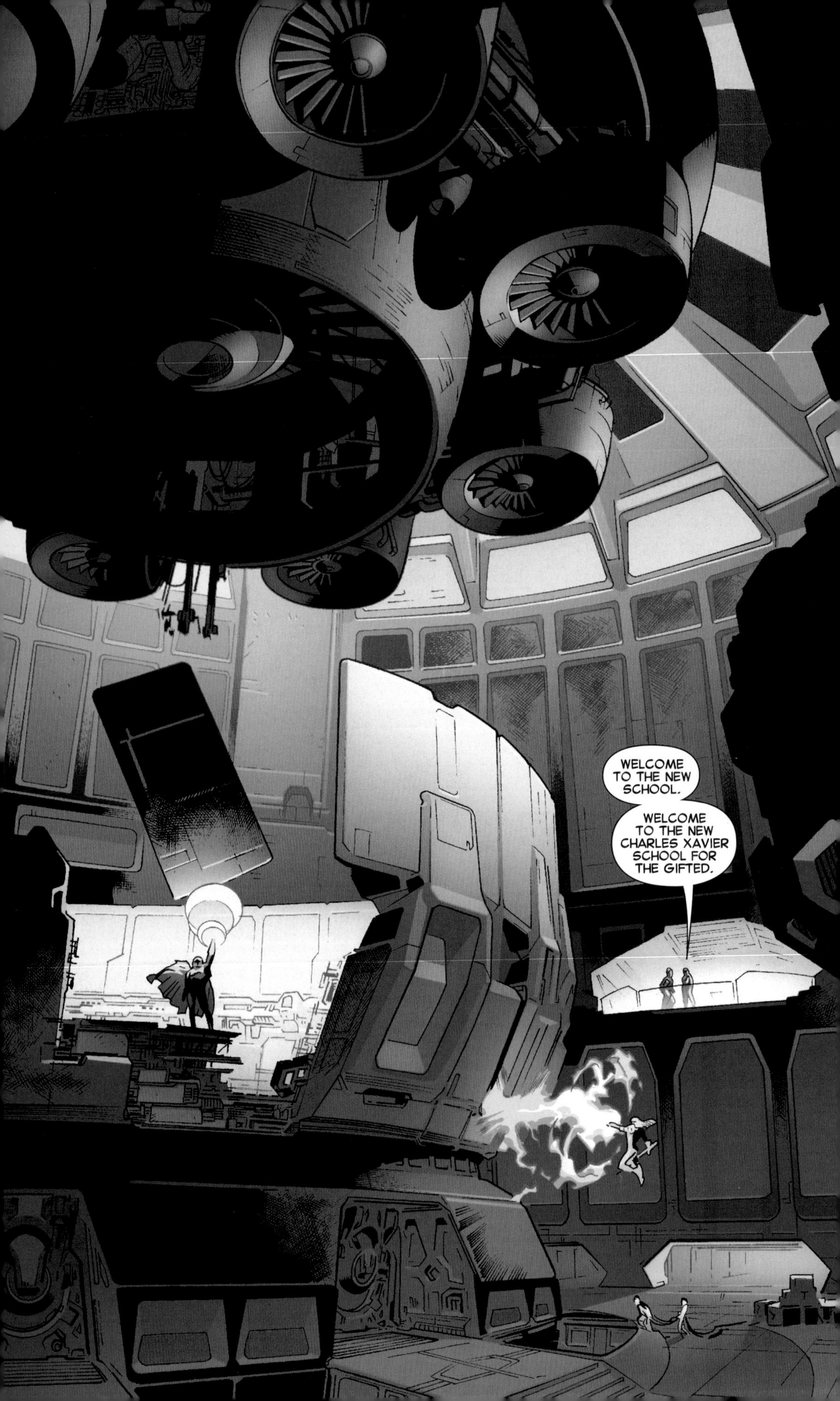
WELCOME TO THE NEW SCHOOL.
WELCOME TO THE NEW CHARLES XAVIER SCHOOL FOR THE GIFTED.

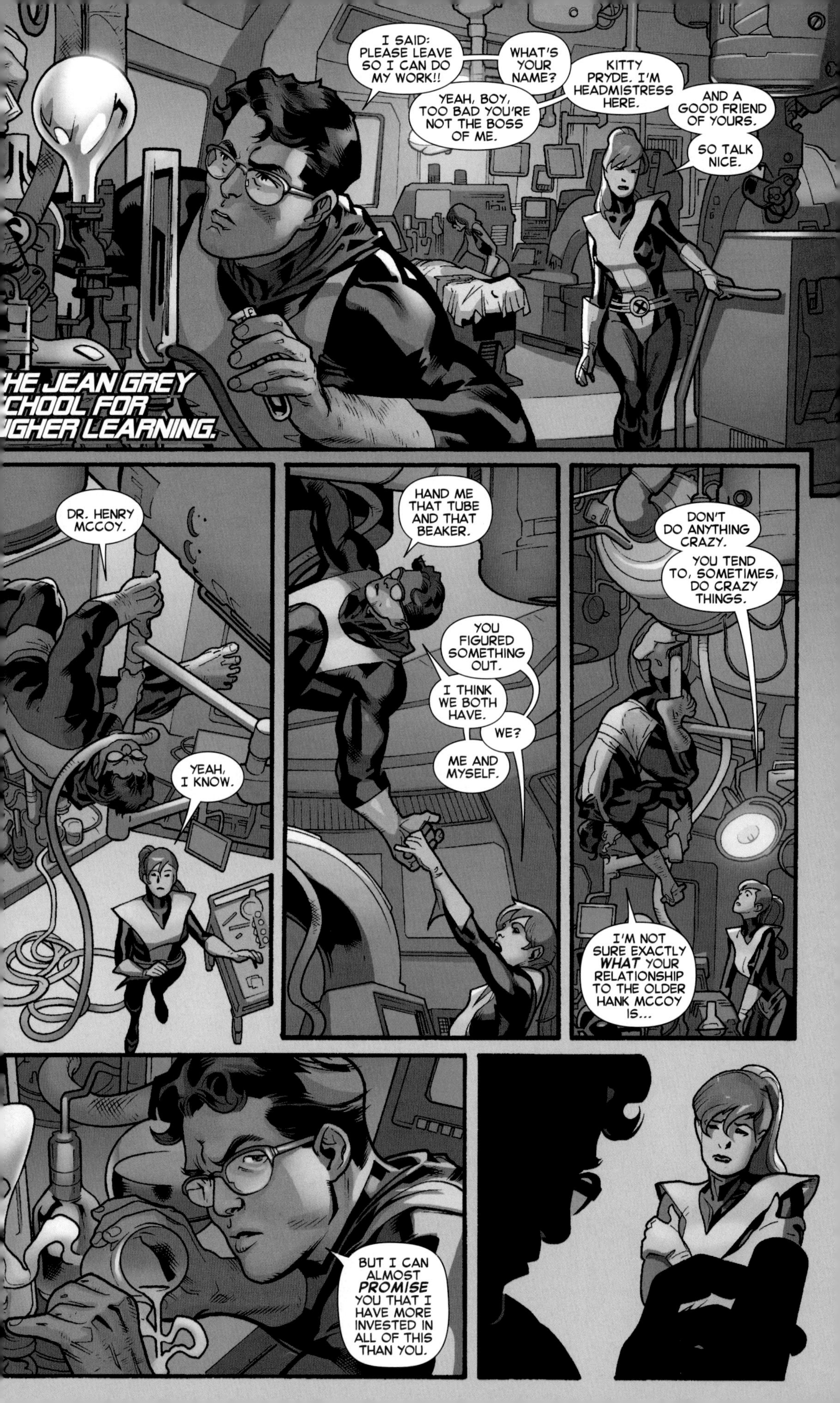
I SAID: PLEASE LEAVE SO I CAN DO MY WORK!!
WHAT'S YOUR NAME?
YEAH, BOY, TOO BAD YOU'RE NOT THE BOSS OF ME.
KITTY PRYDE. I'M HEADMISTRESS HERE.
AND A GOOD FRIEND OF YOURS.
SO TALK NICE.
HE JEAN GREY CHOOL FOR IGHER LEARNING.
DR. HENRY MCCOY.
YEAH, I KNOW.
HAND ME THAT TUBE AND THAT BEAKER.
YOU FIGURED SOMETHING OUT.
I THINK WE BOTH HAVE.
WE?
ME AND MYSELF.
DON'T DO ANYTHING CRAZY.
YOU TEND TO, SOMETIMES, DO CRAZY THINGS.
I'M NOT SURE EXACTLY *WHAT* YOUR RELATIONSHIP TO THE OLDER HANK MCCOY IS...
BUT I CAN ALMOST ***PROMISE*** YOU THAT I HAVE MORE INVESTED IN ALL OF THIS THAN YOU.

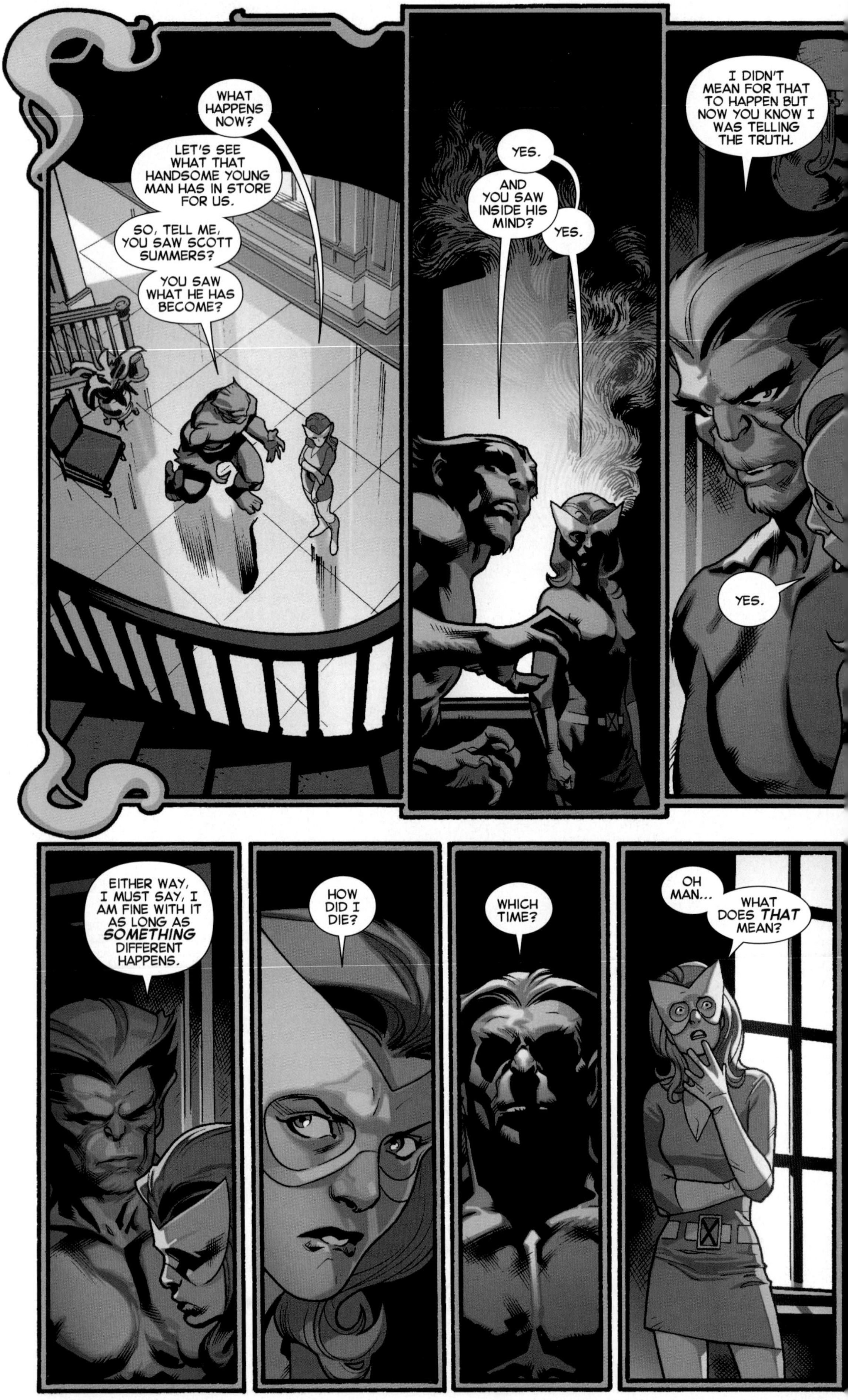

WHAT HAPPENS NOW?
LET'S SEE WHAT THAT HANDSOME YOUNG MAN HAS IN STORE FOR US.
SO, TELL ME, YOU SAW SCOTT SUMMERS?
YOU SAW WHAT HE HAS BECOME?
YES.
AND YOU SAW INSIDE HIS MIND?
YES.
I DIDN'T MEAN FOR THAT TO HAPPEN BUT NOW YOU KNOW I WAS TELLING THE TRUTH.
YES.
EITHER WAY, I MUST SAY, I AM FINE WITH IT AS LONG AS SOMETHING DIFFERENT HAPPENS.
HOW DID I DIE?
WHICH TIME?
OH MAN...
WHAT DOES THAT MEAN?

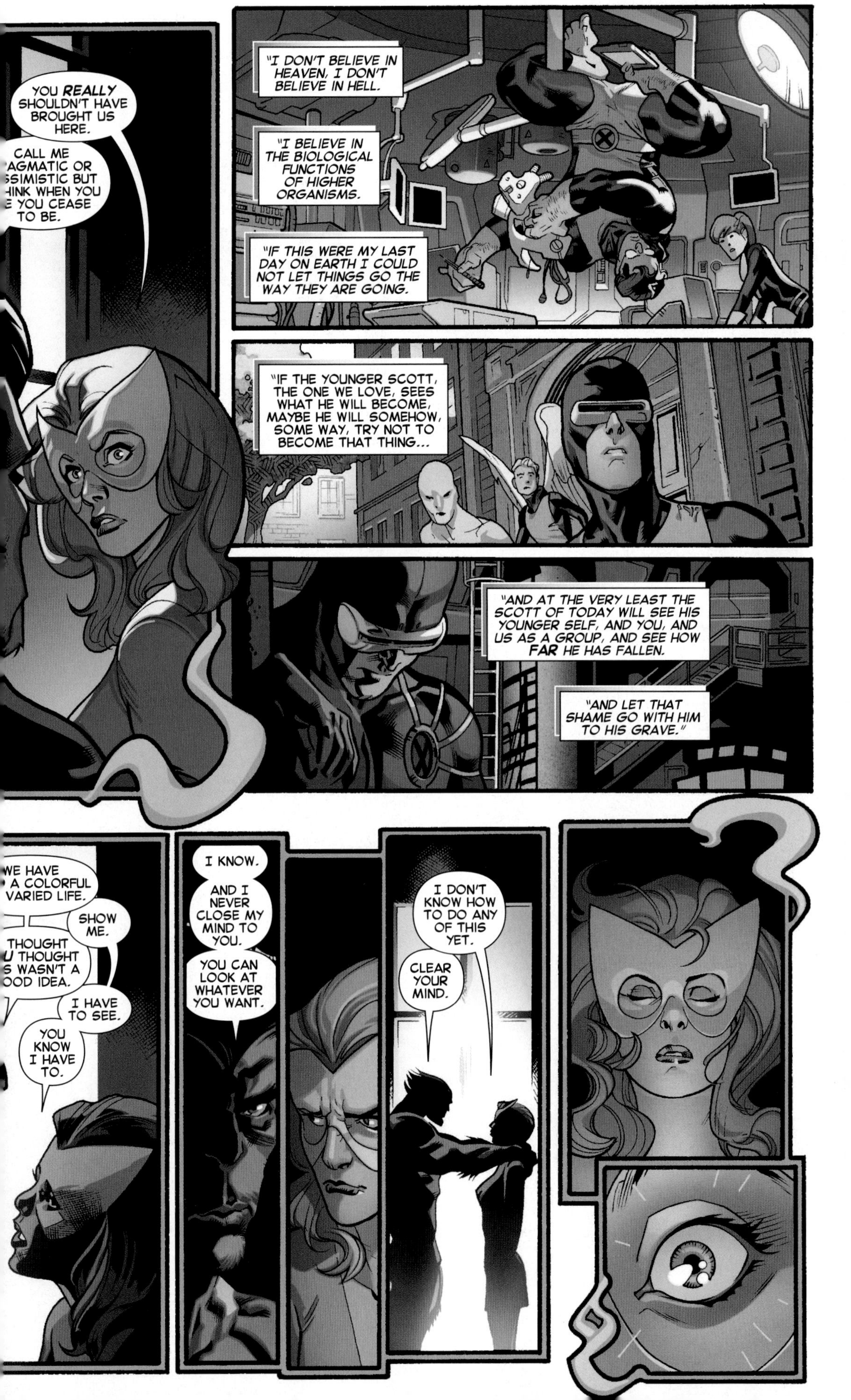

YOU REALLY SHOULDN'T HAVE BROUGHT US HERE.
CALL ME AGMATIC OR SSIMISTIC BUT HINK WHEN YOU E YOU CEASE TO BE.
"I DON'T BELIEVE IN HEAVEN, I DON'T BELIEVE IN HELL.
"I BELIEVE IN THE BIOLOGICAL FUNCTIONS OF HIGHER ORGANISMS.
"IF THIS WERE MY LAST DAY ON EARTH I COULD NOT LET THINGS GO THE WAY THEY ARE GOING.
"IF THE YOUNGER SCOTT, THE ONE WE LOVE, SEES WHAT HE WILL BECOME, MAYBE HE WILL SOMEHOW, SOME WAY, TRY NOT TO BECOME THAT THING...
"AND AT THE VERY LEAST THE SCOTT OF TODAY WILL SEE HIS YOUNGER SELF, AND YOU, AND US AS A GROUP, AND SEE HOW FAR HE HAS FALLEN.
"AND LET THAT SHAME GO WITH HIM TO HIS GRAVE."
WE HAVE A COLORFUL VARIED LIFE.
SHOW ME.
THOUGHT U THOUGHT S WASN'T A OOD IDEA.
I HAVE TO SEE.
YOU KNOW I HAVE TO.
I KNOW.
AND I NEVER CLOSE MY MIND TO YOU.
YOU CAN LOOK AT WHATEVER YOU WANT.
I DON'T KNOW HOW TO DO ANY OF THIS YET.
CLEAR YOUR MIND.

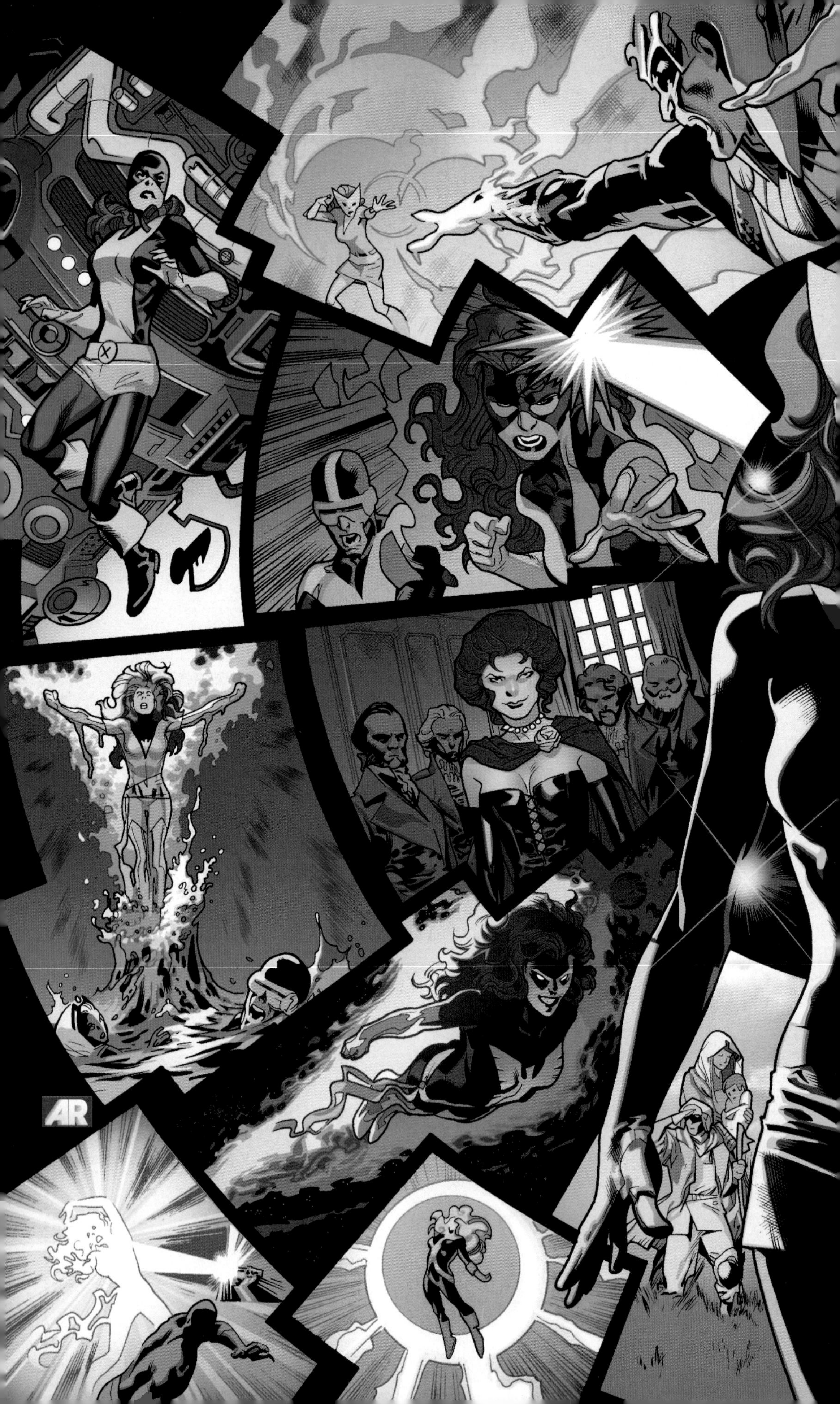

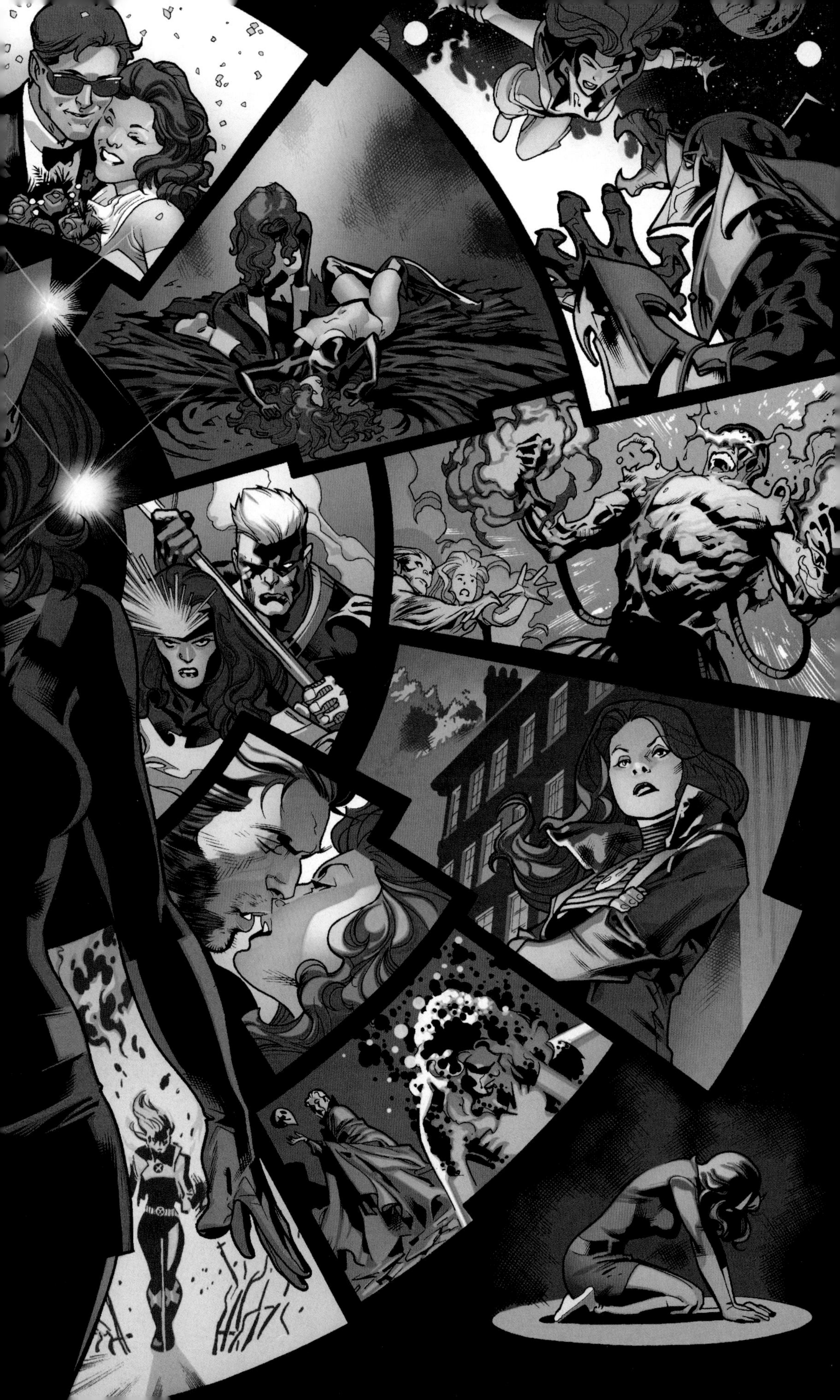

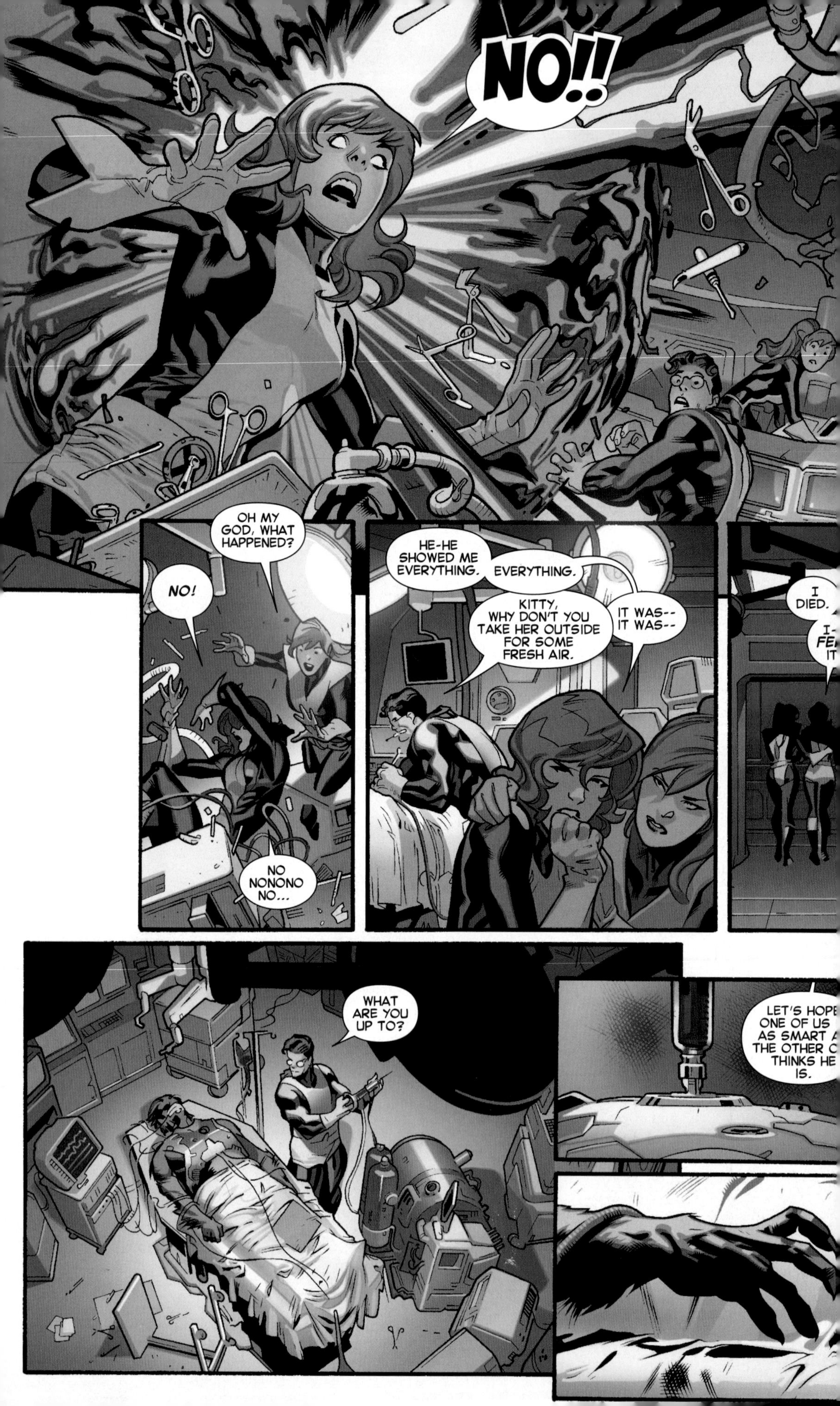

NO!!
OH MY GOD, WHAT HAPPENED?
NO!
NO NONONO NO...
HE-HE SHOWED ME EVERYTHING.
EVERYTHING.
KITTY, WHY DON'T YOU TAKE HER OUTSIDE FOR SOME FRESH AIR.
IT WAS-- IT WAS--
I DIED.
WHAT ARE YOU UP TO?
LET'S HOPE ONE OF US AS SMART THE OTHER THINKS HE IS.

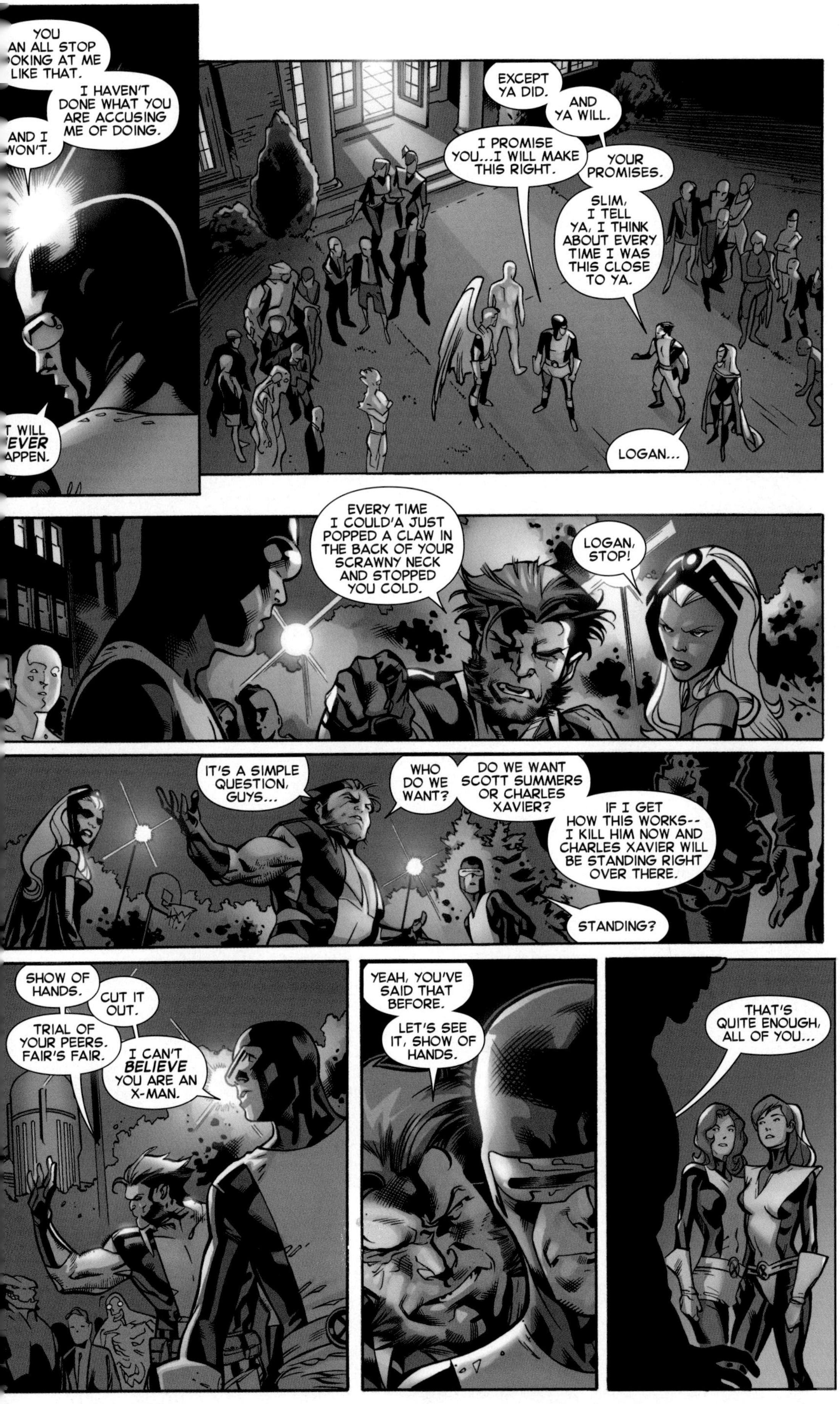
YOU
AN ALL STOP
OOKING AT ME
LIKE THAT.
I HAVEN'T DONE WHAT YOU ARE ACCUSING ME OF DOING.
AND I
WON'T.
T WILL
EVER
APPEN.
EXCEPT YA DID.
AND YA WILL.
I PROMISE YOU...I WILL MAKE THIS RIGHT.
YOUR PROMISES.
SLIM, I TELL YA, I THINK ABOUT EVERY TIME I WAS THIS CLOSE TO YA.
LOGAN...
EVERY TIME I COULD'A JUST POPPED A CLAW IN THE BACK OF YOUR SCRAWNY NECK AND STOPPED YOU COLD.
LOGAN, STOP!
IT'S A SIMPLE QUESTION, GUYS...
WHO DO WE WANT?
DO WE WANT SCOTT SUMMERS OR CHARLES XAVIER?
IF I GET HOW THIS WORKS-- I KILL HIM NOW AND CHARLES XAVIER WILL BE STANDING RIGHT OVER THERE.
STANDING?
SHOW OF HANDS.
CUT IT OUT.
TRIAL OF YOUR PEERS. FAIR'S FAIR.
I CAN'T *BELIEVE* YOU ARE AN X-MAN.
YEAH, YOU'VE SAID THAT BEFORE.
LET'S SEE IT, SHOW OF HANDS.
THAT'S QUITE ENOUGH, ALL OF YOU...

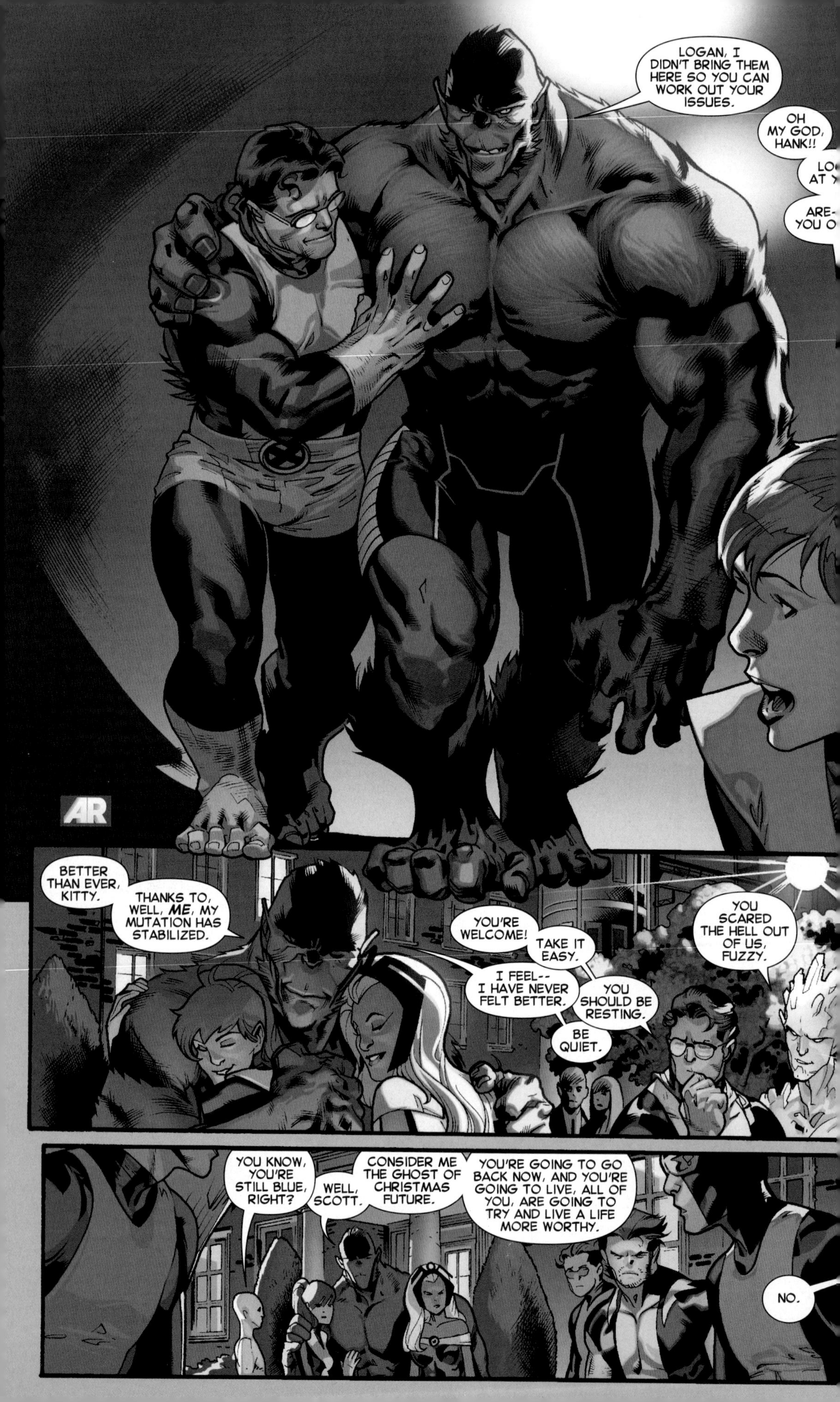
LOGAN, I DIDN'T BRING THEM HERE SO YOU CAN WORK OUT YOUR ISSUES.
OH MY GOD, HANK!!
AR
BETTER THAN EVER, KITTY.
THANKS TO, WELL, ME, MY MUTATION HAS STABILIZED.
YOU'RE WELCOME!
TAKE IT EASY.
I FEEL-- I HAVE NEVER FELT BETTER.
YOU SHOULD BE RESTING.
BE QUIET.
YOU SCARED THE HELL OUT OF US, FUZZY.
YOU KNOW, YOU'RE STILL BLUE, RIGHT?
WELL, SCOTT.
CONSIDER ME THE GHOST OF CHRISTMAS FUTURE.
YOU'RE GOING TO GO BACK NOW, AND YOU'RE GOING TO LIVE, ALL OF YOU, ARE GOING TO TRY AND LIVE A LIFE MORE WORTHY.
NO.

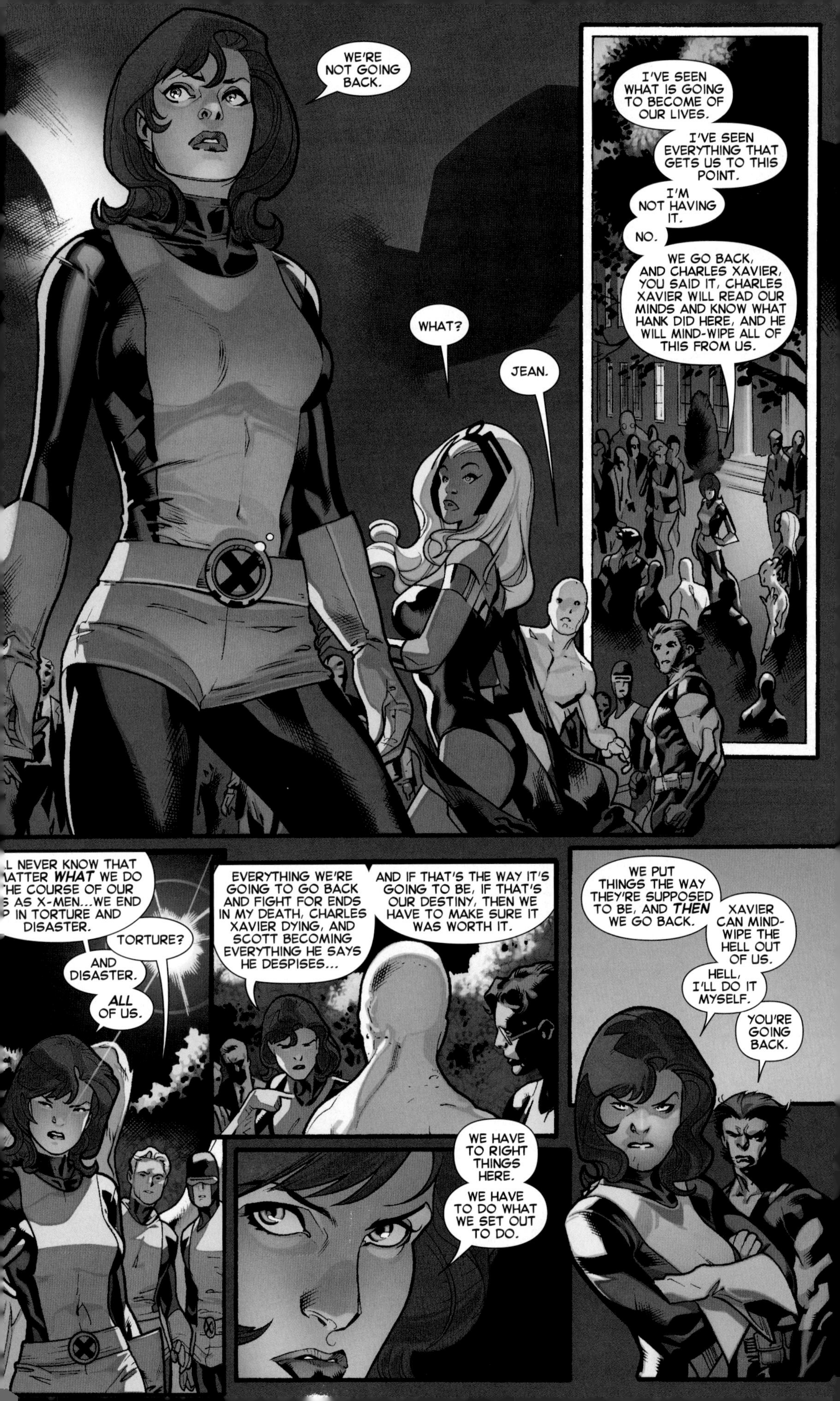
WE'RE NOT GOING BACK.
I'VE SEEN WHAT IS GOING TO BECOME OF OUR LIVES.
I'VE SEEN EVERYTHING THAT GETS US TO THIS POINT.
I'M NOT HAVING IT.
NO.
WE GO BACK, AND CHARLES XAVIER, YOU SAID IT, CHARLES XAVIER WILL READ OUR MINDS AND KNOW WHAT HANK DID HERE, AND HE WILL MIND-WIPE ALL OF THIS FROM US.
WHAT?
JEAN.
L NEVER KNOW THAT ATTER WHAT WE DO HE COURSE OF OUR S AS X-MEN...WE END P IN TORTURE AND DISASTER.
TORTURE?
AND DISASTER.
ALL OF US.
EVERYTHING WE'RE GOING TO GO BACK AND FIGHT FOR ENDS IN MY DEATH, CHARLES XAVIER DYING, AND SCOTT BECOMING EVERYTHING HE SAYS HE DESPISES...
AND IF THAT'S THE WAY IT'S GOING TO BE, IF THAT'S OUR DESTINY, THEN WE HAVE TO MAKE SURE IT WAS WORTH IT.
WE HAVE TO RIGHT THINGS HERE.
WE HAVE TO DO WHAT WE SET OUT TO DO.
WE PUT THINGS THE WAY THEY'RE SUPPOSED TO BE, AND THEN WE GO BACK.
XAVIER CAN MIND-WIPE THE HELL OUT OF US.
HELL, I'LL DO IT MYSELF.
YOU'RE GOING BACK.

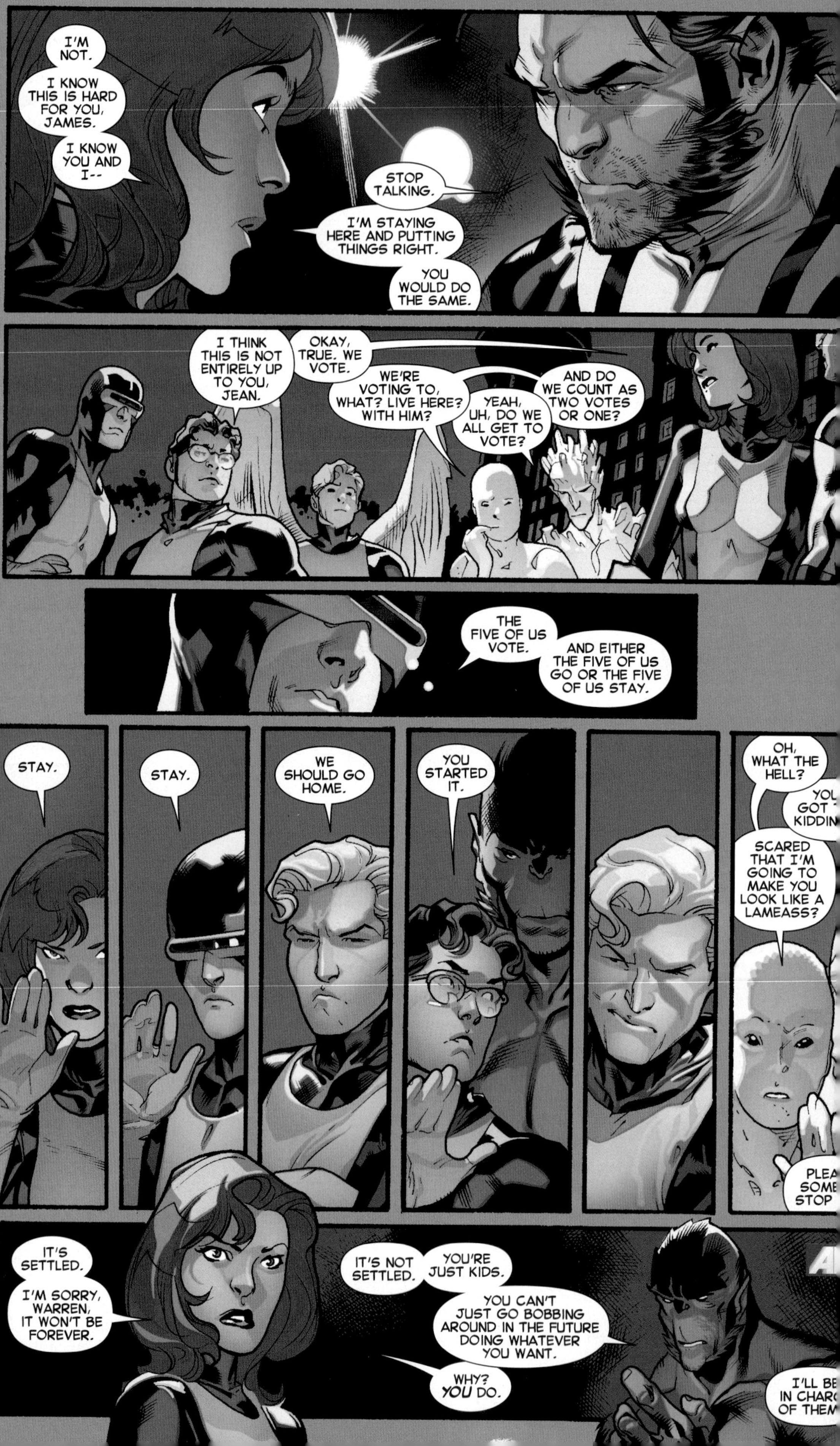
I'M NOT.
I KNOW THIS IS HARD FOR YOU, JAMES.
I KNOW YOU AND I--
STOP TALKING.
I'M STAYING HERE AND PUTTING THINGS RIGHT.
YOU WOULD DO THE SAME.
I THINK THIS IS NOT ENTIRELY UP TO YOU, JEAN.
OKAY, TRUE. WE VOTE.
WE'RE VOTING TO, WHAT? LIVE HERE? WITH HIM?
YEAH, UH, DO WE ALL GET TO VOTE?
AND DO WE COUNT AS TWO VOTES OR ONE?
THE FIVE OF US VOTE.
AND EITHER THE FIVE OF US GO OR THE FIVE OF US STAY.
STAY.
STAY.
WE SHOULD GO HOME.
YOU STARTED IT.
OH, WHAT THE HELL?
YOU GOT KIDDIN
SCARED THAT I'M GOING TO MAKE YOU LOOK LIKE A LAMEASS?
PLEA SOME STOP
IT'S SETTLED.
I'M SORRY, WARREN, IT WON'T BE FOREVER.
IT'S NOT SETTLED.
YOU'RE JUST KIDS.
YOU CAN'T JUST GO BOBBING AROUND IN THE FUTURE DOING WHATEVER YOU WANT.
WHY? *YOU* DO.
I'LL BE IN CHARG OF THEM

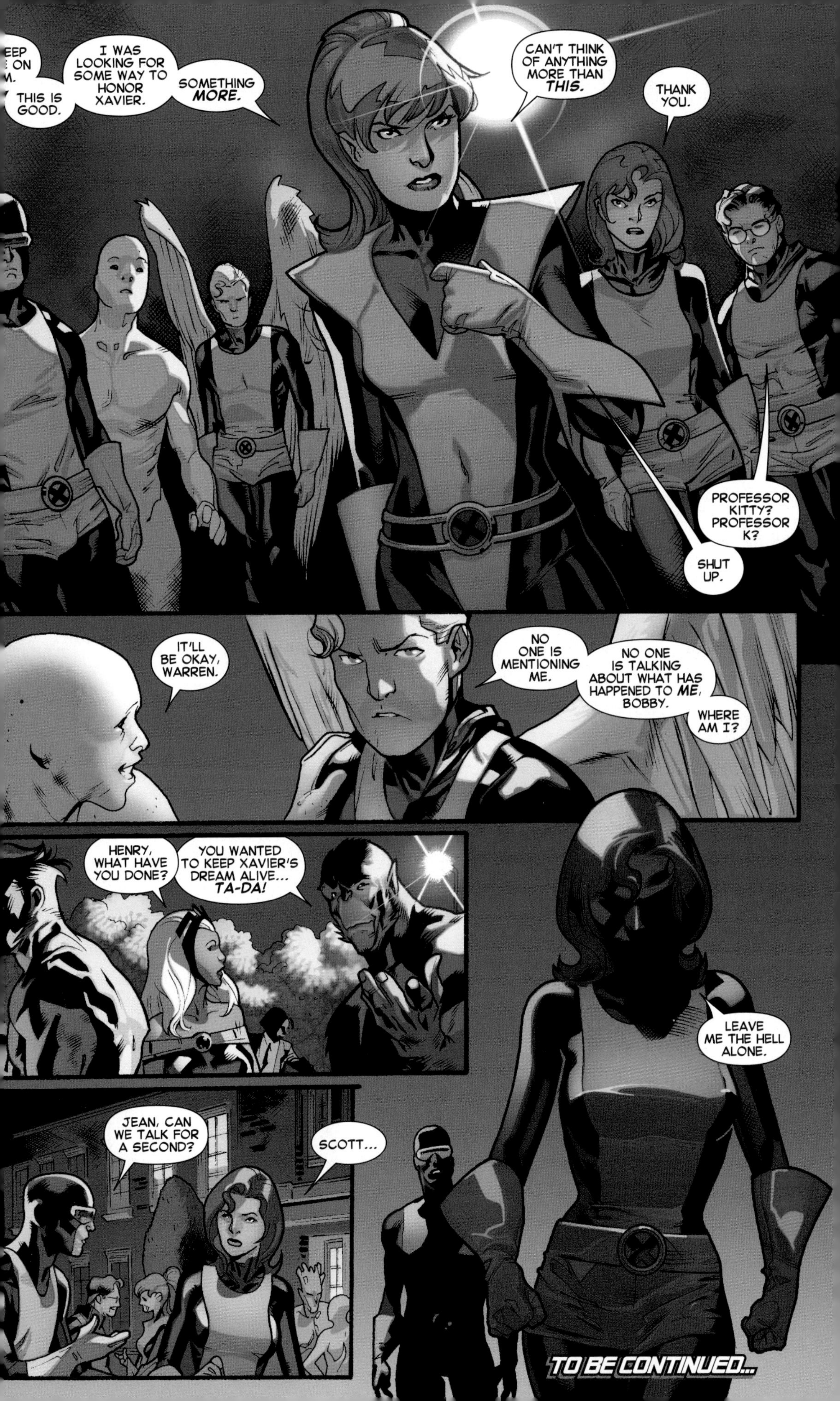

EEP
E ON
M.
THIS IS GOOD.
I WAS LOOKING FOR SOME WAY TO HONOR XAVIER.
SOMETHING MORE.
CAN'T THINK OF ANYTHING MORE THAN THIS.
THANK YOU.
PROFESSOR KITTY? PROFESSOR K?
SHUT UP.
IT'LL BE OKAY, WARREN.
NO ONE IS MENTIONING ME.
NO ONE IS TALKING ABOUT WHAT HAS HAPPENED TO ME, BOBBY.
WHERE AM I?
HENRY, WHAT HAVE YOU DONE?
YOU WANTED TO KEEP XAVIER'S DREAM ALIVE... TA-DA!
JEAN, CAN WE TALK FOR A SECOND?
SCOTT...
LEAVE ME THE HELL ALONE.
TO BE CONTINUED...

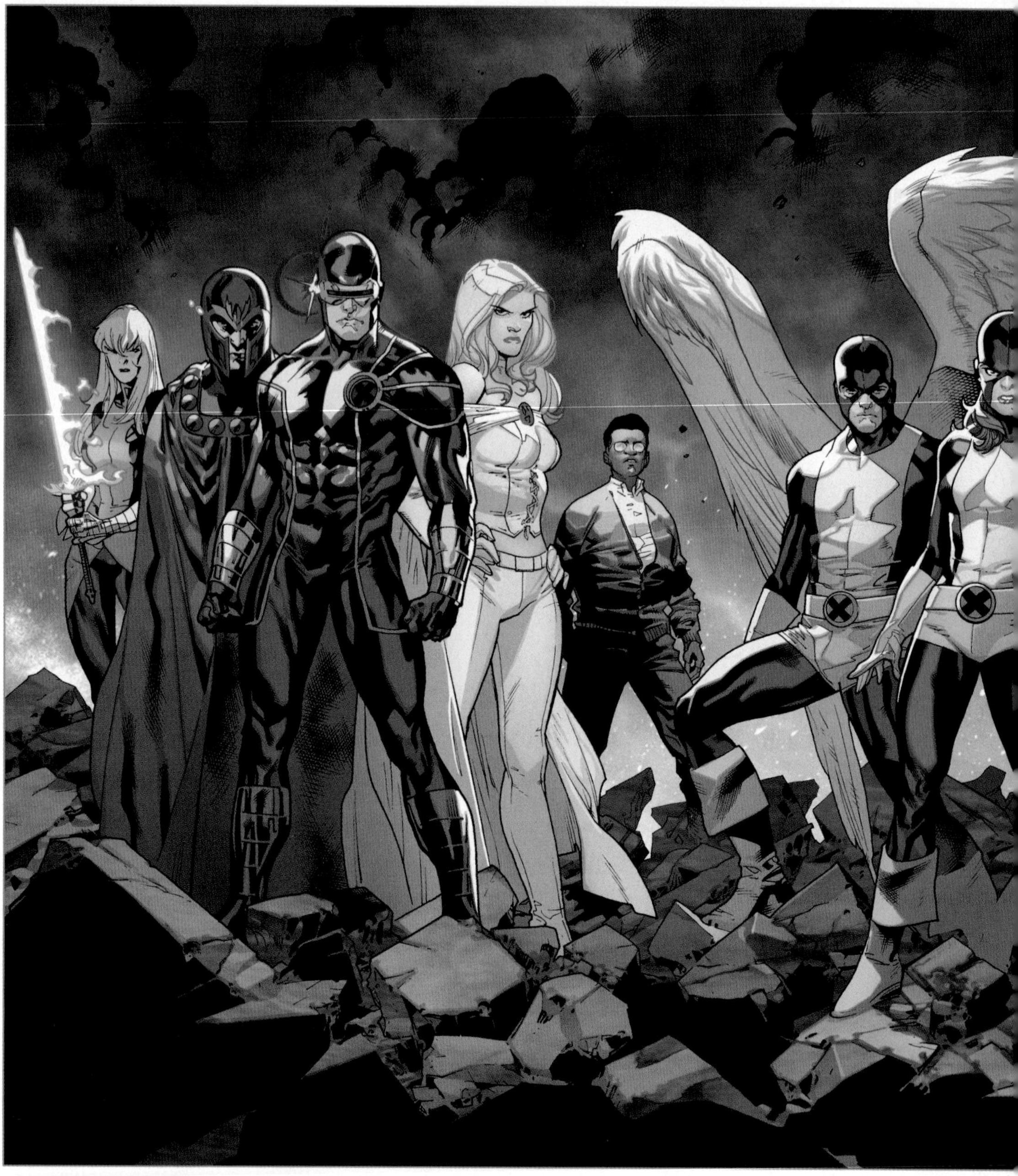

ALL-NEW X-MEN #1-2
COMBINED COVERS
BY STUART IMMONEN, WADE VON GRAWBADGER & MARTE GRACIA

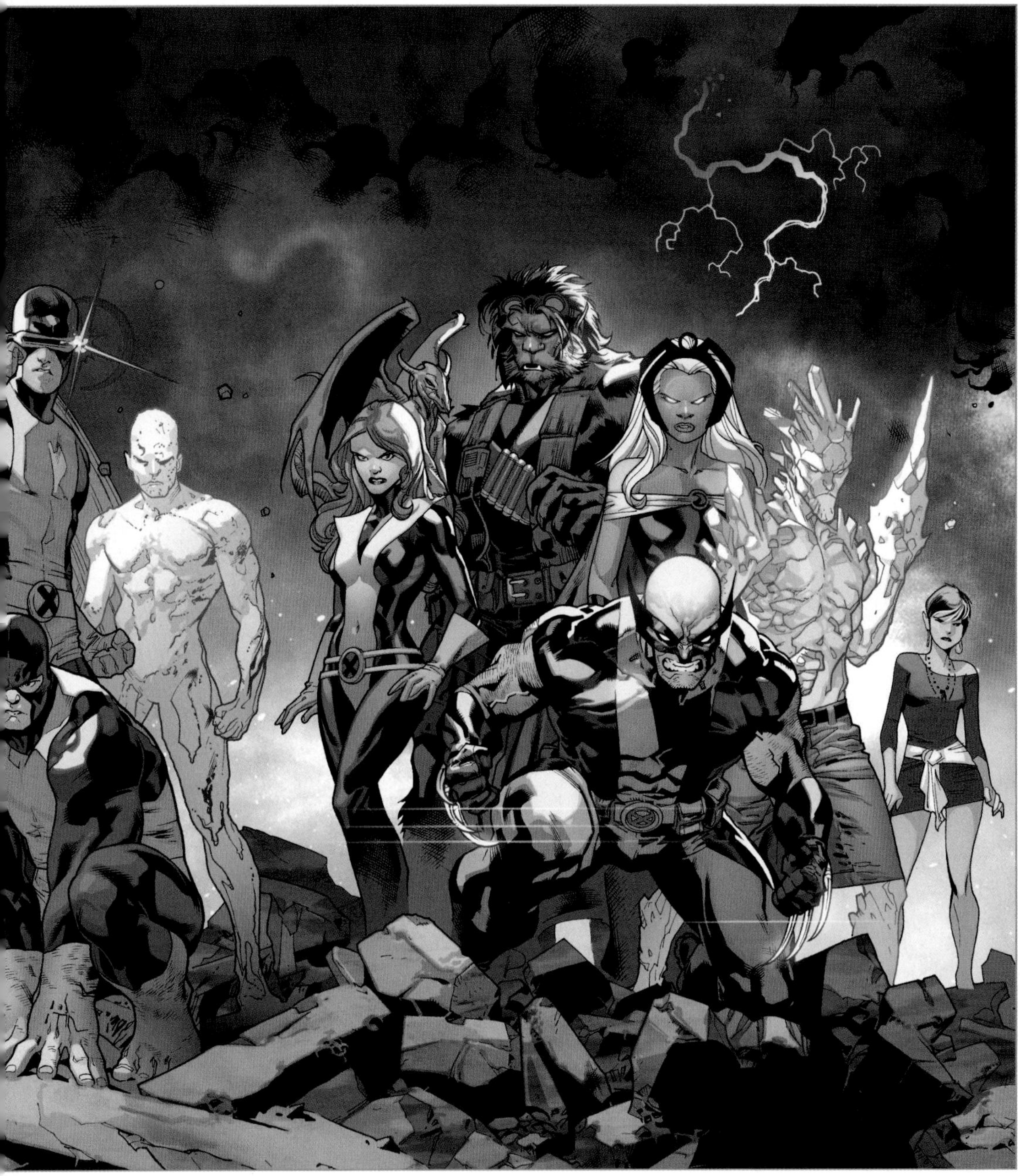

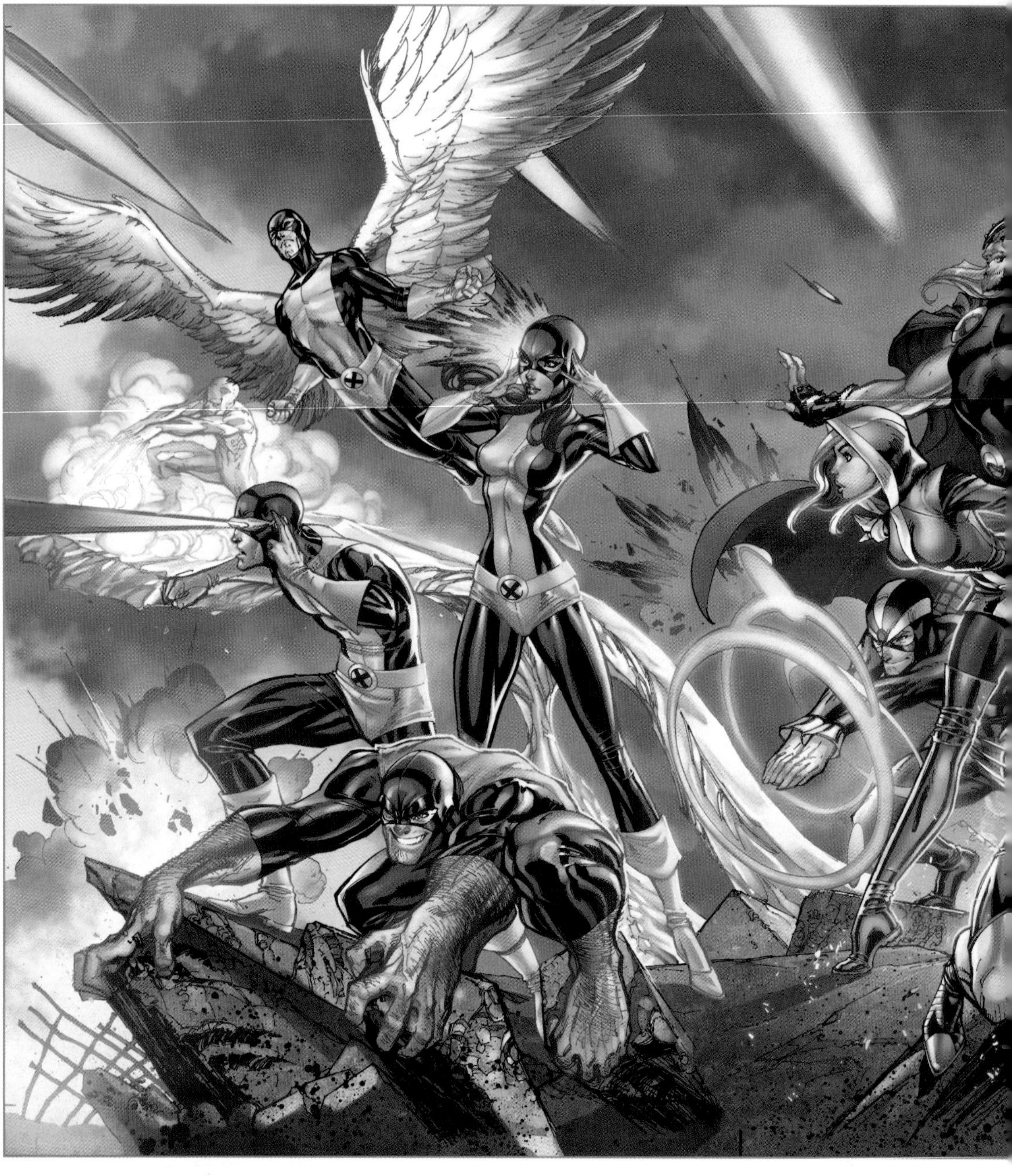

ALL-NEW X-MEN #1
UNCANNY AVENGERS #1
AVENGERS #1

MIDTOWN COMICS EXCLUSIVE COMBINED VARIANTS

BY J. SCOTT CAMPBELL & NEI RUFFINO

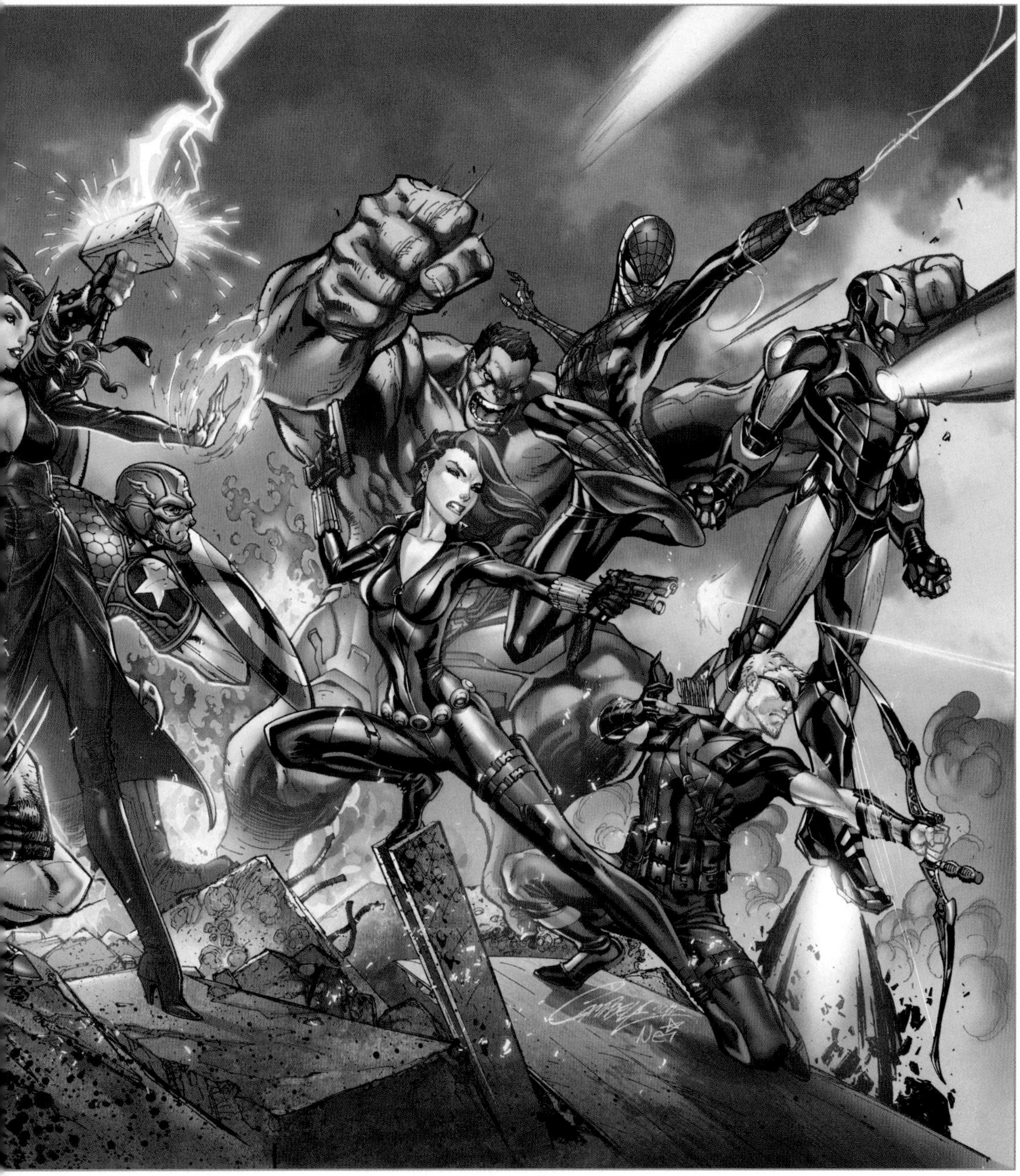

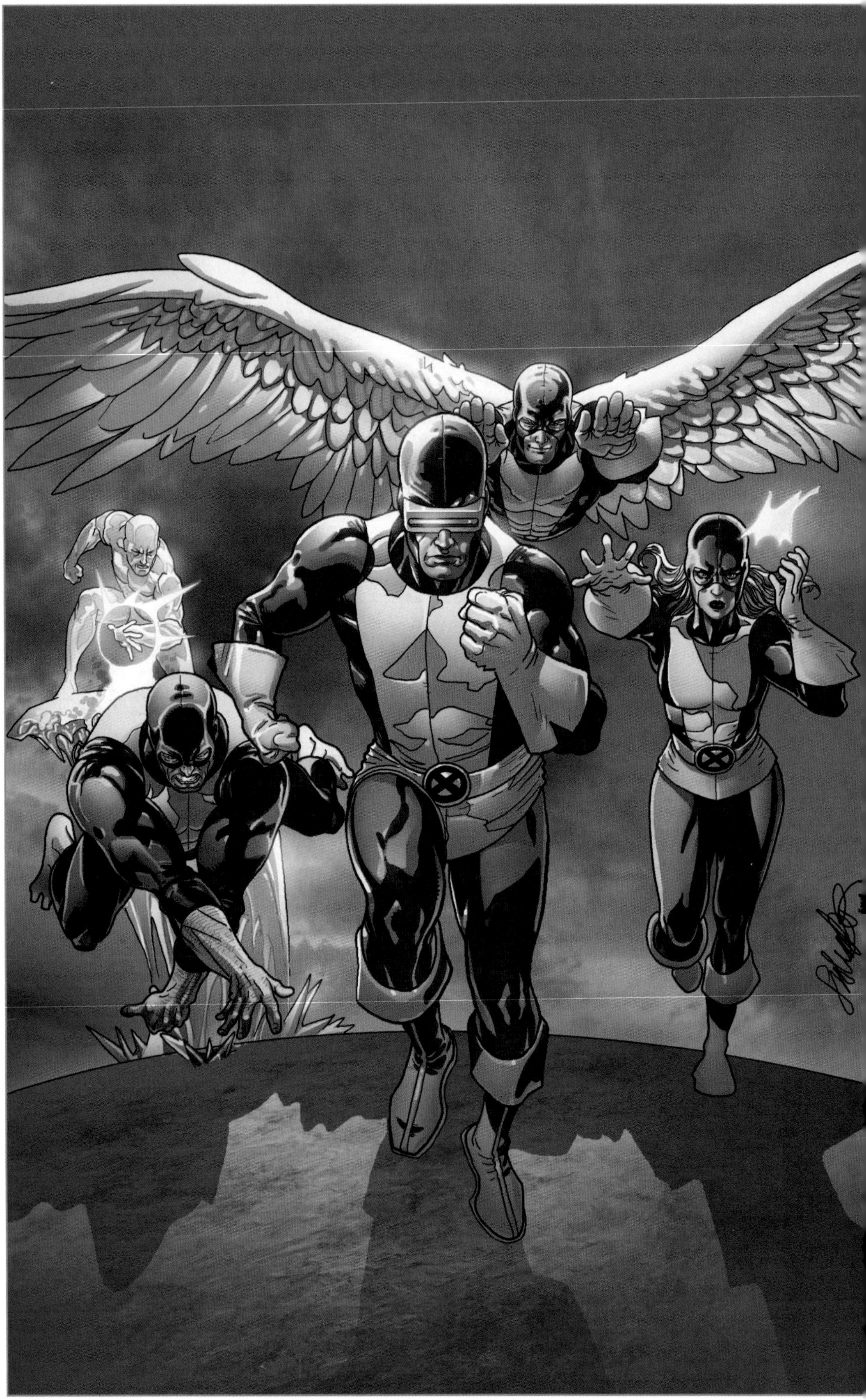

ALL-NEW X-MEN #1 MILE HIGH COMICS VARIANT
BY SALVADOR LARROCA & FRANK D'ARMATA

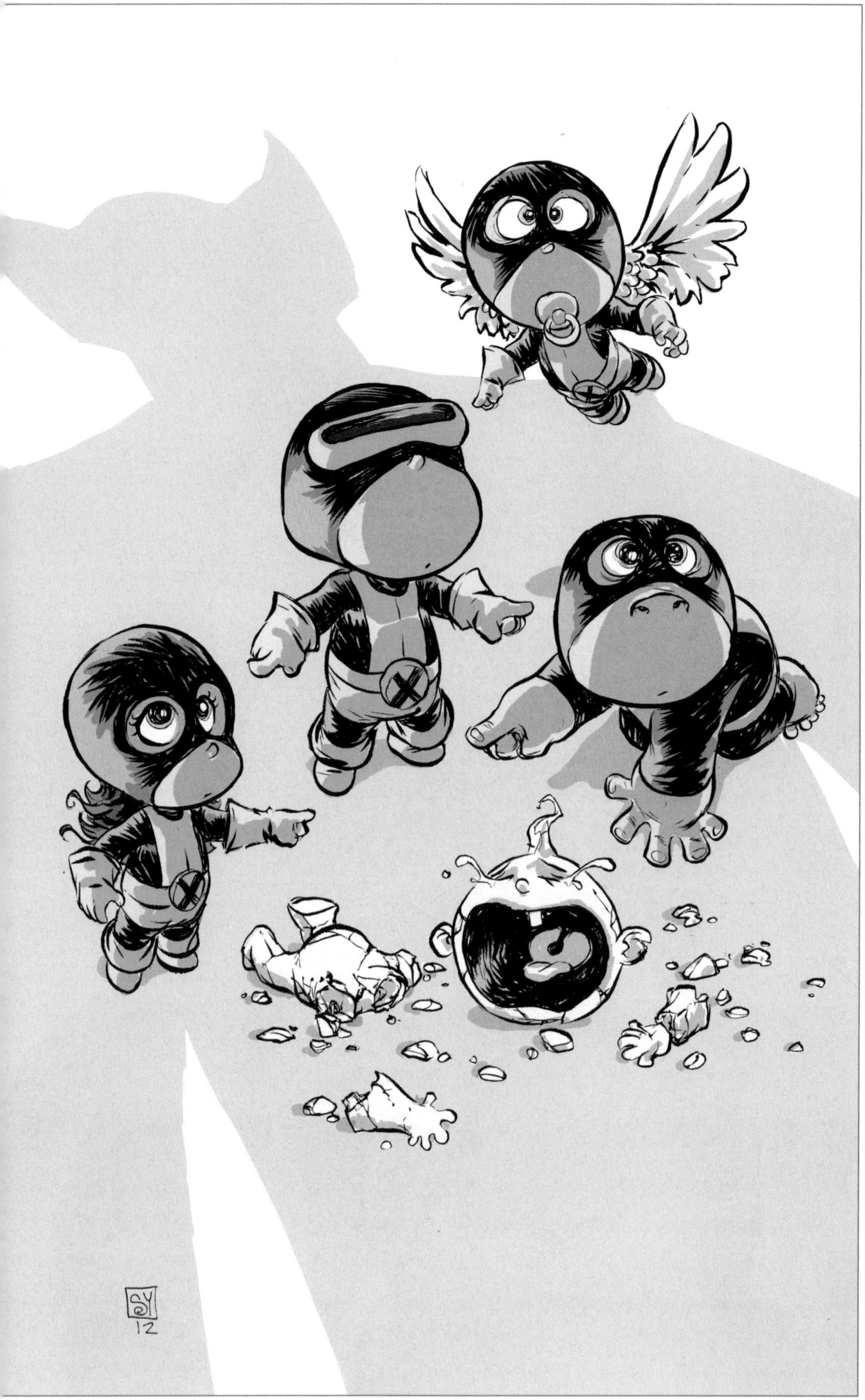
SY
12

ALL-NEW X-MEN #1 BABY VARIANT
BY SKOTTIE YOUNG

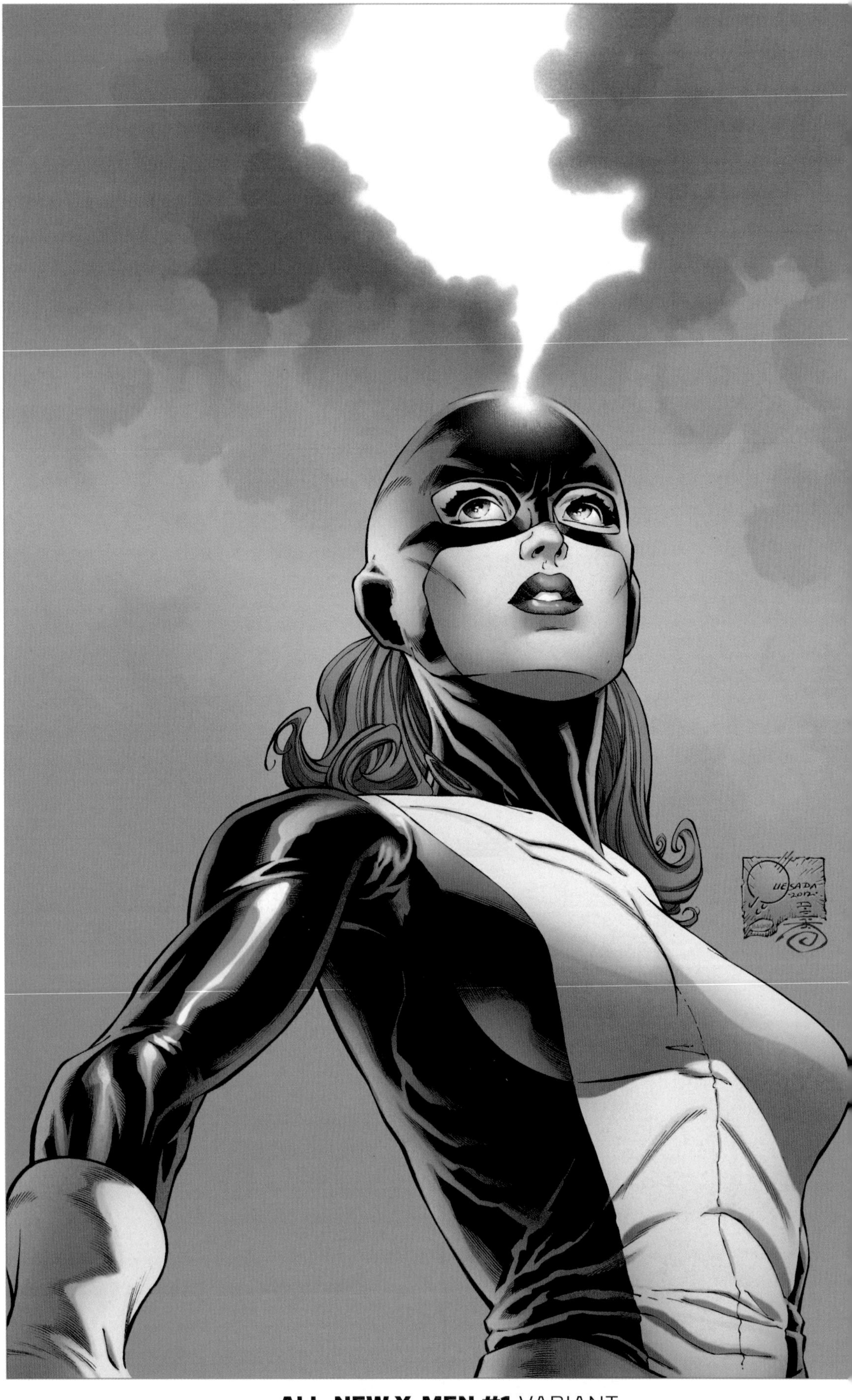
QUESADA 2012

ALL-NEW X-MEN #1 VARIANT
BY JOE QUESADA, DANNY MIKI & RICHARD ISANOVE

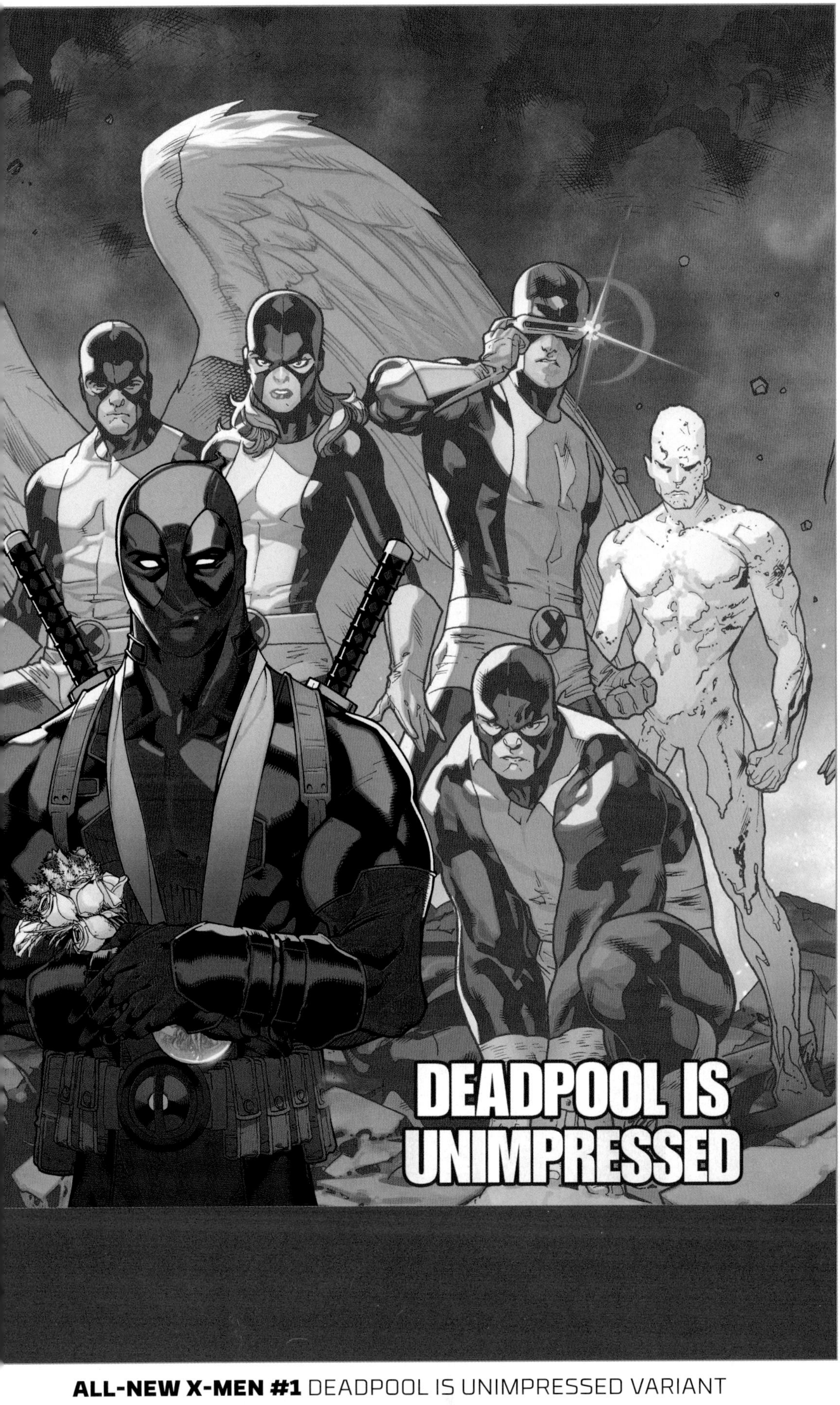
DEADPOOL IS UNIMPRESSED

ALL-NEW X-MEN #1 DEADPOOL IS UNIMPRESSED VARIANT
BY STUART IMMONEN

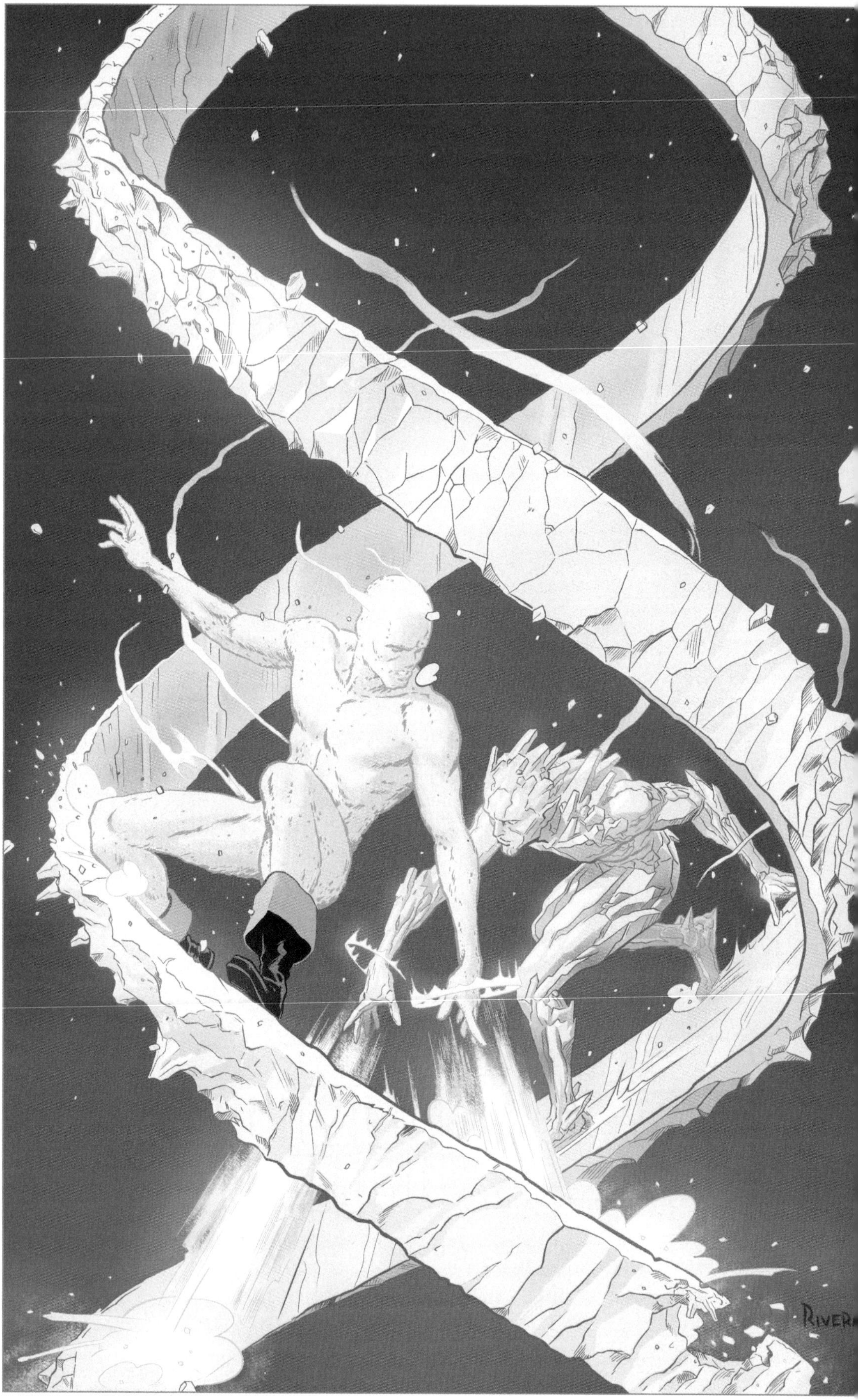
RIVERA

ALL-NEW X-MEN #1 VARIANT

BY PAOLO RIVERA

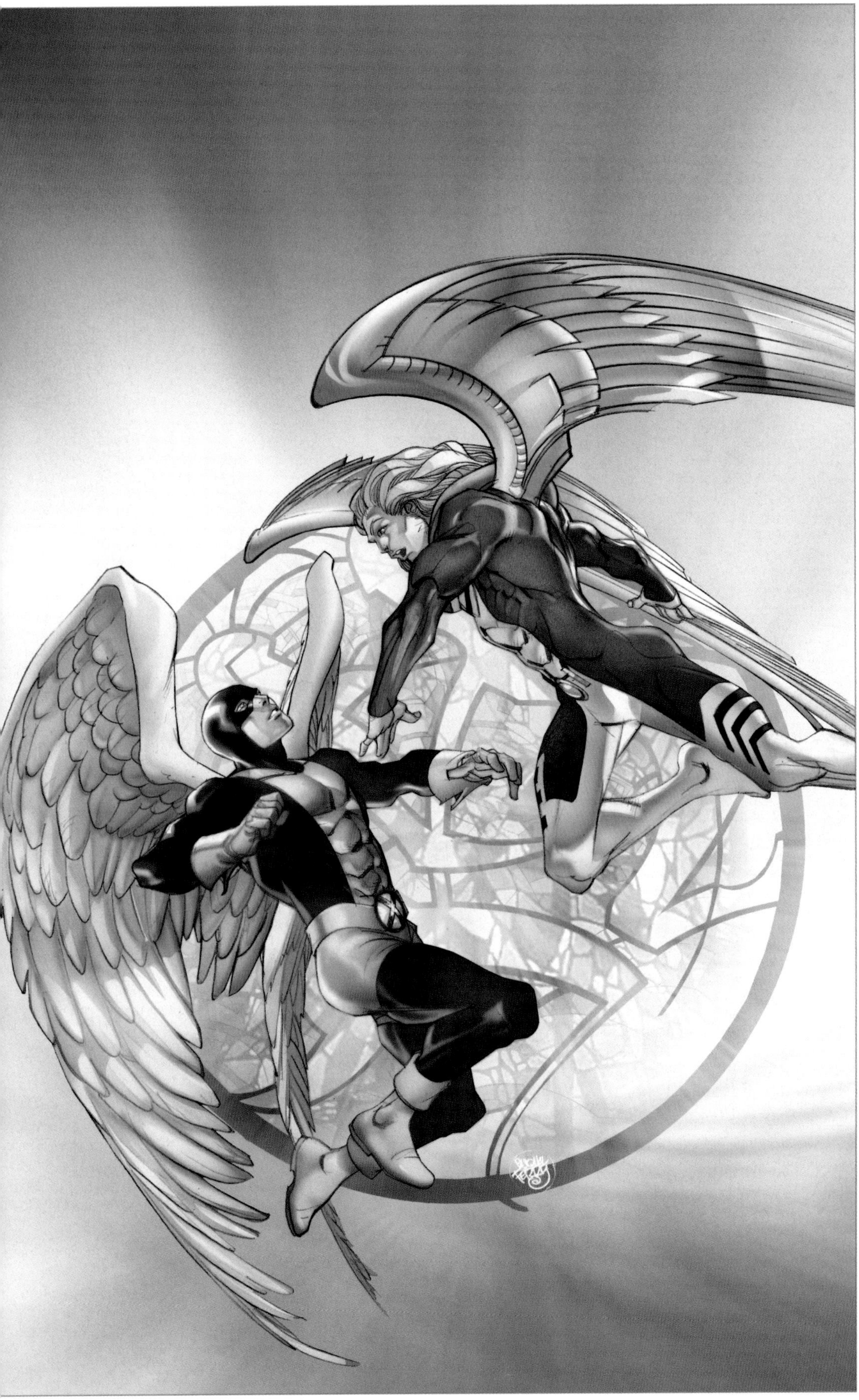

ALL-NEW X-MEN #2 VARIANT
BY PASQUAL FERRY

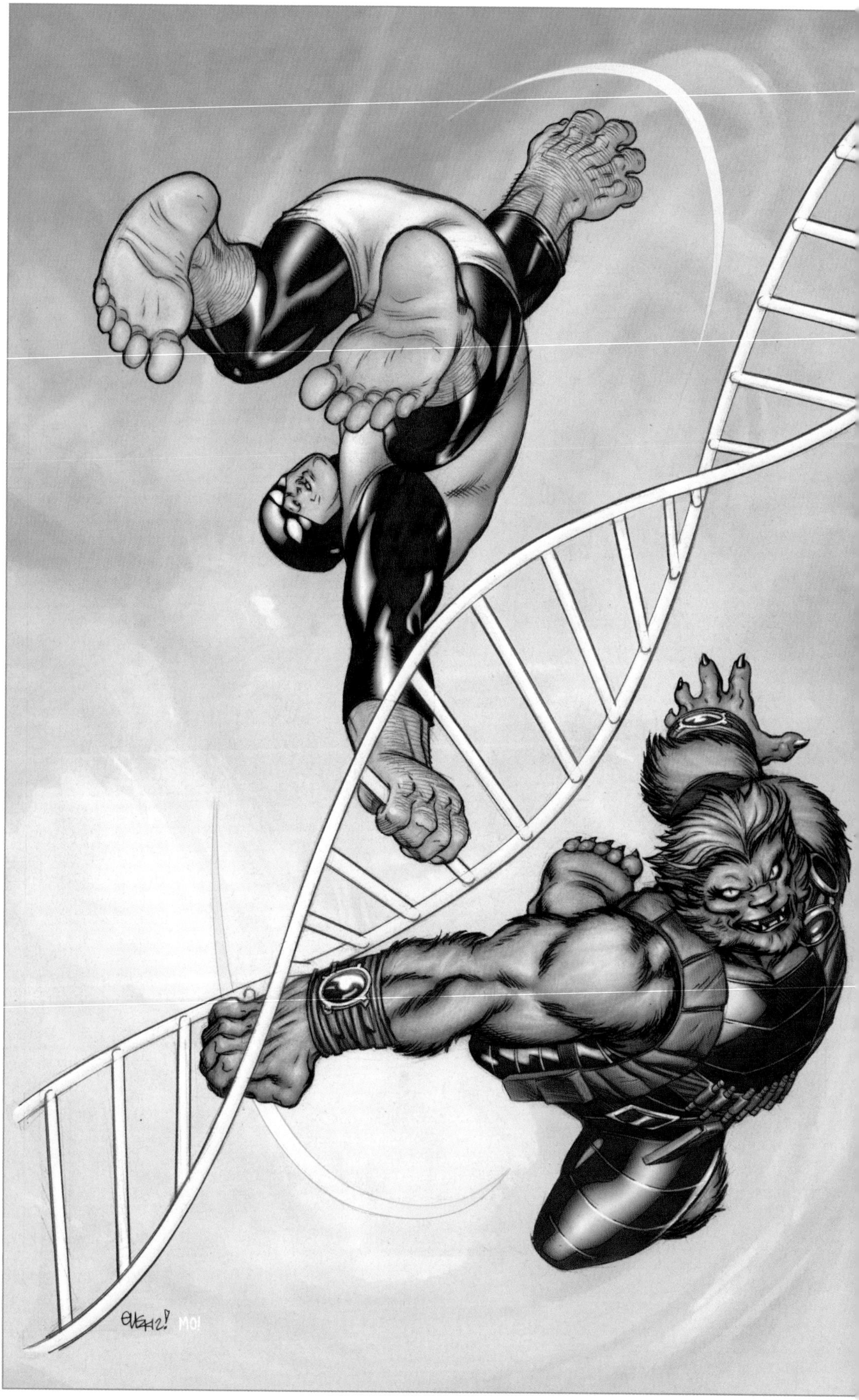

MO!

ALL-NEW X-MEN #3 VARIANT
BY ED McGUINNESS & MORRY HOLLOWELL

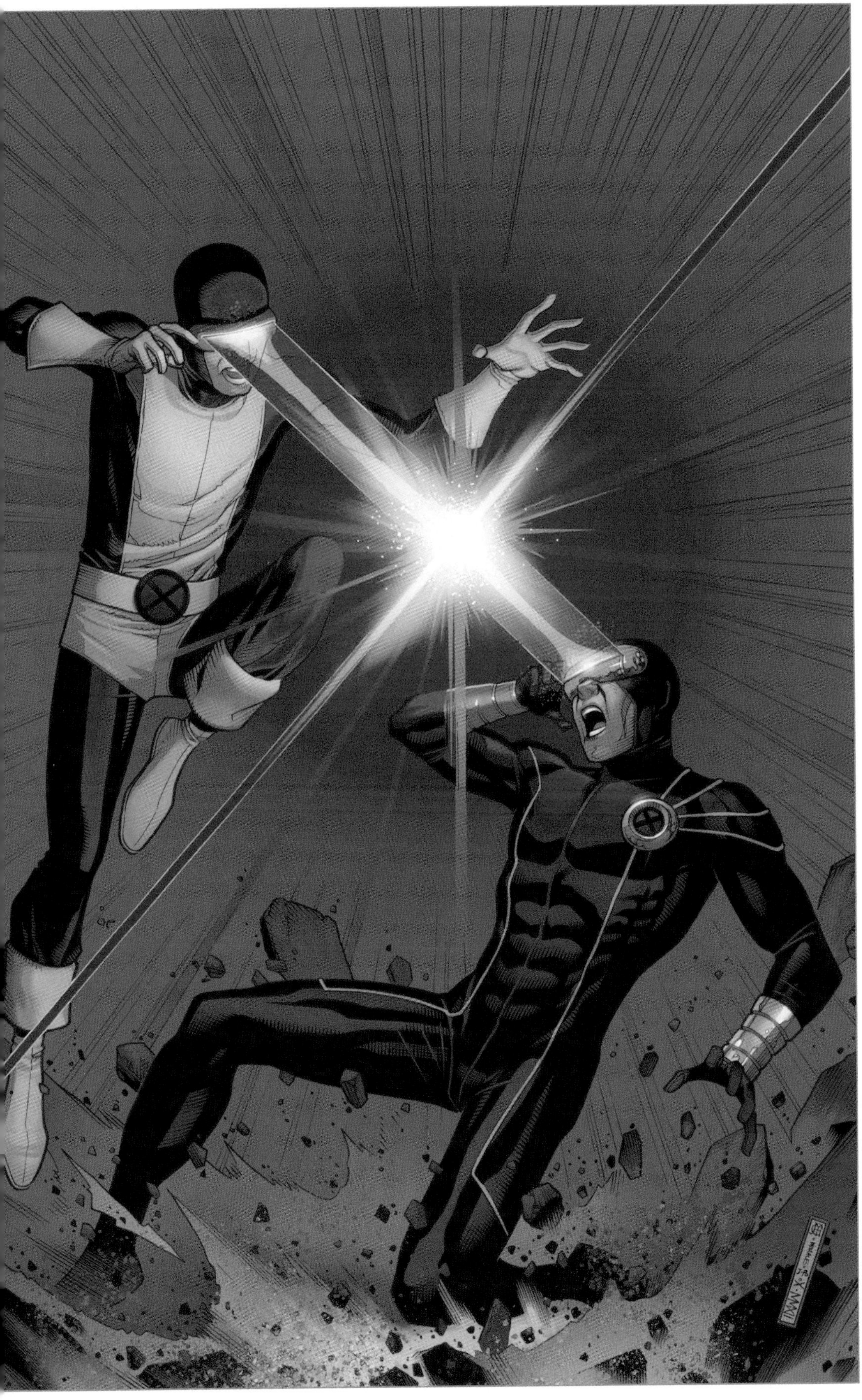

ALL-NEW X-MEN #4 VARIANT
BY JIM CHEUNG , MARK MORALES & JUSTIN PONSOR

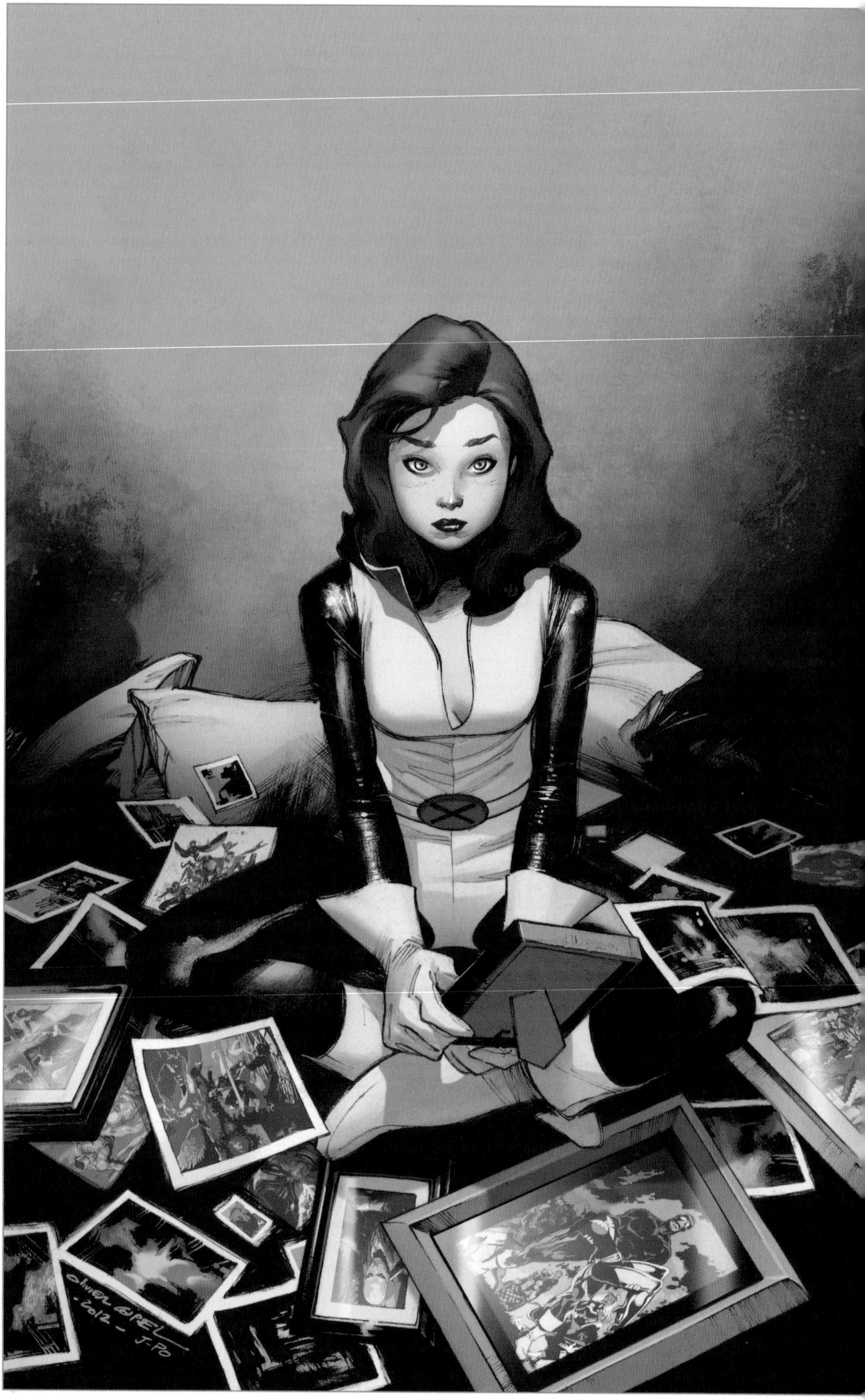
OLIVIER COIPEL
-2012-
J-PO

ALL-NEW X-MEN #5 VARIANT
BY OLIVIER COIPEL & JUSTIN PONSOR

Here's the first document that Brian Bendis wrote for his X-Men run. It was written quite long ago — so long, in fact, you'll notice it was written before the final decision to kill Charles Xavier in *Avengers vs. X-Men #11* was made. There are a few details we needed to redact, but here it is for your edification!

X-Men discussion document

By Brian Michael Bendis

DAYS OF FUTURE NOW

Art- STUART IMMONEN

After the punishing results of Avengers versus X-Men, mutant confusion is at an all-time high. Cyclops, and what is left of the Phoenix 5, have gone full-on mutant revolutionary which is illustrated by a huge set piece where Cyclops makes his 'take no prisoners' attitude very clear.

Hank McCoy, Storm, Wolverine, Iceman, Kitty and the others watch the chaos in disgust. What can they do? If they confront Scott head on then the next step is MUTANT CIVIL WAR.

And if that happens... no one wins.

STORM

> If young Scott Summers saw what he has turned into... he would be sick to his stomach.

ICE MAN

> When we were young we were always worried about a mutant apocalyptic nightmare... if the young us saw what was going on today it would feel worse than an apocalyptic nightmare!!

What the X-Men don't know is that the 'Phoenix 5's' power sets have been severely altered by their time with the Phoenix power.

Scott has to completely re-train himself, Emma is [redacted], Magneto had his powers leveled by the final conflict in AvX. The X-Men revolutionaries' dark secret is that they are as untrained and unprepared for war as they were the first day they got their powers.

Hank McCoy, secretly, hits another secondary mutation. A mutation so severe that he fears for his life. On top of this, Hank is tortured by what has become of their youthful dream of humans and mutants living together and fears that there is no hope.

Storm's words about young Scott haunt him.

He cannot get the idea out of his head that there was no one who can peacefully stop Scott Summers other than the Scott Summers that used to be his friend.

Hank McCoy travels back to the earliest days of the Uncanny X-Men (Uncanny X-Men number 8 for those of you playing at home) and offers them a chance to save the world from themselves.

The original Uncanny X-Men take the offer and travel to the present.

End of 1st issue

Rest of the story–

Throughout the first arc the original Uncanny X-Men will see everything that has happened to them. They will see that the Xavier school is now the Jean Grey School.

Young Jean will be rattled to her core as she hears how she sacrificed herself for the greater good of mankind.

Young Scott will come face-to-face with the future self that in many ways represents everything he's sworn to fight against.

Older Scott is PARTNERED with Magneto?

Everyone is shocked to find out that Bobby Drake ended up turning out the best. Bobby, humorously, is a little disappointed.

And young Hank McCoy is eventually able to figure out how to turn The Beast back into the fun-loving, blue, furry friend to everyone.

The original Uncanny X-Men and the X-Men of today will go head-to-head in a very large set piece.

At the end of it the original X-Men will decide to stay.

JEAN GREY

This is where we are needed most.

Then...

Three months later this project will split into 2 monthly books.

ALL-NEW X-MEN will continue and will star the original Uncanny X-Men coming to terms with the world as it is today and fighting to make it better.

The book will star the original Uncanny X-Men and members of the X-Men today. New friendships, new relationships, new drama, new dedication towards an ideal as fresh as it was originally stated.

Plus we have a book full of fish out of water Capt. America types dealing with the new.

The other book, launching in February will be called, UNCANNY X-MEN and will star, primarily, the Phoenix 5 as they deal with their uphill battles, their new powers and their new struggles.

ALL NEW X-MEN will be youthful and exuberant. Think of it as a cross between the original idea of the X-Men and the best version of the runaways. This is where Stuart will remain.

UNCANNY X-MEN will be, in many ways, similar in function to the DARK AVENGERS. While nowhere near as twisted, because of the nature of the characters, it will be a more mature look at a revolutionary's dedication to making the world a better place at all costs.

What is the world like when the people decide they have to rise up against their oppressors?

The original 5 X-Men [redacted]. QUESTIONS TO BRING UP IN THE RETREAT Where does Xavier fit into all of this?

I don't want to take him off the table. I want him to be furious at Hank McCoy for abusing technology for his own selfish purposes. Maybe it pushes him so far as to side up with Scott. Maybe he can't abandon his star pupil.

The Wolverine of it all.

I know that you, Nick, have ideas about [redacted] but I don't think we should do it right away. [redacted]. I do think we should do it, I'm just saying I don't think we need right now.

Where does Hope fit into all of this?

Can Kitty be the modern Xavier to the original Uncanny X-Men? Does that mess up the New Mutants book?

When is the right time to put all this together for a [redacted]?

CHARACTER SKETCHES

BY STUART IMMONEN

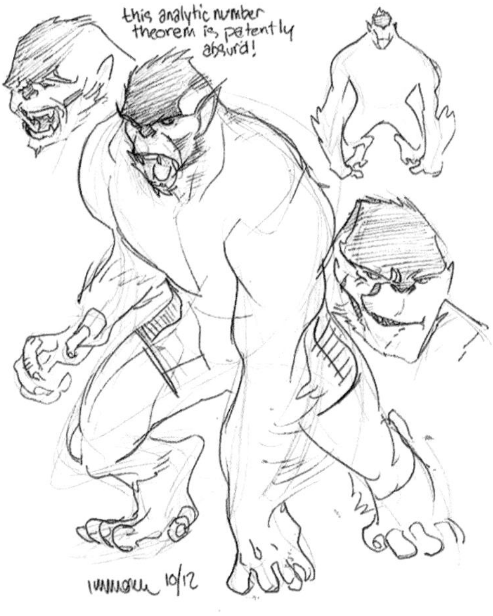
this analytic number theorem is patently absurd!

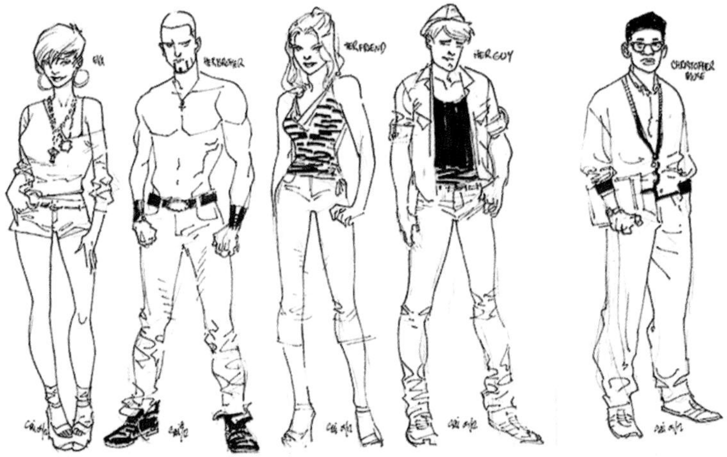
HER FRIEND
HER GUY

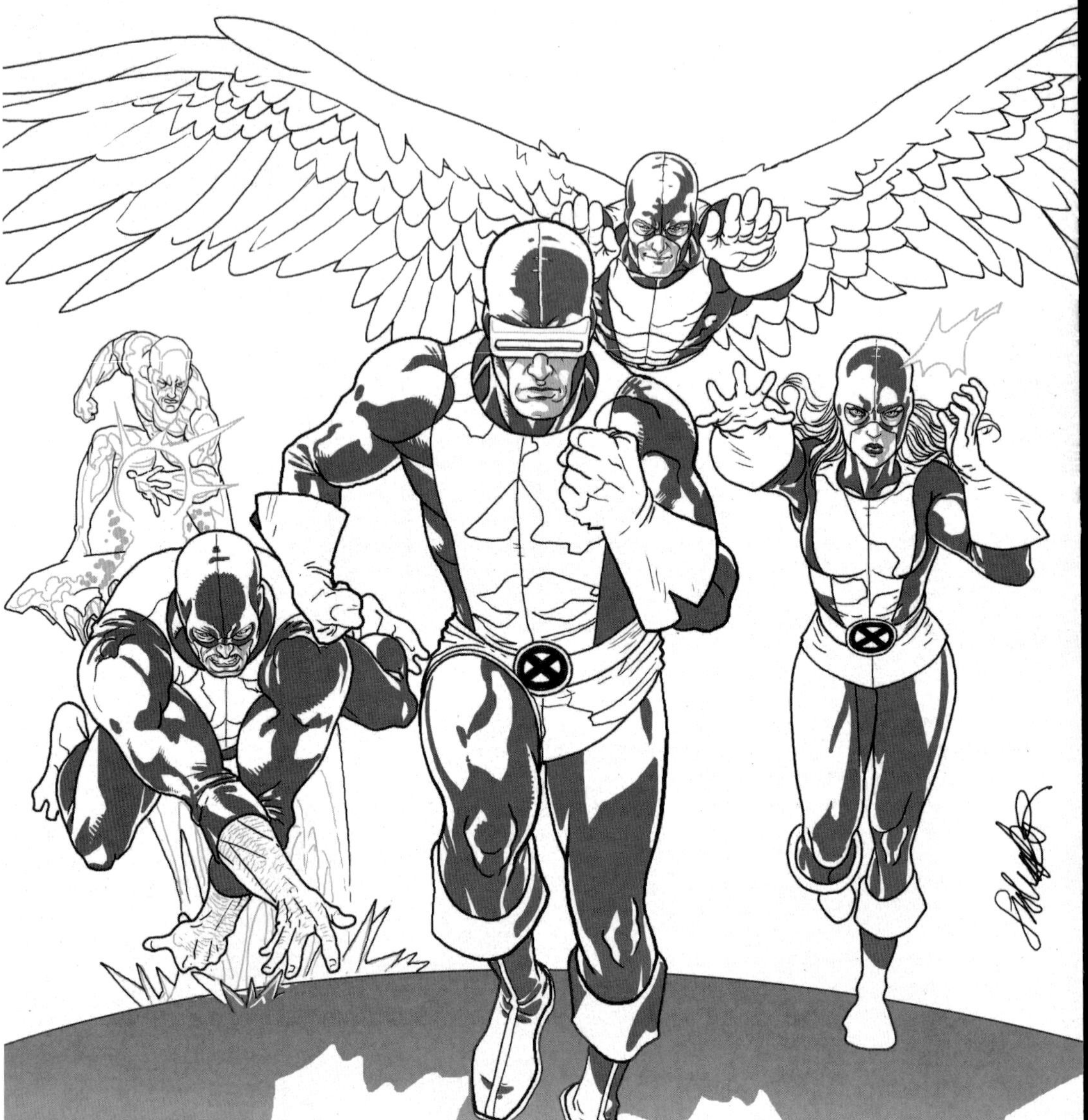

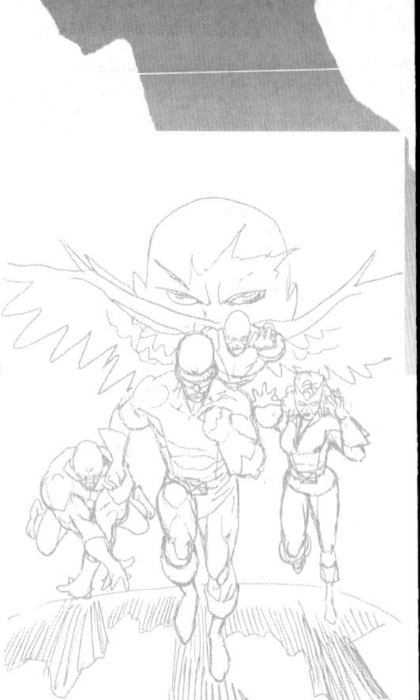

#1 VARIANT
BY SALVADOR LARROCA

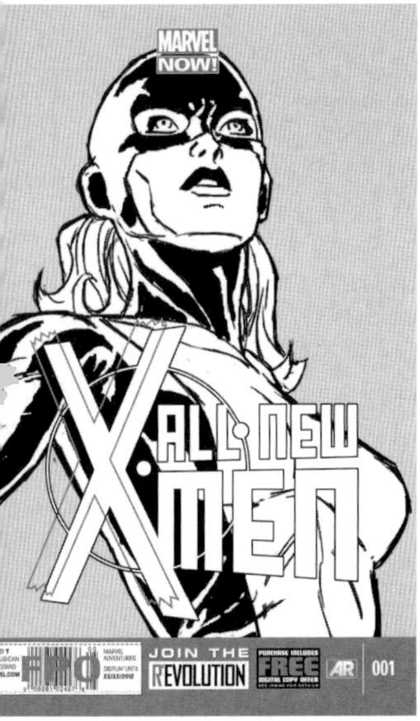
MARVEL NOW!
ALL NEW X-MEN
JOIN THE REVOLUTION
001

#1 VARIANT
BY JOE QUESADA

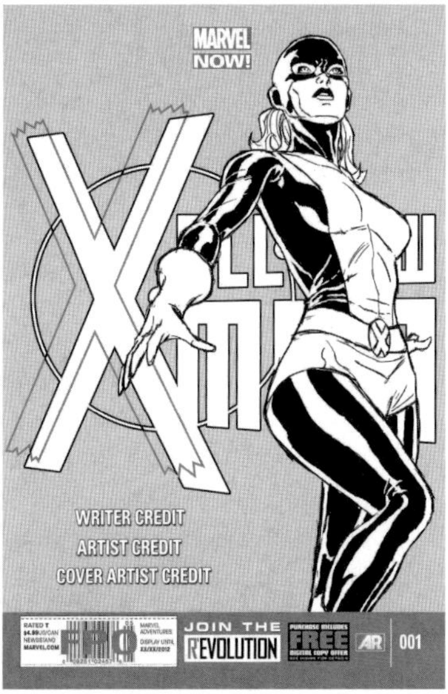
MARVEL NOW!
ALL NEW X-MEN
WRITER CREDIT
ARTIST CREDIT
COVER ARTIST CREDIT
JOIN THE REVOLUTION
001

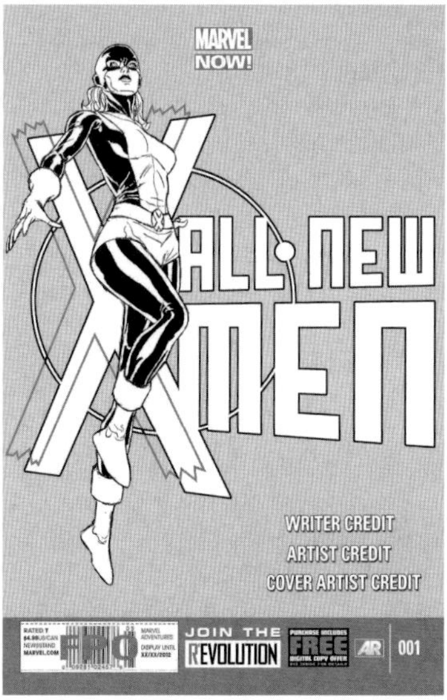
MARVEL NOW!
ALL NEW X-MEN
WRITER CREDIT
ARTIST CREDIT
COVER ARTIST CREDIT
JOIN THE REVOLUTION
001

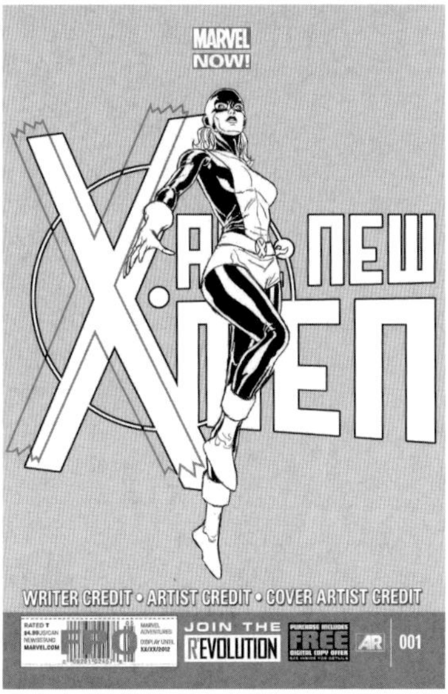
MARVEL NOW!
ALL NEW X-MEN
WRITER CREDIT • ARTIST CREDIT • COVER ARTIST CREDIT
JOIN THE REVOLUTION
001

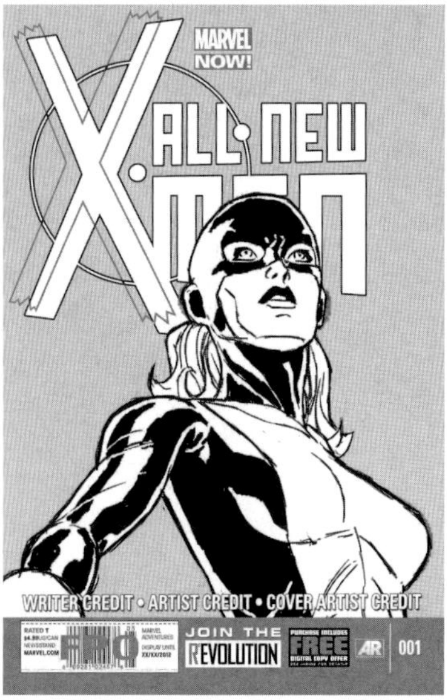
MARVEL NOW!
ALL NEW X-MEN
WRITER CREDIT • ARTIST CREDIT • COVER ARTIST CREDIT
JOIN THE REVOLUTION
001

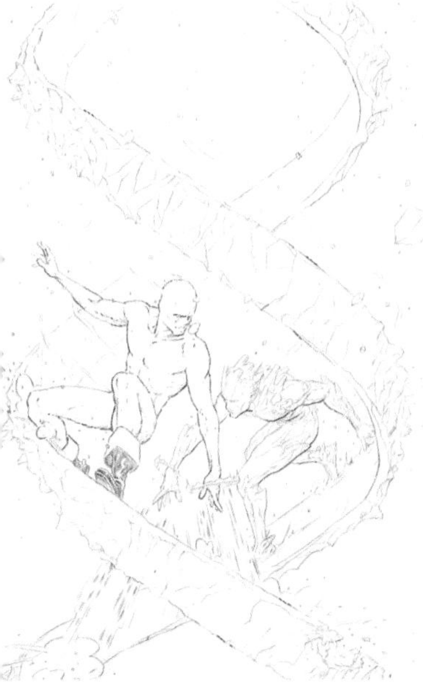

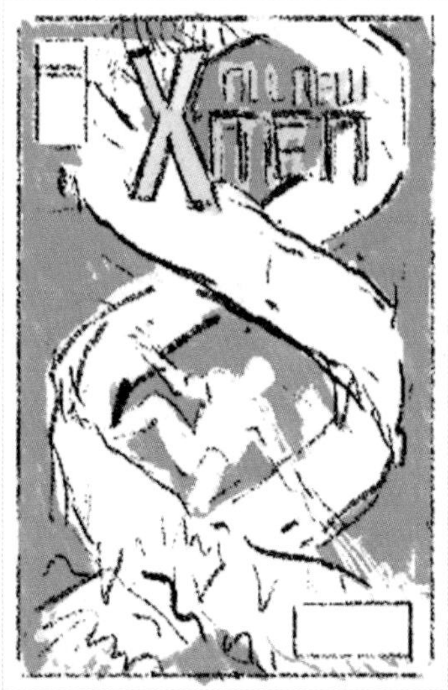
ALL NEW X-MEN

#1 VARIANT
BY PAOLO RIVERA

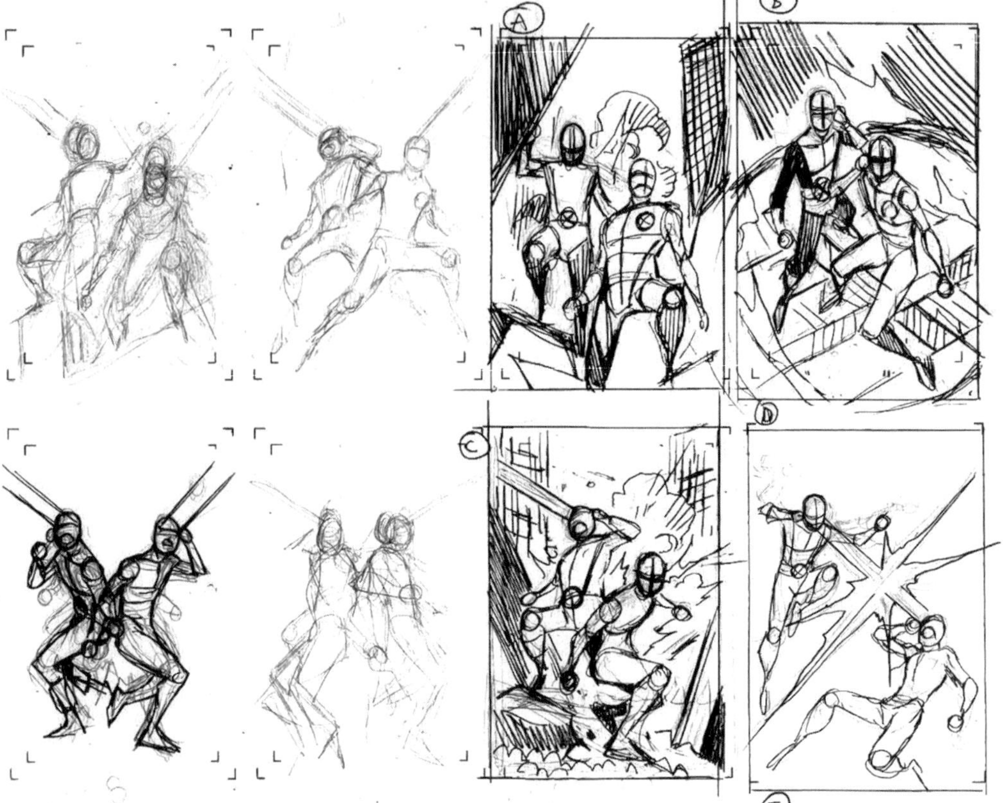
A
B
C
D

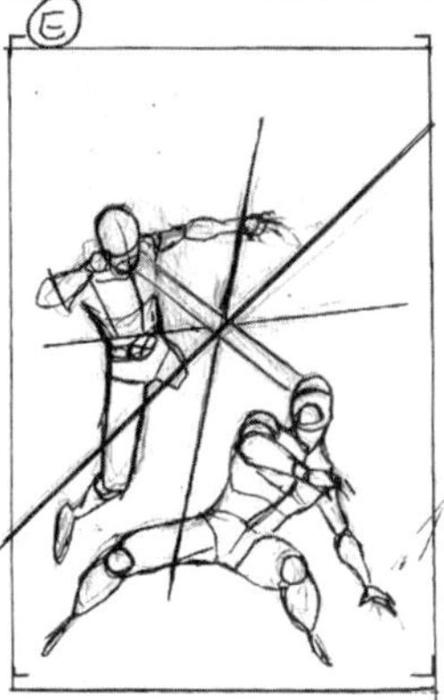
E

#4 VARIANT
BY JIM CHEUNG

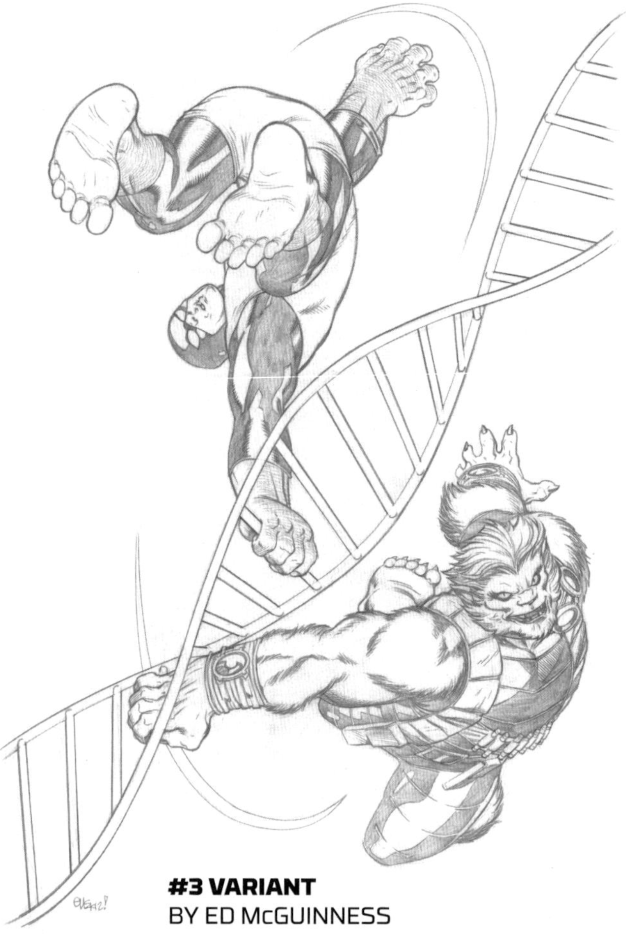

#3 VARIANT
BY ED McGUINNESS

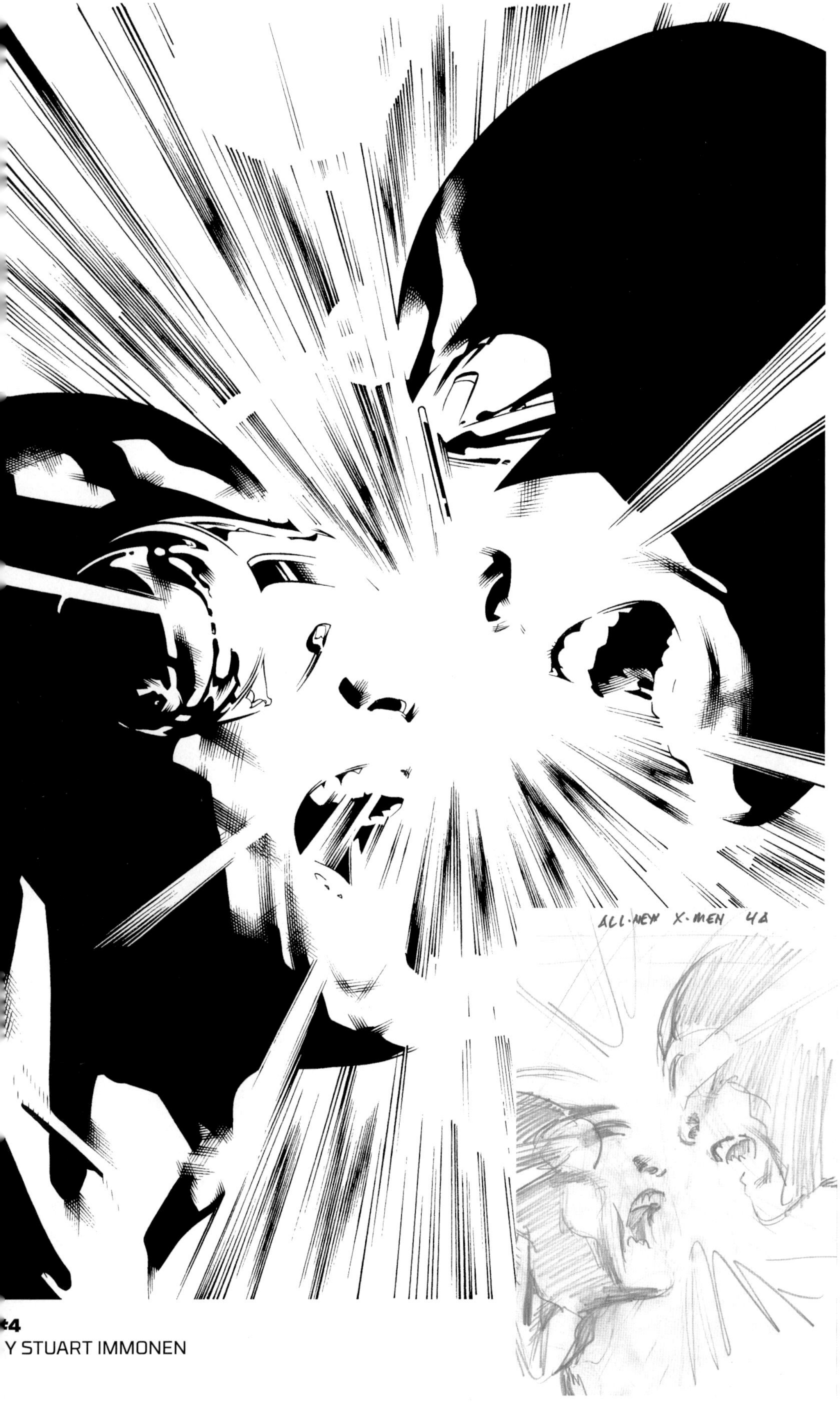
ALL-NEW X-MEN 4A

4
Y STUART IMMONEN

#5 VARIANT
BY OLIVIER COIPEL

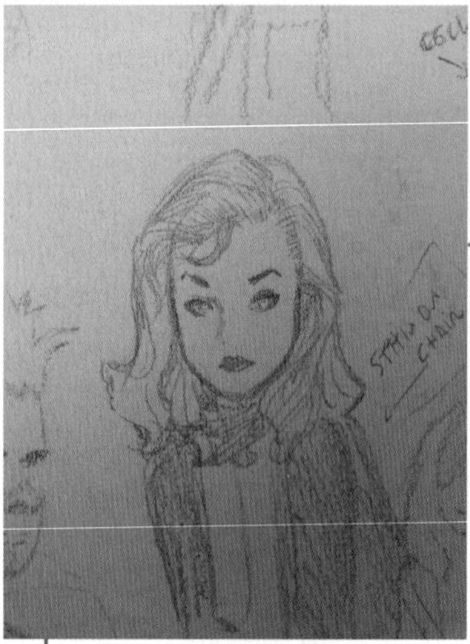

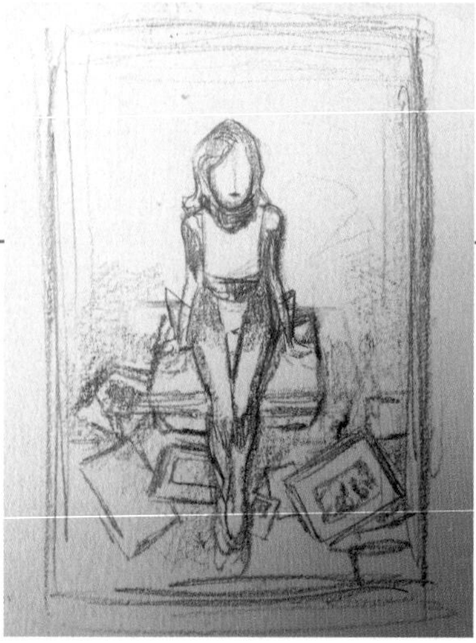

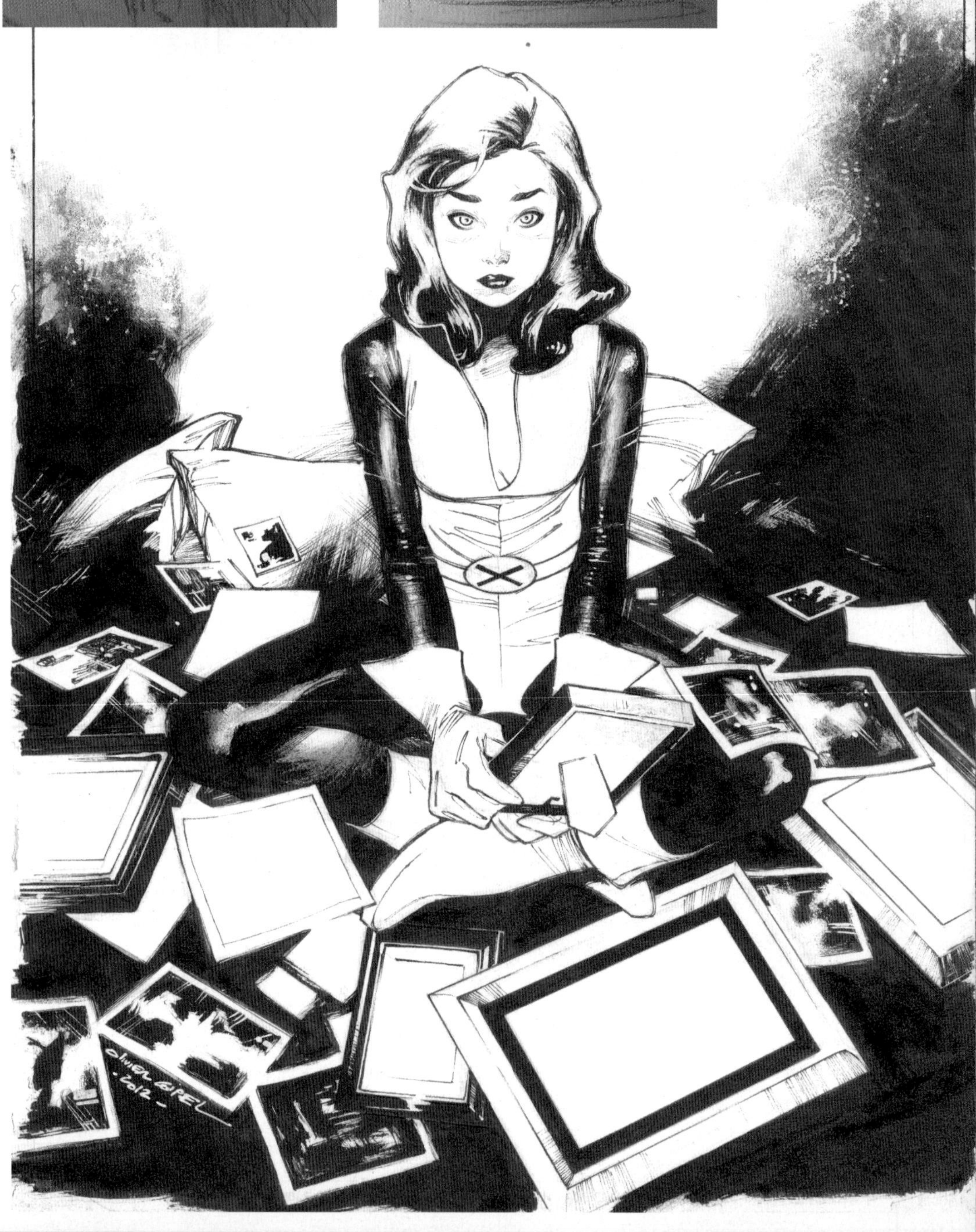

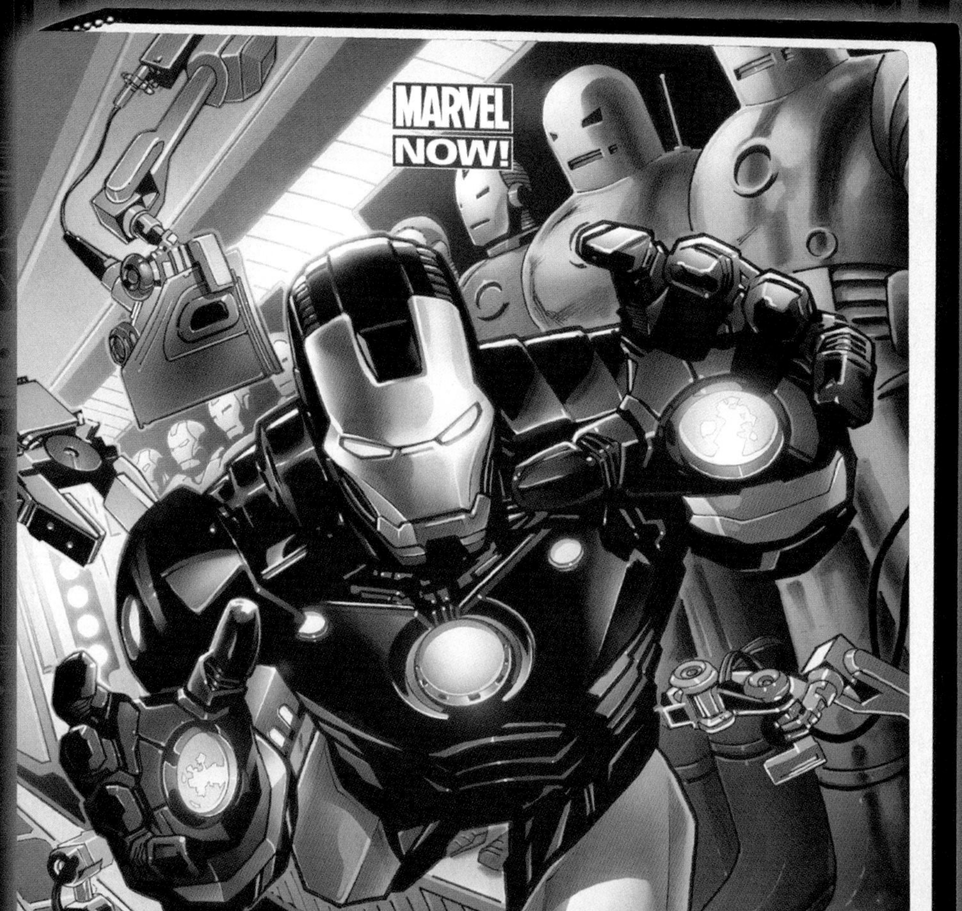
MARVEL
NOW!
IRON MAN

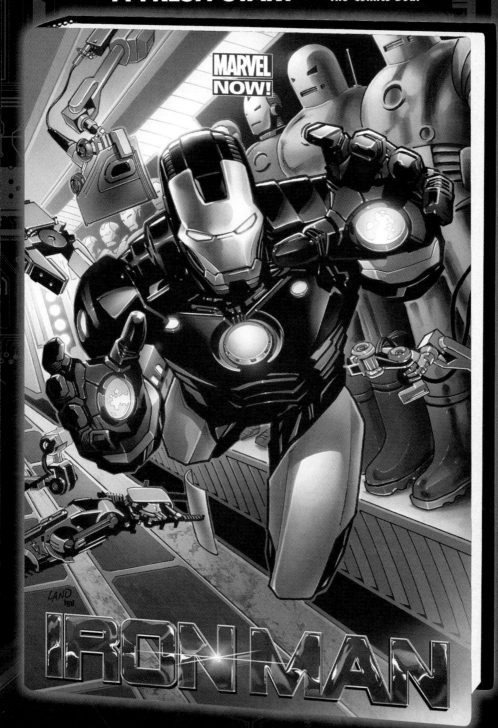

ALL·NEW X·MEN **AR** INDEX